The practice of cannibalism is in certain cultures rejected as evil, while in others it plays a central part in the ritual order. Anthropologists have offered various explanations for the existence of cannibalism, none of which, Peggy Sanday claims, is adequate. In this book she presents a new approach to understanding the phenomenon. Through a detailed examination of ritual cannibalism in selected tribal societies, and a comparison of those cases with others in which the practice is absent, she shows that cannibalism is closely linked to people's orientation to the world, and that it serves as a concrete device for distinguishing the "cultural self" from the "natural other."

Combining perspectives drawn from the work of Ricoeur, Freud, Hegel, Jung, and symbolic anthropology, Sanday argues that ritual cannibalism is intimately connected both with the constructs by which the origin and continuity of life are understood and assured from one generation to the next and with the way in which that understanding is used to control the vital forces considered necessary for the reproduction of society. She reveals that the presence or absence of cannibalism in a culture derives from basic human attitudes toward life and death, combined with the realities of the material world.

As well as making an original contribution to the understanding of a significant human practice, Sanday also develops a theoretical argument of wider relevance to anthropological analysis in general. The book will appeal to anthropologists, psychologists, sociologists, and other readers interested in the function and meaning of cannibalism.

Divine hunger

Divine hunger

Cannibalism as a cultural system

PEGGY REEVES SANDAY

University of Pennsylvania

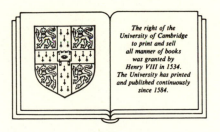

The right of the
University of Cambridge
to print and sell
all manner of books
was granted by
Henry VIII in 1534.
The University has printed
and published continuously
since 1584.

CAMBRIDGE UNIVERSITY PRESS

Cambridge
London New York New Rochelle
Melbourne Sydney

Published by the Press Syndicate of the University of Cambridge
The Pitt Building, Trumpington Street, Cambridge CB2 1RP
32 East 57th Street, New York, NY 10022, USA
10 Stamford Road, Oakleigh, Melbourne 3166, Australia

First published 1986

Printed in the United States of America

Library of Congress Cataloging-in-Publication Data
Sanday, Peggy Reeves.
Divine hunger.
Bibliography: p.
Includes index.
1. Cannibalism – Cross-cultural studies. I. Title.
GN409.S25   1986   394'.9   85–21322
ISBN 0 521 32226 X hard covers
ISBN 0 521 31114 4 paperback

British Library Cataloging-in-Publication applied for

TO *Frank* AND *Dorothy Reeves*
WITH LOVE AND GRATITUDE

Contents

Preface   ix
Acknowledgments   xv

Introduction

1   Cannibalism cross-culturally   3

2   Analytic framework   27

The symbols that give rise to a cannibalistic consciousness

3   The mysteries of the body: Hua and Gimi
    mortuary cannibalism   59

4   The androgynous first being: Bimin-Kuskusmin
    cannibalism   83

5   Cannibal monsters and animal friends   102

The mythical chartering and transformation of cannibal practice

6   The faces of the soul's desires: Iroquoian torture
    and cannibalism in the seventeenth century   125

7   Raw women and cooked men: Fijian cannibalism
    in the nineteenth century   151

8   Precious eagle-cactus fruit: Aztec human
    sacrifice   169

9   The transformation and end of cannibal
    practice   196

Contents

10 Conclusion: Other symbols and ritual
    modalities   214

Notes   233
References   253
Index   261

Preface

The brothers went on. When they arrived at the shore of the main island, Atu'a'ine said: "Aturamo'a, how shall we go? Shall we look towards the sea?" Said Aturamo'a; "O, no, let us look towards the jungle." Aturamo'a went ahead, deceiving his brother, for he was a cannibal. He wanted to look towards the jungle, so that he might eat men. Aturamo'a went ahead, and his eyes turned towards the jungle. Atu'a'ine turned his eyes, looked over the sea, he spoke: "Why did you deceive me, Aturamo'a? Whilst I am looking towards the sea, you look towards the jungle." Aturamo'a later on returned and came towards the sea. He spoke, "Good, you Atu'a'ine, look towards the sea, I shall look to the jungle!" This man, who sits near the jungle, is a cannibal, the one who sits near the sea is good.

Trobriand Island myth[1]

The Trobriand Island myth of the two brothers was told to Malinowski as an explanation for why some of the peoples of the kula ring are cannibals and others are not. The association between the jungle and cannibalism, on the one hand, and between the sea and abstention from human flesh, on the other, is similar to another myth in which two sisters settle down on an island. One of them faces toward the noncannibal people of the north and she is said to be averse to cannibalism. The other faces toward the cannibal people of the south and she is said to be a cannibal.

This myth and the area from which it comes (the Massim area of Papua New Guinea) touch on the central puzzles addressed in this book. Cast as morally wrong in the Trobriand myth, elsewhere cannibalism is indulged by humans or projected to the realm of the gods whose appetite for human flesh constitutes the ritual order. Thus, a central question here concerns the basis on which the practice of cannibalism is rejected as evil in some cases or incorporated in the cycle of ritual in others.

The Trobriand myth differentiates cannibals from noncannibals in terms of a basic orientation to the physical and moral worlds. The brother who looks toward the jungle is a cannibal; the brother who sits on the beach and looks toward the sea "is good." Because cannibalism cannot be separated from a people's orientation to their physical and moral worlds, the second question, closely tied to the first, asks how cannibalism is incorporated in a cultural system so that it is inextricably interwoven with worldview and ethos.

Finally, the islands of the Massim, where the brothers are traveling, are all exposed to occasional periods of drought or famine. The bifurcation in the brothers' orientation illustrates an actual bifurcation in traditional islander responses to hunger and famine. Some are known to react to famine by mounting interisland raids for cannibal victims, a practice that is regularized and that may occur in the absence of famine. Others, like the Trobrianders, understand famine cannibalism but reject its regular practice. Thus, the third question is, Why these different responses to similar circumstances?

The answers to these questions are complex and have led me beyond the usual dialectic of materialist or culturalist interpretations that have characterized the anthropological examination of cannibalism. In this Preface I briefly sketch my overall approach, which is more fully explained in Chapters 1 and 2.

In Chapter 1, I examine some basic issues from a cross-cultural perspective. First, cannibalism is clearly not a unitary phenomenon but varies with respect to both cultural content and meaning. As Poole notes (see Chapter 1), cannibalism may be displayed in the anguish of mourning, it may mark aspects of the life cycle, or it may be projected outwardly to the realm of the gods or inwardly as an idiom of dreams. Additionally, cannibalism may be defined as a monstrous act against society or as a sacred moral duty in the interest of social well-being. Explanations of cannibalism are also diverse. There are psychogenic, materialist, and culturalist interpretations of cannibalism, each of which tends to ignore or reject both the data and the conclusions offered by the others. The significant association I establish in Chapter 1 between the regular experience of hunger, famine, or protein deficiency and cannibal practice suggests that material forces cannot be ignored. However, the fact that hunger is just as likely to characterize societies that do not practice cannibalism, such as some of the societies of the Massim, suggests that the materialist explanation is insufficient.

I suggest that ritual cannibalism expresses the ontological structures for being-in-the-world in terms of which humans understand the forces of life and death and use this understanding to control vital forces deemed necessary for the reproduction of society. This approach is guided by Ricoeur's analysis of the primary symbols of evil in his book *The Symbolism of Evil* (see Chapter 2). Just as Ricoeur argues that "symbols give rise to thought," I argue that certain symbols and myths predicate cannibalism. In Chapter 2, I describe the kinds of symbols and myths that predicate the practice of cannibalism. The remaining chapters present the data on which my argument is based. These chapters are divided in two sections. The first section considers the symbolic oppositions that predicate cannibal practice. The second section looks at the myths that charter, transform, or end cannibal practice. This format is similar to that of Ricoeur's book, which is separated into an analysis, first, of the primary symbols of evil and, second, of the myths "of the beginning and the end." This is a workable format for analyzing cannibalism as a cultural system, because the fifteen case studies on which I rely for the empirical analysis can be divided into those in which cannibalism is predicated by symbolic oppositions that are not specifically chartered in the language of myth and those in which cannibalism is chartered or transformed by mythical statements.

In addition to being influenced by Ricoeur's analytic framework in *Symbolism of Evil,* I have been guided by Freud's theory of instincts, Jung's emphasis on the power of certain symbols to formulate and channel inchoate psychological energy, and the symbolic anthropologists' emphasis on the social power of symbols. I suggest that ritual cannibalism is part of a system of symbols that predicates social and individual consciousness by transforming inchoate psychological energy into social channels through the mechanism of identification.

Any attempt to move from the particular to the generic or to take analytic guidelines from diverse explanatory and interpretive paradigms, as I do in this book, requires a note of explanation. Contrary to some current trends in anthropological discourse, my approach is to use the comparative method and to seek generalizations. I am as much concerned with explaining cannibal practice as I am with exploring its cultural meaning. In the pursuit of explanation I deduce certain patterns from a reading of the ethnographic particulars in a dialogue with theory. In the pursuit of cultural meaning I draw extensively on a series of fifteen case studies that illuminate the logic of cannibalism. In Chapters 3–9 I first present the ethnographic particulars in a context that illuminates the logic of cannibalism and then from this context I derive a more general explanatory statement.

I suggest that rituals of cannibalism summarize and express an ontology, provide a model for individuation, and control violent emotions. In these rituals the human body is the medium for a conceptual framework – a physiologically based ontology that regulates as it regenerates social, psychological, and, sometimes, cosmological categories. The somatically based ritual symbols of cannibalism stamp the psyche and the social order in ritual acts that transform inchoate psychic energy, formulate self- and social-consciousness and, in some cases, transmit vital essence into social categories. The basic psychological mechanism that seems to be involved here is individuating by physically differentiating oneself from primordial, inchoate energy. Inchoate psychic energy is transformed by projecting inner feelings onto outer persons where the feelings can be clarified and given social form. Usually the rituals are motivated by concerns about the replacement of personnel or about transmitting psychobiological substances from the dead to the living or from humans to the gods.

As for the relationship between cannibalism and hunger or other sources of stress, many societies can be observed in which hunger is severe or there is occasional famine but cannibalism is absent (see Chapters 9 and 10). I suggest that we must look first at the key symbols and oppositions that predicate being. These symbols and oppositions express the postulates by which self is related to the other. In Chapter 2, I describe postulates that imply cannibalism and compare these postulates with others that do not lead to cannibalism.

Because the data are too thin or conjectural, I cannot specify the material realities that participate in the structuring of the innate. It is interesting to note that in protein-deficient areas of New Guinea, men connect the more rapid growth of the female body with the idea that the female body is endowed with superior biological power. This idea influences the cultural phrasing of male gender identity formation and has direct bearing on the practice of mortuary cannibalism. I can also say that where humans prey on animals for much of their subsistence needs, the idea of the cannibal predator is likely during times of famine, when parents may prey on children, or during times of social upheaval, when the normal relationships of reciprocity are transgressed. The idea of the cannibal monster seen in some cases suggests the projection of inner fears produced by stressful outer circumstances.

In my argument, ontological considerations take precedence over the utilitarian concerns given priority in the materialist point of view. Such considerations frame a people's response to stress. This is not to say that the environment plays a passive role; indeed, it plays a most active role. As people express a language of emotions in communicating with one another, the lexicon for this language may be inspired by attributes of the external environment as well as by attributes of significant others. It is from this process of communication that the symbols predicating the relationship between self and other emerge. Thus, I suggest that attributes of the environment play largely a symbolic, not utilitarian, role in rituals of cannibalism.

In rendering cannibalism comprehensible, I found it necessary to balance the divergent styles of hermeneutics and hypothetico-deductive explanation. Although I use the basic format of Ricoeur's *Symbolism of Evil,* I go beyond this format when I examine the role of certain symbols in predicating institutionalized cannibalism. In my discussion of the symbolic and psychological phrasing of cannibalism, my use of Freudian and Jungian theory will be evident. Here too, however, I only draw guidelines. It is not my intention to integrate the theories of these diverse thinkers, but to turn to them for inspiration as I forge a framework that is internally consistent and that provides a lens for comprehending the logic of a powerful human image.

Acknowledgments

I owe a great deal to the ethnographers whose work is cited in this book. In particular, I want to thank Marshall Sahlins, who sent me a prepublication version of his paper on Fijian cannibalism; Anna Meigs, who shared her then unpublished manuscript on Hua food rules; and Fitz John Porter Poole, who gave me a prepublication version of his analysis of Bimin-Kuskusmin cannibalism. Sahlins's ability to see the social messages and the cultural meaning in the outpouring of blood on the Aztec sacrificial stone or in the traffic of Fijian cannibal victims; Meigs's understanding of the ontological meaning of Hua food; and Poole's firsthand observation of mortuary cannibalism together with his brilliant reconstruction of the Great Pandanus Rite (a ritual involving exocannibalism) significantly shaped my approach.

Early on, when I was struggling through Ricoeur's *Symbolism of Evil*, Stephen Dunning shared with me his then unpublished paper on this book, and we discussed its applicability to my project. Those discussions and his later reading of Chapter 2 helped me to bring Ricoeur's complex thinking into an anthropological focus.

Demaris Wehr's feminist critique of Jung in her Ph.D. dissertation showed me the value of Jung for this project. David Hart's invitation to speak at the Jung Center in Philadelphia provided the opportunity to air and clarify my evolving ideas. Dorothy Reichard patiently listened when I got particularly fed up. I am grateful for the interest these friends showed in this project.

Fitz Poole graciously consented to read drafts, a labor which resulted in several rewritings on my part and much reading on his. I am also grateful to Arjun Appadurai and Anna Meigs, who took time out of busy schedules to read and comment on early drafts. The anonymous reviewers, of course, always help.

Despite what I owe to so many others, the final product is my own construction and I, alone, am responsible for its failings. My children, Julie and Eric, endured another round of book writing with their usual zest and again participated in the naming of the final product. I dedicate this product to my parents, who are in some ways responsible for it.

Introduction

1 · Cannibalism cross-culturally

In recent years . . . cultural anthropologists have . . . begun to give the topic [cannibalism] serious analytic attention. This development stems partly from the discovery of new facts and partly from the realization that cannibalism – like incest, aggression, the nuclear family, and other phenomena of universal human import – is a promising ground on which to exercise certain theoretical programs.[1]

Anthropological debate on the subject of cannibalism has revolved around three theoretical programs, each of which provides a distinctly different lens for viewing the details of cannibalism. Psychogenic hypotheses explain cannibalism in terms of the satisfaction of certain psychosexual needs. The materialist hypothesis presents a utilitarian, adaptive model – people adapt to hunger or protein deficiency by eating one another. The third approach follows a hermeneutical path rather than a hypothetico-deductive model in conceptualizing cannibal practice as part of the broader cultural logic of life, death, and reproduction.

In this chapter I show that cannibalism is not a unitary phenomenon but varies with respect to both cultural meaning and cultural content. Cannibalism is never just about eating but is primarily a medium for nongustatory messages – messages having to do with the maintenance, regeneration, and, in some cases, the foundation of the cultural order. In statistical terms, cannibalism can be tied to hunger, but hunger is not necessarily tied to cannibalism (see discussion of Table 5 in this chapter). The job of analysis, I suggest, requires a synthetic approach, one that examines how material and psychogenic forces are encompassed by cultural systems. We must look, as Geertz says, at how generic potentialities (and, I

3

would add, concerns stemming from material realities) are focused in specific performances.[2]

The complexity of cannibal practice cross-culturally

The discussion that follows is based on an examination of the sample of 156 societies I employed in an earlier study of female power and male dominance. This group offers scholars a representative sample of the world's known and best-described societies. The time period for the sample societies ranges from 1750 B.C. (Babylonians) to the late 1960s. These societies are distributed relatively evenly among the six major regions of the world as defined by cross-cultural anthropologists. Additionally, the societies represented vary in level of political complexity and type of subsistence technology.[3]

Of the 156 societies examined, 109 yielded information that I deemed sufficient enough to judge whether cannibalism could be classified as present or absent. One-third (34 percent) of this sample yielded information indicating the presence of cannibalism. Descriptions of cannibalism come from several types of sources: interviews with people who have observed cannibalistic practices in their own society; eyewitness accounts left by missionaries; tribal traditions; and accounts of travelers. Reports of cannibalism are unevenly distributed in various cultural areas of the world. Most come from North America and the Pacific Islands, with reports from Africa and South America being next in the order of frequency. Only two cases have been reported in the Circum-Mediterranean area and no cases have been reported for the whole of East Eurasia (see Table 1).

The descriptions of cannibalism can be classified according to three general categories: (1) ritual cannibalism is practiced, that is, human flesh is regularly consumed in ritual settings; (2) ritual cannibalism is not reported but institutionalized cannibalism is mentioned in other contexts (i.e., reports of famine, reports of past practice, legend, or hearsay); (3) ritual cannibalism is not reported, but fantasized incidents of cannibalism are feared and take the form of belief in cannibal sorcerers or witches.

A variety of themes appear in reports of cannibalism. The role of hunger is frequently mentioned, and most people believe that cannibalism may occur during times of extreme hunger and fa-

Table 1.   *Geographical distribution of reports of cannibalism*

| | Cannibalism | | | | | |
| | Present | | Absent | | Row totals | |
Geographical area	No.	%	No.	%	No.	%
Sub-Saharan Africa	7	47	8	53	15	100
Circum-Mediterranean	2	15	11	85	13	100
East Eurasia	0	0	23	100	23	100
Insular Pacific	11	52	10	48	21	100
North America	11	48	12	52	23	100
South and Central America	6	43	8	57	14	100
Column totals	37 (34%)		72 (66%)		109 (100%)	

mine. However, hunger cannibalism is generally treated as revolt-ing and reprehensible, the ultimate antisocial act, in some cases punishable by death. Tuzin provides an excellent description of this attitude in his discussion of the Arapesh response to Japanese hunger cannibalism as the ultimate unthinkable act, one that im-plied a deranged, anguished abandonment of humanity.[4] Tuzin also mentions, however, that other groups in New Guinea treated hunger cannibalism as commonplace.[5]

The food value of human flesh is referred to in many reports from the Pacific. It is not clear, however, whether such reports are the authors' fantasy or actual fact. Quoting from a nineteenth-century account, Sahlins notes that Fijian chiefs of the last century did not regard the human victim "in the shape of food," since cannibalism was "a custom intimately connected with the whole fabric of their society." Nevertheless these chiefs told the Europe-ans "that they indulged in eating (human flesh) because their coun-try furnished nothing but pork, being destitute of beef and all other kinds of meat."[6] Reports from the Pacific commonly equate human with animal flesh. The Orokaiva gave as their reason for consuming human flesh their "desire for good food." All victims acquired in an intertribal raid were consumed. Human corpses were handled as if they were animals slain in the hunt. Corpses of grown men were tied by their hands and feet to a pole and carried face downward. Slain children were slung over the warrior's shoulder in the manner of a hunter carrying a dead wallaby, with each hand of the body tied to each foot.[7] Lindenbaum reports that the Fore equated pigs and humans and applied the Melanesian pigdin term for meat and small game to the human flesh consumed by women.[8] Despite the reputed equation of human flesh with meat in some cases, the actual consumption in these cases has cultural connotations beyond gustatory considerations. For example, among the Orokaiva the primary reason for acquiring cannibal victims in intertribal raids was to compensate for the spirit of an Orokaiva man killed in such a raid. Fore concepts revolved around the notion that human meat, like pig flesh, helps some humans regenerate.

In many reports, the events associated with cannibalism refer not to hunger but to the physical control of chaos. For example, the victim is cast as the living metaphor for animality, chaos, and the powers of darkness – all those things people feel must be tamed, destroyed, or assimilated in the interest of an orderly social life. Cannibalism is then associated with a destructive power that must be propitiated or destroyed, and the act of propitiation or destruction is directly tied to social survival. The power is variously located. It may be within animals or enemies, or may be harbored as a basic instinct in humans. When projected onto enemies, cannibalism and torture become the means by which powerful threats to social life are dissipated. To revenge the loss of one's own, the victim taken in warfare is tortured and reduced to food in the ultimate act of domination. At the same time, by consuming enemy flesh one assimilates the animus of another group's hostile power into one's own.

Other reports tie cannibalism to a basic human instinct that must be controlled for the sake of internal social survival. In these cases cannibalism provides an idiom for deranged and antisocial behavior. For example, in their most secret and supernaturally powerful ritual society, the Bella Coola performed a Cannibal Dance in which they enacted their view of human nature. The Bella Coola believed that during the performance of this ritual the cannibal dancer became possessed by an animal force that caused the dancer to want to bite people and filled him or her with an insatiable desire for human flesh.[9] This force was controlled in the dancer with ropes, bathing, and a droning kind of singing.[10] The close connection between the cannibal dancer and the Bella Coola gods adds a supernatural dimension to the Bella Coola perception of the cannibal instinct of humans. In staging the cannibal ritual, the Bella Coola found a way to channel powerful forces into society and to order those forces for social purposes.

Human sacrifice with its associated cannibalism was the means by which the Aztec gained access to the animating forces of the universe. For the Aztec "the flowing of blood [was] equivalent to the motion of the world." "Human sacrifice," Sahlins says, "was . . . a cosmological necessity in the Aztec scheme, a condition of the continuation of the world."[11] The Aztec feared that when the gods became hungry their destructive powers would be unleashed against humanity. To keep the mystical forces of the universe in balance and to uphold social equilibrium, the Aztec fed their gods human flesh. By the act of consecration the sacrificial victims were incarnated as gods. Through eating the victim's flesh, men entered into communion with their gods, and divine power was imparted to men.

Exocannibalism (the cannibalism of enemies, slaves, or victims captured in warfare), characterizes the majority of cases. In the few instances of endocannibalism (the cannibalism of relatives) human flesh is a physical channel for communicating social value and procreative fertility from one generation to the next among a group of humans tied to one another by virtue of sharing certain substances with common ancestors. Endocannibalism recycles and regenerates social forces that are believed to be physically constituted in bodily substances or bones at the same time that it binds the living to the dead in perpetuity.

These sketchy descriptions illustrate the diversity in the cultural content of cannibal practice. More recent ethnographic descriptions of cannibalism reach the same conclusion. Even within the same society, cannibalism may be diversely constituted, as Poole's description of Bimin-Kuskusmin cannibalism illustrates. For Bimin-Kuskusmin,

the idea of cannibalism implicates a complex amalgam of practice and belief, history and myth, and matter-of-fact assertion or elaborate metaphor. The subject enters into crass sexual insults, ribald jokes, and revered sacred oratory. It is displayed in the plight of famine, the anguish of mourning, and the desperation of insanity. It marks aspects of the social life-cycle from the impulses of the unborn to the ravages of the ancestors. It is projected outward as a feature of the ethnic landscape and

7

inward as an idiom of dreams, possession states, and other personal fantasy formations. In different contexts it may be seen as an inhuman, ghoulish nightmare or as a sacred, moral duty. But always it is encompassed by the order of ritual and the tenor of ambivalence. The Bimin-Kuskusmin have no single term for "cannibalism," for the ideas that are implicated are constructed for particular purposes of discourse that emphasize different dimensions of the phenomenon.[12]

The complexity of cannibalism as a cultural practice means that to reduce it to a dichotomous variable robs it of all cultural content.[13] Nevertheless I proceed with this exercise as a means for determining whether the kinds of exogenous forces posited by material and psychogenic hypotheses are statistically associated with the practice of consuming human flesh. In doing so I do not intend to suggest that culture must conform to material constraints, but rather, as Sahlins states, "that it does so according to a definite symbolic scheme which is never the only one possible."[14] Thus, if hunger is a material force to be reckoned with in societies practicing cannibalism, as Table 5 suggests, I argue that we must look at the effects of hunger and ask how these effects are culturally constituted. The fact that hunger is just as likely to be present in societies that do not practice cannibalism demonstrates Sahlins's point that more than one symbolic order may constitute the effects of a given material force. Thus, hunger is encompassed by a cultural order that includes cannibal practice in some cases and by some other symbolic scheme, which may or may not include a physical referent to eating, in others.

The information presented in Tables 1–5 is based solely on reports of cannibalism falling in the category of institutionalized cannibalism. Reports of cannibalism as fantasy, as a past event, or as a periodic occurrence during times of famine are not included. The reason for limiting the cases to the purported regular consumption of human flesh derives from the stipulations on the data posed by the materialist hypothesis. Since the main causal variable posited by the materialist explanation is the ongoing satisfaction of hunger or protein deficiency, obviously the data must reflect actual as opposed to fantasized or infrequent consumption of human flesh. (In subsequent chapters, this restriction on the data will not apply and the discussion will include the fear of cannibalism, whether or not cannibalism is thought to be actually practiced. Additionally, in these chapters I will not be concerned with whether the consumption of human flesh actually takes place, because my focus will be on interpreting the rituals in which human flesh is purportedly consumed.)

The requirement that the data reflect actual instances of cannibalism brings to mind Arens's charge that since "no one has ever observed this purported cultural universal," we must be skeptical about its actual existence.[15] A search of the literature convinces me that Arens overstates his case. Although he is correct in asserting that the attribution of cannibalism is sometimes a projection of moral superiority, he is incorrect in arguing that cannibalism has never existed. Contrary to his assertion that no one has ever observed cannibalism, reliable eyewitness reports do exist. In response to Arens, Sahlins excerpts some of the nineteenth-century eyewitness reports from the journals of Pacific travelers.[16] Additionally, eyewitness reports presented in *The Jesuit Relations* contradict Arens's assertion that "[t]he collected documents of the Jesuit missionaries, often referred to as the source for Iroquois cruelty and cannibalism, do not contain an eyewitness description of the latter deed."[17]

One of the most compelling eyewitness reports I have encountered was penned in 1879 by a native of the Cook Islands who was among the first Polynesian missionaries. Upon learning to write from European missionaries, he kept a log of his travels and wrote many letters, some of which described the consumption of human flesh. One particularly lurid but descriptive example comes from a report of a war that broke out in New Caledonia soon after his arrival there as a missionary.

I followed and watched the battle and saw women taking part in it. They did so in order to carry off the dead. When people were killed, the men tossed the bodies back and the women fetched and carried them. They chopped the bodies up and divided them. . . . When the battle was over, they all returned home together, the women in front and the men behind. The womenfolk carried the flesh on their backs; the coconut-leaf baskets were full up and the blood oozed over their backs and trickled down their legs. It was a horrible sight to behold. When they reached their homes the earth ovens were lit at each house and they ate the slain. Great was their delight, for they were eating well that day. This was the nature of the food. The fat was yellow and the flesh was dark. It was difficult to separate the flesh from the fat. It was rather like the flesh of sheep.

I looked particularly at our household's share; the flesh was dark like sea-cucumber, the fat was yellow like beef fat, and it smelt like cooked birds, like pigeon or chicken. The share of the chief was the right hand and the right foot. Part of the chief's portion was brought for me, as for the priest, but I returned it. The people were unable to eat it all; the legs and the arms only were consumed, the body itself was left. That was the way of cannibalism in New Caledonia.[18]

More recent eyewitness evidence is reported by Poole, who witnessed acts of Bimin-Kuskusmin mortuary cannibalism and by Tuzin, who describes eyewitness evidence given him by Arapesh informants.[19]

The fact that Arens overstates his case should not be taken to mean that the thirty-seven cases of cannibalism reported in Table 1 represent undisputed examples of actual cannibalism. The ethnographies upon which I relied are the best available for use in cross-cultural research based on a standard sample. The data on cannibalism, however, are uneven, ranging from lengthy descriptions of ritual cannibalism reconstructed from informants' recollections of the past to a few sentences describing the consumption of the hearts of enemies. Keeping in mind the problematic nature of the data, the reader is cautioned to look for suggestive trends in the tables rather than irrefutable demonstrations of relationships.

Sagan's psychogenic hypotheses

I begin by considering the hypotheses in Sagan's study of cannibalism that can be examined within a cross-cultural framework. These are not the only dimensions to Sagan's argument. For example, he builds a good case for the role of emotional ambivalence in cannibal practice, an argument I shall return to in Chapter 2, where I suggest that, although Sagan's contribution is important and useful, it is limited by his particular reading of Freud.

Sagan contends that cannibalism "is the elementary form of institutionalized aggression."[20] Employing the Freudian frustration-aggression hypothesis and the idea that oral incorporation is the elementary psychological response to anger and frustration, Sagan hypothesizes that cannibalism is characteristic of a primitive stage of social development. "The undeveloped imagination of the cannibal," he says, will deal with frustration through oral aggression, because the cannibal "is compelled to take the urge for oral incorporation literally. He eats the person who, by dying, has abandoned him."[21] Or, he eats the enemy whose very existence may deny him strength in order to incorporate that strength into his own body. When it occurs in more advanced social systems, Sagan suggests that cannibalism is a regressive response to social disintegration, for in these cases, he says, "it is inevitable that the satisfaction of aggressive needs sinks to a more primitive level." This happened in Nazi Germany, "a society in a state of psychotic breakdown." The civilizing forces broke down under the strain Germany experienced before the Nazis took power. Although not true cannibalism, Sagan says, the destruction of millions of people, the lamp shades of human skin, and similar practices concentrated on the body, exemplify the reversion to primitive aggression.[22]

Citing the work of the Whitings, Sagan hypothesizes that extended nursing, a long period of sleeping with the mother, and father absence yield children who are overly dependent on their mothers and hence more prone to frustration and oral aggression. The adult male who carries this unconscious dependence upon infantile and childhood supports and who is also expected to be masculine and brave will need to display his masculinity and his independence of feminine support: "He will eat people, he will kill people, he will make war, he will enslave others, and he will dominate and degrade women."[23]

Sagan's discussion suggests that as the elementary form of institutionalized aggression, cannibalism will occur among the simpler societies, in advanced societies faced with a disintegrating social identity, and in societies in which infant dependence upon the mother is prolonged. We can frame these suggestions in terms of several variables and correlate them with reports of the presence or absence of cannibalism, admitting, however, that this exercise does not do justice to Sagan's more complex ideas.

The first variable measures the level of political complexity. Twenty-five of the thirty-seven societies with reported cannibalism are politically homogeneous, meaning that the highest level of jural authority is the local community. Thus, cannibalism is more likely to be present in politically homogeneous than heterogeneous societies (see Table 2). However, this information does not support Sagan's hypothesis that cannibalism is a primitive form of aggression because of the fact that more than half (56 percent) of

11

Table 2.   *Relationship between level of political sovereignty and cannibalism*

Levels of political sovereignty	Cannibalism				Row totals	
	Present		Absent			
	No.	%	No.	%	No.	%
Nothing above local community	25	44	32	56	57	100
One jural level above community	4	23	13	77	17	100
Two jural levels above community	4	44	5	56	9	100
Three or more jural levels above community	4	15	22	85	26	100
Column totals	37 (34%)		72 (66%)		109 (100%)	

the simpler societies do not practice cannibalism. The most that can be said from the information presented in Table 2 is that cannibalism is more likely to be found in the simpler societies.

From Sagan's discussion of maternal dependency and oral aggression, it is reasonable to assume that cannibalism is associated with such factors as a lengthy postpartum taboo against sexual intercourse and male aggression, including aggression against women. However, these variables are not associated with the cross-cultural incidence of cannibalism in simple societies. There is no statistically significant relationship between the length of the postpartum sex taboo, the variable usually employed as an indicator of maternal dependency, and the occurrence of cannibalism in politically homogeneous societies. Neither is there any relationship between the number of indicators of male aggression and the incidence of cannibalism in these societies (see Tables 3 and 4).

However, in politically heterogeneous societies (with at least one jural level above the local community), a significant association between the length of the postpartum sex taboo and cannibalism emerges. In Sagan's terms, this means that maternal dependency is related to oral aggression (as measured by the presence of cannibalism) in more complex societies. It is also true that in more complex societies there is a significant relationship between male aggression against women and cannibalism (see Tables 3 and 4).

Table 3.   *Relationship between length of postpartum sex taboo and cannibalism in politically homogeneous and heterogeneous societies*

| | Cannibalism | | | | |
| | Present | | Absent | | |
Length of postpartum sex taboo	No.	%	No.	%	Row total
Politically homogeneous societies					
Up to 6 Months	12	63	16	67	28
From 6 Months to more than 2 years	7	37	8	33	15
Column totals	19	100	24	100	43
Politically heterogeneous societies					
Up to 6 months	3	30	22	73	25
From 6 months to more than 2 years	7	70	8	27	15
Column totals	10	100	30	100	40

Note: For politically homogeneous societies phi = .04, not significant. For politically heterogeneous societies phi = .39, p = .007. No information for twenty-six societies.

Elsewhere I have shown that male aggression against women is significantly associated with food stress. I argue that male aggression is a reaction to stress as males seek to dominate controlling material forces by dominating the bodies of women and female reproductive functions. However, I qualify this conclusion by showing that male aggression against women is more likely to be a solution to stress in societies displaying a symbolic orientation to the male creative principle. Thus, adaptation to stress does not always include the subjugation of women and I argue for the necessity of examining cultural factors that may shape a people's reaction to stress.[24] The same comments apply to the results displayed in Tables 3 and 4. Although male aggression and maternal dependency are related to the presence of cannibalism in politically heterogeneous societies, it is clear from these tables that both of these variables may occur in the absence of cannibalism, suggesting that we must look beyond the behaviors measured by these variables in order to comprehend the incidence of cannibalism.

A similar argument is called for when examining Table 5, which

Table 4. *Relationship between male aggression and cannibalism in politically homogeneous and heterogeneous societies*

| Male aggression scale[a] | Cannibalism | | | | Row total |
| | Present | | Absent | | |
	No.	%	No.	%	
Politically homogeneous societies					
0–3 indicators of					
male aggression	7	32	11	42	18
4 or 5 indicators of					
male aggression	15	68	15	58	30
Column totals	22	100	26	100	48
Politically heterogeneous societies					
0–3 indicators of					
male aggression	2	25	15	68	17
4 or 5 indicators of					
male aggression	6	75	7	32	13
Column totals	8	100	22	100	30

Note: For politically homogeneous societies phi $= .11$, not significant. For politically heterogeneous societies phi $= .39$, $p = .02$. No information for thirty-one societies.
[a] A Guttman scale formed by five indicators: (1) men's houses, (2) machismo, (3) interpersonal violence, (4) rape, (5) raiding other groups for wives. See Sanday (1981, Appendix F) for details.

indicates a significant relationship between cannibalism and food stress. Most (29, or 91 percent) of the societies for which there are reports of cannibalism experience occasional hunger or famine or protein deficiency. Although hunger is intimately associated with the practice of cannibalism, we cannot conclude that hunger constitutes cannibal practice. As Table 5 demonstrates, many societies (43, or 60 percent) that experience food stress show no evidence of cannibalism; thus, here again, we must look to culture to understand the constitution of cannibal practice.

The data are inconclusive with respect to Sagan's psychogenic hypotheses. Sagan's claims are reductionist and, like the materialist approach, ignore the symbols mediating the experience of oral frustration and the act of oral aggression in cannibalism. Sagan's stress on cannibalism and male aggression as a reaction to oral frustration (as measured by maternal dependency and food stress)

Table 5. *Relationship between food stress and cannibalism in politically homogeneous and heterogeneous societies*

| Food stress | Cannibalism | | | | Row total |
| | Present | | Absent | | |
	No.	%	No.	%	
Politically homogeneous societies					
Food is constant	2	9	9	31	11
Occasional hunger or famine or protein deficiency	19	91	20	69	39
Column totals	21	100	29	100	50
Politically heterogeneous societies					
Food is constant	1	9	16	41	17
Occasional hunger or famine or protein deficiency	10	91	23	59	33
Column totals	11	100	39	100	50

Note: For politically homogeneous societies phi $=$ .26, p $=$ .03. For politically heterogeneous societies phi $=$ .28, p $=$ .02. No information for nine societies.

is relevant, as the results shown in Tables 3–5 illustrate. However, I argue that we must examine the underlying ontological structures that render maternal dependency, food stress, and associated acts of male aggression relevant to the practice of cannibalism in some cases and not in others since, as Tables 3–5 also indicate, these factors are just as likely to be present in the absence of cannibalism. In Chapter 2, I present the analytic framework that incorporates these considerations. In the remaining part of this chapter I examine the materialist hypothesis, Sahlins's culturalist response, and several other approaches that are useful for comprehending the social and cultural context of cannibal practice.

The materialist approach of Michael Harner and Marvin Harris

The materialist hypotheses proposed by Harris and Harner to explain the scale of Aztec human sacrifice focus on hunger and protein deficiency. Harner claims that ecological and demographic facts explain the scale of Aztec human sacrifice. In the Aztec case Harner sees

an extreme development, under conditions of environmental circum-scription, very high population pressure, and an emphasis on maize ag-riculture, of a cultural pattern that grew out of a Circum-Caribbean and Mesoamerican ecological area characterized by substantial wildgame degradation and the lack of a domesticated herbivore. . . . Intensification of horticultural practices was possible and occurred widely; but for the necessary satisfaction of essential protein requirements, cannibalism was the only possible solution. . . . From the perspective of cultural ecology and population pressure theory, it is possible to understand and respect the Aztec emphasis on human sacrifice as the natural and rational re-sponse to the material conditions of their existence.[25]

Citing an unpublished estimate by a leading authority on the demography of Central Mexico around the time of the Conquest, Harner says that 1 percent of the total population, or 250,000, were sacrificed per year in Central Mexico in the fifteenth century. As to what was done with the bodies, Harner relies on accounts writ-ten by conquistadores such as Bernal Diáz and Cortés and on the post-Conquest description penned by Sahagún.[26]

Some reports refer to eating human flesh in a nonsacrificial con-text. Cortés writes that one of his men leading a punitive expedi-tion came across "loads of maize and roasted children which they [Aztec soldiers] had brought as provisions and which they left be-hind them when they discovered the Spaniards coming."[27] Simi-larly, Sahagún mentions that Aztec merchants discovered traveling in enemy territory were killed and served "up with chili sauce." According to Durán, the flesh of the captive eaten after sacrifice was not part of the rite itself but "was considered [to be] 'leftovers' and was returned to the captor as a reward for having fed the deity."[28]

Such rewards were important because captors were recruited from the ranks of commoners who rarely ate meat or poultry. They got their protein from a "floating substance" on the surface of lakes, from amaranth, and from the regular diet of maize and beans. Famines were common and every year people faced the threat of shortage. A prolonged famine in 1450, for example, forced the rulers of the Three-City League to distribute the surplus grain that had been stored for ten years.[29]

The scarcity of fats caused another dietary problem. Although it is not known what amount of fatty acids is required by the human body, fats are thought to provide a longer-lasting energy source and assure the utilization of the essential amino acids for tissue building. In this connection, Harner notes that the Aztecs kept prisoners in wooden cages prior to their sacrifice and may sometimes have fattened them there.[30]

In contrast to the commoners, the nobility and the merchant class fed on a rich diet of protein in the form of wild game. Human flesh, too, was reserved for "illustrious and noble people." Thus, during good times human flesh may not have been nutritionally essential for the nobility. Harner suggests, however, that the consumption of human flesh probably fluctuated and made its greatest contribution to the diet when protein resources were at their lowest ebb. The privilege of eating human flesh provided good insurance against hunger during times of famine, when the nobility as well as the commoners could suffer significantly.[31]

Commoners could partake of human flesh and wild game by taking captives single-handedly in battle. Upon capturing a total of three war prisoners, commoners received the gustatory privileges of the nobility and were raised to the position of "master of the youths." They also became eligible to host a cannibal feast for their blood relatives and dine at Moctezuma's palace on imported wild game. These were the rewards in an economy of scarce meat. By rewarding successful warriors in this manner, the Aztec rulers motivated the poor to participate in offensive military operations. They pumped up an aggressive war machine with the promise of meat. "[U]nderlying the competitive success of that machine," Harner says, "were the ecological extremities of the Valley of Mexico."[32]

Marvin Harris describes preconquest political necessities in the Valley of Mexico along with several other examples to demonstrate a more general relationship in human society "between material and spiritual well-being and the cost/benefits . . . for increasing production and controlling population growth."[33] In the case of the Aztecs, their material well-being was threatened by occasional periods of famine caused by depletion of the Mesoamerican ecosystem after centuries of intensification and population growth. Their spiritual well-being depended on sacrifice and cannibalism. The severe depletion of animal protein resources in the Valley of Mexico, he claims,

17

made it uniquely difficult for the Aztec ruling class to prohibit the consumption of human flesh and to refrain from using it as a reward for loyalty and bravery on the battlefield. It was of greater advantage to the ruling class to sacrifice, redistribute, and eat prisoners of war than to use them as serfs or slaves. Cannibalism therefore remained for the Aztecs an irresistible sacrament, and their state-sponsored ecclesiastical system tipped over to favor an increase rather than a decrease in the ritual butchering of captives and the redistribution of human flesh.[34]

Sahlins's culturalist rejoinder to Harris and Harner

Sahlins sees the "Western business mentality" at the heart of Harris's view of Aztec cannibalism. In Harris's utilitarian view, everything in the social superstructure is governed by its economic function so that the meanings other people give to their lives are nothing more than the material rationalizations we give to our own. "Once we characterize meaningful human practices in these ideological terms," Sahlins says, "we shall have to give up all anthropology, because in the translation everything cultural has been allowed to escape."[35]

The cultural content Harris ignores is the stupendous system of Aztec sacrifice. Sahlins approaches this content head on: He does not attempt to dodge its complexities. Staying close to his subject matter, he illuminates the logic of sacrifice and shows how cannibalism fits within this logic. Aztec cannibalism can only be understood within the broader system of Aztec sacrifice for by itself cannibalism did not exist for the Aztec. It is true that human flesh was consumed, but neither was it ordinary human flesh nor was it eaten in an ordinary meal. Cannibalism as a cultural category among the Aztec was invented by anthropologists. For the Aztec, the consumption of human flesh was part of a sacrament bringing humans into communion with the gods. The Aztec focused not on the consumption of flesh but on the sacred character of the event.[36]

Sahlins points out that the logic of Aztec sacrifice is not unique. It is found in many other societies and conforms to Hubert's and Mauss's classic explanation of the nature and function of human sacrifice. Aztec sacrifice brought the sacrificer, "sacrifier," and the victim into union with the divine. The consumption of the consecrated victim transmitted divine power to man. Underlying this transmission was the notion of regeneration and reproduction. The gods were renewed through the offering, and the sacrifier (the one who has provided the victim but not necessarily the one who sacrifices it) gained divine power by giving up his claim to the victim. The entire process began with mutual adoption between Aztec victim and sacrifier. When the warrior took a prisoner, he declared: "He is as my beloved son." The captive replied: "He is as my beloved father."[37] Thus, the victim offered up by the Aztec sacrifier was his own child.

The reproductive imagery is manifest in the parallelism drawn between the mother and the warrior. The warrior's job was to nourish the sun with the blood of adopted captives borne by the warrior to the sacrificial altar. The mother in childbirth was likened to the warrior engaged in battle. If she died, she shared the warriors' fate and went to the House of the Sun. When the mother bore a child, the midwife shouted war cries, "which meant that the woman . . . had taken a captive."[38] Thus, male and female alike contributed to the physical reproduction of the Aztec universe.

Giving their children to the gods was a cosmological necessity: It was a condition for the continuation of the world. Without proper nourishment the gods could not work on behalf of humans. The gods depended on sacrifice for energy. Without it the sun would not come up, the sky would fall down, and the universe would return to its original state of chaos. The gods depended on humans and humans depended on the gods. The steepness of the Aztec pyramid steps paralleled the course of the sun from dark to light and back to dark. As the victim climbed the steps, he or she was the sun climbing to its midday zenith. Rolled down the western steps of the temple, the victim, like the sun, was going to his or her grave. The sustenance given to the gods in the offering and to humans in their houses ensured the regeneration of everyone.[39]

Sacrifice was also a sociocultural necessity. It was so implicated in the particulars of social relations, politics, and economics, that without sacrifice, the web of human social interactions would come apart. Fundamentally, "Aztec culture *was* reproduced by human sacrifice." Just as the main relations of the Aztec universe were renewed by the blood of captives, so were the relations on the social plane, for in the sacrificial act the logic of both was represented. Men were like the gods whose original self-destruction set the sun in motion. According to the principle of sacrifice, the flowing of blood was equivalent to the motion of the world. Without it all would come to an end.[40]

Enemies could not be subjugated or exterminated because they supplied the lifeblood of the state. Sahlins agrees that the structure of the empire was conditioned by the system of human sacrifice. But his explanation goes beyond material considerations or cost-benefit analysis. He notes that the high Aztec god Tezcatlipoca has as another name, "Enemy." The figure of this god embodied the power of the enemy. Supernatural power was often conceived as being external to society: "What is beyond society, escaping its order, is precisely what is greater than it." The ritual value of enemies lay in the greater spiritual power they brought to society. To have annexed and subjugated enemy territory would have meant destroying the lifeblood of the state. The greater supernatural power of the enemy helps to explain the initial ease of the conquest and why the subsequent hostilities were so bloodthirsty. The Spanish were conceived as different, more powerful enemies, and hence more powerful gods. The Spanish were unaware of their own worth as victims.[41]

The physical production and reproduction of cosmological and social categories

Sahlins's analysis of Aztec cannibalism is at once a critique of the idea that human cultures are formulated out of practical activity and utilitarian interests and an example of another approach to the study of culture. Harner and Harris believe that culture is precipitated from the rational activity of individuals pursuing their own best interest. The assumption underlying such utilitarianism is that humans seek to maximize benefits relative to costs. Sahlins's reasoning instead focuses on the symbolic and the meaningful. The distinctive quality of man is "not that he must live in a material world . . . but that he does so according to a meaningful scheme of his own devising." The decisive quality of culture is not that it "must conform to material constraints" but that it constitutes these constraints in a meaningful symbolic order:

[N]ature is to culture as the constituted is to the constituting. Culture is not merely nature expressed in another form. Rather the reverse: the action of nature unfolds in the terms of culture; that is, in a form no longer its own but embodied as meaning. Nor is this a mere translation.

The natural fact assumes a new mode of existence as a symbolized fact, its cultural deployment and consequence now governed by the relation between its meaningful dimension and other such meanings, rather than the relation between its natural dimension and other such facts.[42]

A striking feature of Sahlins's analysis of Aztec cannibalism is his illumination of the role of the sacrificial complex in the social and cosmological reproduction of the Aztec universe. Men and women contributed to the physical reproduction of the cosmos in a variety of ways: They (along with children) contributed their lifeblood to nourish hungry gods; men conveyed the victim to the sacrificial stone; and women bore new victims in childbirth. The relations of the social order were sustained and regenerated through the idiom of sacrifice and cannibalism. For example, noble titles were conferred on those who contributed sacrificial victims, humans became gods through the sacrificial rites, and the states supplying victims were politically separated from those counted as allies.

More than an idiom for regenerating order and structure, the sacrificial complex was also deeply implicated in the founding of Aztec society (see Chapter 8). The dialectic between submission in sacrifice and dominance in the gruesome rites that followed ritually marked the development of the Aztec state from its beginning, when the migrating hunters who were the ancestors of the Aztec first settled in the Valley of Mexico. When the Aztec nobility felt defeated, as they did during the famine of 1450, they admitted their submission by increasing the scale of sacrifice and asserted their dominance in arrogantly pretentious cannibal feasting. In myth and history, the Aztec social and political order was constituted in terms of struggle. Sacrifice and cannibalism, I suggest, were the primordial metaphors symbolizing dominance and submission.

The chartering of a social order and its reproduction are an important part of Sahlins's analysis of Fijian cannibalism as well (see Chapter 7). Sahlins presents a myth of the origin of cannibalism that has to do with the origin of culture. Like Aztec cannibalism, Fijian cannibalism is part of the mythical charter for society. In practice, Fijian cannibalism could not be separated from the ordered circulation of the principal sources of social reproduction, which established and perpetuated the developed Fijian chiefdom. The chiefdom was organized "by an elaborate cycle of exchange of raw women for cooked men between a basic trio of social cum cosmic categories: foreign warriors, immigrant chiefs, and indigenous members of the land."[43] Wives and cooked men are both reproductive. The wives are directly "life-giving"; the cannibal victims are life-giving in that their bodies provide a tangible channel for the exchange of *mana* between men and gods.[44] The system of exchange culminating in sacrifice and cannibalism constituted "an organization of all of nature as well as all society, and of production as well as polity."[45] Sahlins concludes that "the historical practice of cannibalism can alternately serve as the concrete referent of a mythical theory or its behavioral metaphor."[46] Thus, Fijian cannibalism, like that of the Aztec, is part of the foundation of the social order. Fijian cannibalism also served as a tangible symbol of dominance. The Fijian chief who offered victims to his people legitimated his chiefly dominance. In the gruesome rites that followed the chiefly offering, his male and female subjects gave vent to more lurid displays of dominance.

Although Annette Weiner does not address the issue of cannibalism, her analysis of reproduction is relevant to this discussion because of her emphasis on the specific resources that "objectify the general societal process of reproduction, documenting and legitimizing the fundamental condition whereby ego and 'others' are tied together."[47] By reproduction, Weiner means "the way societies come to terms with the processes whereby individuals give social identities and things of value to others and the way in which these identities and values come to be replaced by other individuals and regenerated through generations."[48] The specific resources that mark relations across the generations must be material objects with some physical property of durability. Possibilities mentioned by Weiner are substances or objects taken from the corpse itself, or material objects used in formal exchange events.[49] Weiner's comparison of the Bimin-Kuskusmin use of bones as the concrete referent in acts of social reproduction with the Trobriand employment of bundles of banana leaves raises some interesting hypotheses regarding the social concomitants of cannibalism.

The fundamental problematic posed by social reproduction, Weiner says, is "[H]ow can one draw on the resources and substances of others while maintaining and regenerating one's own resources and substances" without becoming "other"?[50] The Bimin-Kuskusmin essentially cut off relations with the other after the reproductive potential of the other has been employed to beget children. For them the other always remains essentially suspect, and the substances of the other (namely, affines) are rigidly separated from the substance of the lineage.[51]

Poole's analysis of Bimin-Kuskusmin models of procreation, death, and personhood supports Weiner's discussion of reproduction and regeneration. Through acts of mortuary cannibalism, the procreative powers of the dead are recycled within the Bimin-Kuskusmin lineage and clan, whereas the spirit of the newly dead, provided that it meets the test for proper ancestorhood, takes its place among the clan ancestral spirits that are responsible for nurturing the manifestation of the clan spirit in the bodies of future generations.[52] When a man or woman becomes an ancestor, Poole says, "the mortal individual is substantially dissolved in most respects, and the wider social bonds founded on eroding substance are significantly sundered."[53] The person who becomes an ancestor leaves a legacy in the form of children, departed ancestral (called *finiik*) spirit, bone, bone marrow, and procreative power. This legacy "constitutes the substantial core of the cycle of birth, death, and rebirth, *and this cycle turns inward on the clan as the social category that is forever reconstituted in the Bimin-Kuskusmin ideology of societal regeneration*" (emphasis mine).[54] Thus, the clan stands alone in the symbolism of death and rebirth – it is the clan that is perpetuated. The symbol of the continuity and perpetuity of the clan "is cast in the substantial symbols of bone in and on living persons, in shrines, cult houses, and ossuaries, and in ritual performance," including ritual anthropophagy.[55] This inward-turning character of Bimin-Kuskusmin acts of social reproduction can be compared – providing that the quite different level of political complexity is taken into account – with the Aztec state, which, as noted earlier, adopted a policy of nonexpansion. The inward-turning nature of the Aztec state was the means by which its hegemony was maintained.

The Trobriand solution does not display the exclusive inward orientation of the Bimin-Kuskusmin. Labor and production of yams and women's wealth are directed within the lineage, but relationships are not cut off with others, such as affines, fathers, and spouses. Bundles of banana leaves objectify the reproductive significance of women at the same time that they give economic validation to relations between individuals of different lineages. Thus, "bundles provide for the linking of networks of relationships that last for three or more generations."[56] Trobriand bones, like Bimin-Kuskusmin bones, remain within the ritual contexts of ancestors. As significant objects, however, bones "never enter the economic or political domain, for bones do not validate relations external to the ancestral domain."[57]

This difference between turning inward as opposed to connecting ties with affines in mortuary ceremonies is one of the social concomitants Strathern relates to the presence of cannibalism in New Guinea Highlands and Fringe Highlands societies. Focusing on marriage exchange and prominence of pig herds, Strathern notes that, where cannibalism is present, two factors are also present: (1) "the idea of 'turning back' or of repeating marriage" is accepted just as "the idea of 'turning back' to eat one's own kind is not regarded as wrong"; (2) "herds of domestic pigs, which could be used as substitutes for the exchange and consumption of persons, are less prominent."[58]

Most Bimin-Kuskusmin marriages are intratribal. Marriages between tribes are usually marriages with women from enemy groups. The fear and antagonism between groups is accentuated because no attempt is made to regenerate these relationships through time, as Weiner notes in the Trobriand case.[59]

Bimin-Kuskusmin cannibalism and endogamous structure can be contrasted with the marriage system of the Melpa of the Western Highlands. The Melpa abhor cannibalism, relegating it to the secret practices of evil witches. The Melpa have elaborate rules against marrying kin, and against repeating marriages between small groups. These prohibitions occur in conjunction with an obvious stress "on proliferating exchange ties, on facing outwards to an expanding network, and on a continuous substitution of wealth items, pork and shell valuables (or nowadays cash), for the person. In this context, cannibalism stands for an unacceptable 'turning back', and is thus symbolically equated with incest."[60]

Bimin-Kuskusmin pig herds are tiny by highland standards, according to Poole, and there certainly is not the elaborate network of exchange documented for the Melpa.[61] Nor do pigs figure prominently in Bimin-Kuskusmin mortuary rituals, as they do among the Melpa. Melpa mortuary rites transfer the spirit of the corpse into the world of the ghosts by means of a pig sacrifice designed to ensure the goodwill of the new ghost and the com-

munity of ghosts. Eating the pig flesh coincides with the release
of the deceased's soul. The pigs, Strathern concludes, are substitutes for the person's body: "[T]he pork is eaten *instead of* the deceased." The funerary pig sacrifices are presented to the ghosts "in
order to persuade them to accept a new ghost, and to the deceased's maternal kin, in substitution for the flesh which will rot
and return to the earth," where it fertilizes and thereby regenerates
the soil of the clan territory.[62] The bones of the corpse are kept by
the paternal kin and placed in special houses. Thus, through the
medium of pig flesh, the deceased's spirit is replaced; what the
Bimin-Kuskusmin accomplish through mortuary cannibalism the
Melpa accomplish through pig sacrifices.

Strathern notes that the practice of cannibalism in the New
Guinea Highlands is associated with sparsely populated fringe regions where large herds of domestic pigs are absent. However, he
cautions against jumping to the conclusion that protein-hunger is
causally related to the practice of cannibalism, because where pigs
are absent, alternative sources of protein are available in wild
game, including feral pigs. Furthermore, the Hua, the Gimi, and
the Fore are reported to have practiced cannibalism and all of these
groups keep herds of domestic pigs. However, in areas where agricultural intensification has proceeded to its greatest lengths, cannibalism is absent.[63]

Conclusion

As the most recent ethnographic studies of cannibalism confirm,
cannibalism is not a unitary phenomenon but varies both in meaning and cultural content. The cross-cultural data point to at least
six patterns in the practice of cannibalism:

1. Famine cannibalism is frequently mentioned.
2. Cannibalism may be motivated by competition between
   groups and the desire to avenge the death of someone lost
   in war.
3. Mortuary cannibalism is part of the physical regeneration
   of fertile substances required to reproduce future generations and maintain ties with the ancestors.
4. Cannibalism is a behavioral referent of a mythical charter
   for society and, with other social and cosmological cate-

gories, is a condition for the maintenance and reproduction of the social order.

5. Cannibalism is a symbol of evil in the socialization of persons.
6. Cannibalism is part of the cultural construction of personhood.

As Poole's ethnography of Bimin-Kuskusmin cannibalism shows, several patterns may characterize the expression of cannibalism in one society; or, only one of the patterns described above may be represented.

The explanations of cannibalism are also diverse. The data presented in this chapter are inconclusive with respect to the claims of psychogenic and materialist hypotheses. However, I do not discount the role of psychogenic and materialist forces and in the following chapters I examine the interrelationship between material forces and the psychological states predicated by rituals of cannibalism. The relationship between food stress and cannibalism leads me to suggest that, like male control of female bodies, cannibalism is part of a hegemonic strategy developed in reaction to a perception of controlling natural or political forces in some cases. This strategy, however, cannot be separated from the system of symbols that predicates a people's understanding of their being-in-the-world and formulates their strategies vis-à-vis social regeneration, reproduction, and dominance. More than just a reaction to external conditions, cannibalism is a tangible symbol that is part of a system of symbols and ritual acts that predicate consciousness in the formulation of the social other and reproduce consciousness in the ritual domination and control of the social other. Where domination and control are subordinate to accommodation and integration, however, cannibalism is absent regardless of the nature of the food supply.

2 · Analytic framework

[I]nsist as we may upon the distinct character of cultural action, we are invariably forced to the conclusion that the cultural, too, is merely a part of nature. Whatever we do, we do as warm-blooded, mammalian animals, exemplifying natural effect in all of our actions. In our own terms, then, culture is nature harnessing nature, understanding nature, and coming to know itself.[1]

This chapter introduces the conceptual framework that guides the analysis and presentation of data in the following chapters. Fifteen case studies provide the material for the more detailed discussion. These case studies are identified in Table 6 by the name and location of the society; and by whether cannibalism is social (that is, under the control of group decisions) or is antisocial (that is, outside group control). Table 6 also identifies the type of data on which my analysis is based, the type of cannibalism practiced, and the chapters that treat the case studies in more detail.

The fifteen cases were chosen because of the reliability and detailed nature of the data. Some are drawn from the fieldwork conducted by ethnographers in the past decade. In one case, that of the Bimin-Kuskusmin, instances of mortuary cannibalism were observed by the ethnographer. In three cases (the Hua, Gimi, and Goodenough Islanders), the ethnographer provides detailed information on the practice of cannibalism, as reported by informants, before it was prohibited by government and missionary officials. Three additional examples of ritual cannibalism are drawn from descriptions reconstructed by anthropologists from the accounts of missionaries and travelers. Although these descriptions are detailed and vivid, the data are not specific on such topics as the theory of procreation and conception, which is essential for under-

Table 6. *Case studies*

Society	Location	Source of data	Type of cannibalism	Chapter
Hua	New Guinea	Ethnography	Mortuary	3
Gimi	New Guinea	Ethnography	Mortuary	3
Melpa	New Guinea	Ethnography	Absent (antisocial)	3
Bimin–Kuskusmin	New Guinea	Ethnography	Mortuary, enemies	4
N. E. Algonkians	North America	Reports of informants	Endocannibalism (antisocial)	5
Beaver	North America	Reports of informants	Endocannibalism (antisocial)	5
Kwakiutl	N. W. coast, North America	Myth, reports of informants	Ceremonial, endocannibalism (antisocial)	5
Iroquois	North America	Missionary traveler	Enemies	6
Fijians	Oceania	Missionary traveler	Enemies	7
Aztec	Mexico	Missionary reports of informants	Enemies	8
Dobu	Massim	Reports of informants	Enemies, endocannibalism (antisocial)	9
Goodenough Islanders	Massim	Reports of informants	Enemies (antisocial)	9
Trobriand Islanders	Massim	Reports of informants	Absent (antisocial)	9
Navajo	North America	Ethnography	Absent (antisocial)	10
Mbuti	Africa	Ethnography	Absent (antisocial)	10

standing cannibalism as a cultural system. I have included these cases (the Aztec, Fijians, and Iroquois) because the analyses by Sahlins (who treats the first two groups) and by Wallace (who deals with the third) have guided some aspects of my general approach.

For the other groups identified in Table 6, cannibalism is a focal symbol for thinking about evil. Three of these groups – the Northern Algonkians, the Beaver, and the Kwakiutl – practiced cannibalism. The data for these cases are based on fieldwork conducted in this century and on reports from previous centuries. In four additional cases cannibalism is not practiced. The Melpa substitute pig flesh for human flesh in rituals that are structurally analogous to rituals of cannibalism. Trobriand Island legends tell of famine and cannibalism in the past and one myth suggests at least a symbolic equivalence between a human victim and items of wealth. However, as with the Melpa, there is no evidence of the systematic practice of cannibalism. The Navajo and the Mbuti provide examples of symbolic orders that do not employ cannibalism as a modality for acquiring wealth or communicating with essential life forces.[2]

The following discussion is based solely on the case studies presented in Table 6. An obvious bias introduced by the selection of these particular cases (based as it was on the best sources available) is that examples from Africa and Eurasia are lacking. References to cannibalism are reported in ethnographies of the Sherbro and Tiv from Africa and of societies in northern Eurasia. Because these descriptions do not present the kind of detail reported in the cases listed in Table 6, however, I have chosen not to include this information. Were such detail available from Africa and northern Eurasia, perhaps the symbolic oppositions I identify as underlying cannibal practice might be increased in number (see section entitled "The dialectical structure of the symbols of cannibalism").

Some remarks on the relationship between cannibalism, ritual, and ecological stress

Before describing the general theoretical framework, I want to review some common assumptions about the relationship between ritual and ecological stress. Laughlin and d'Aquili define ecological stress as "any threat to the survival of all or most of the members of a society posed by a decrement in the quantity or quality of basic resources."[3] The decrement in resources may be caused by a change in the environment or by competition with other groups. Where the actual and conceived probability of ecological stress is high, they suggest, the society will rely heavily on collective action, particularly on ritual, because ritual models social and cosmological organization and thereby provides a forum for antic ipating change and controlling social action. In a similar vein, referring to myths of famine on the Northwest Coast of North America, Cove argues that these myths prepare people for the experience of famine by providing them with a set of behavioral responses.[4]

Laughlin and d'Aquili distinguish between prolonged, regular deprivation and deprivation due to fluctuating conditions. Whereas prolonged hunger has an atomizing effect on group behavior and sociality, action in response to fluctuating periods of hunger is mediated by myth and ritual. When prolonged hunger and deprivation are the only predictable feature of the environment, adaptation takes the form described by Holmberg for the Siriono or by Turnbull for the Ik.[5] In these cases, reciprocity and reciprocal altruism decline. Marginally productive members of society are expected to fend for themselves and are allowed to perish. It is interesting to note that neither Holmberg nor Turnbull report cannibalism of those who die of starvation whereas others frequently report cannibalism in societies faced with fluctuating periods of prolonged famine or drought.

Turnbull argues that, in adapting to deprivation, the Ik have developed a system that enables them to survive with predictability. He notes that this is preferable to the hazards of adapting to better conditions that might prove temporary.[6] Having revised their concept of normalcy to fit the immediacy of unremitting deprivation, the Ik do not see themselves as being under stress.[7] Their cognition

coincides with the operational reality of their situation. The reality is stark but cold and clear; the cognitive model is similarly devoid of imaginative frills and is essentially pragmatic. There is no room for ideals, no need to explain the inexplicable by reference to gods or spirits. There is no need for ritual to mediate between the cognized and operational environments.[8]

The Ik's acceptance of their situation is mirrored in the relative lack of physical violence or hostility among them. In Chapter 10, I suggest that this acceptance is due to the Ik's perception of the nature of existence and not to ecological necessity.

Laughlin and d'Aquili note that most human societies experience some degree of fluctuation in their food supply. Although many are able to avoid debilitating deprivation during these periods, others may experience deprivation for brief periods each year or may have to contend with extreme deprivation frequently, although not necessarily annually.[9] Cyclical stress may be anticipated in the annual ritual cycle, as can be seen in the Aztec calendrical cycle of sacrifices, or ritual and sometimes mythology may provide models for behavioral responses during periods of crisis. Such responses, Laughlin and d'Aquili say, "facilitate the maximization of basic resource availability, social unity, and collective action and the minimization of psychological stress."[10]

Rappaport's analysis of the Maring ritual cycle illustrates the feedback relationship between ecology and ritual by showing that "it is the increase in pig population to intolerable limits, as indicated by complaints concerning labor and conflicts resulting from porcine depredations, that triggers the regulatory reaction of the ritual cycle."[11] The Maring ritual cycle is more than a corrective response. As Rappaport makes clear, the ritual cycle must also be understood as a system of processing culturally encoded information: "It is founded upon cultural perceptions of natural processes which may, of course, be 'objectively' inaccurate and which are also likely to be shaped by social factors."[12]

My approach conceptualizes cannibalism as a cultural system, that is, a system of symbols and ritual acts that provides models of and for behavior. I suggest that ritual cannibalism facilitates the flow of life-generating substances and power, expresses social unity, and programs psychological reactions. Additionally there is evidence that, in some cases at least, cannibalism is triggered by and models extreme circumstances (see discussion of the Algonkian Windigo monster in Chapter 5 and the Goodenough Islanders in Chapter 9). Like the Maring ritual cycle, ritual cannibalism is more than a corrective response. It is a system of processing culturally encoded information that is founded on conceptualizations of the innate in humans, animals, and the nonhuman world – in other words, in nature. These conceptualizations form the ontological structures for being-in-the-world in terms of which humans invent and reproduce society and the self. By "ontological structures for being-in-the-world" I mean the myths, symbols, and rituals by which a people explore their relationship to the world, to other beings, and to being itself.[13]

Introduction

Cannibalism and the analysis of ethno-ontologies

Whether it is a symbol of evil or is actually practiced, ritual cannibalism makes a statement about the sources of life and death and suggests how these sources are to be controlled and dominated by humans in the perpetuation of social and biological life. Mortuary cannibalism, for example, passes on the vital essence of the newly dead so that it will not be lost from the general pool available to society. In Aztec sacrificial rites, the gods had to be nourished with human blood to ensure social and cosmological well-being. The Fijian quest for cannibal victims nourished and reproduced the Fijian chiefdom. Iroquoian torture rituals regenerated the spent energy of victims lost at war and at the same time provided the community with a forum for restating its dominance in a world torn by conflict. Even as a symbol of evil, cannibalism is about control and reproduction – because, by providing a map of the unthinkable, people affirm the expected in the socialization of new generations.

The above remarks clarify the social function of cannibalism. In the following I attempt a somewhat deeper level of analysis by discussing the relationship between cannibalism and the ontological structures for being-in-the-world in terms of which humans invent and reproduce self and society.

The suggestion that symbols predicate and formulate psychological and social consciousness is central to Geertz's discussion of religion as a cultural system. Geertz argues that the extreme generality, diffuseness, and variability of the innate response capacities of humans means that without the assistance of symbols we would be "functionally incomplete, not merely a talented ape who had, like some underprivileged child, unfortunately been prevented from realizing his full potentialities, but a kind of formless monster with neither sense of direction nor power of self control, a chaos of spasmodic impulses and vague emotions."[14]

Human beings escape the anxiety of inchoateness, Fernandez says, "through various concrete predications upon themselves."[15] Consciousness is born, inchoate psychic energy takes perceptible form, in the use humans make of metaphor. The movement accomplished by metaphor "is from the abstract and inchoate in the subject to the more concrete, ostensive, and easily graspable in the metaphoric predicate." Metaphor obtains an "'objective correlative' of what is subjectively inchoate in perception and reflection."[16] The inchoate subject finds direction and perceptible form by likening objects in the external environment to itself. Such an intellectual exploitation of natural objects, as Lévi-Strauss has shown, is also used by humans for purposes of social categorization and differentiation.[17]

In addition to looking at the structures that predicate being, we must also determine how symbolic vehicles are bound up with cognitive and affective processes by which information from external objects is employed to give social and psychological form to an inner sense of being. Analogic reasoning is one of the cognitive processes that has been mentioned. Dialectical opposition between the internal self and the external other is another process by which the inchoate subject is formulated. Wagner says that the invention of self in tribal societies is conceptualized in dialectical terms.[18] For example, writing about the dualistic character of Iatmul actions and institutions, he says that this dualism "corresponds to the fact that the Iatmul think and act – and therefore invent themselves and their society – dialectically."[19]

The fact that dialectical opposition is evident in the symbolic ordering of cannibalism leads me to suggest that ritual cannibalism is intimately connected with the cultural construction of self and society. The importance of opposition in the construction of consciousness is argued by Lévi-Strauss and Ricoeur, although in quite different terms. Lévi-Strauss says "no act of consciousness constitutive of the self would be possible" in the absence of an opposition between the self and the other apprehended as an opposition.[20] If it is not apprehensible as a relationship,

Being . . . would be equivalent to nothingness. . . . since thought itself cannot be other than thought about an object, and since an object, however starkly and simply it is conceived, is an object only in so far as it constitutes the subject as subject, and consciousness itself as the consciousness of a relationship.[21]

Ricoeur's analysis of the symbolism of evil provides a model for my analysis of the predicating symbols and oppositions associated with the practice of cannibalism. Following his example, I discuss the following topics: (1) the primary symbols and oppositions of

ritual cannibalism and their formulation in the language of myth;
(2) the predication of the self by the physical; and (3) the progressive internalization of predicating symbols by the self.

Ricoeur begins his discussion of the symbolism of evil with a typology of the primary symbols and oppositions associated with the experience of fault. The manner in which I employ this typology in my analysis of the key symbols of cannibalism will soon become evident. Defilement, sin, and guilt are his three primary symbols. In each type he assumes a dialectical tension between objective and subjective poles and suggests that the objective and subjective poles of each type are retained and transformed by the next type.[22]

In defilement, the physical and the ethical are merged and the physical provides an externalized map for the internal experience of good and evil. The stage of defilement introduces self-consciousness for the first time, according to Ricoeur, because an objectively impure object produces dread of pollution in the subject and this tension is taken up into the language of confession of stain. The confession of stain removes pollution from the subject and provides a means for reconciliation. Reconciliation is necessary because the objective event of defilement is experienced subjectively as dread or "ethical terror." Dread originates in "the primordial connection of vengeance with defilement," that is, in the presupposition that all suffering is punishment for becoming defiled, a variant of the "lex talion" principle.[23] By projecting destructive wishes, humans find the means for controlling these wishes in themselves by controlling them in others – an example of the budding superego. Ritual recognition of defilement sublimates dread and becomes the instrument by which the defiled self not only becomes conscious of itself, as Ricoeur suggests, but finds the means for control.

In sin, the experience of dread goes beyond objective pollution and involves the transgression of some objective demand. Sin does not "so much signify a harmful substance as a violated relation."[24] Here the subjective dread of defilement is transformed into the fear of the wrath of God (Ricoeur's discussion is based on sacred images of Western culture). The symbolism of defilement and purification is taken up, reaffirmed, and even amplified in the expiatory rite of the blood sacrifice. As the consciousness of defilement leads from mere object-consciousness to the birth of subject-consciousness, the subject-consciousness of sin leads back to the objective rite of blood sacrifice. The sacrifice, in contrast to defilement, expresses the consciousness of the subject objectively, just as sin revealed its own objectivity to consciousness.[25] Thus, the subjective awareness of sin, defined as a violated relationship, leads to objective expressions of reconciliation. These expressions exteriorize ontological models and the problems they entail. By being expressed in tangible symbolic acts, subjective experience is both acted out and controlled.

The final synthesis (*Aufheben*, to use the Hegelian term) of Ricoeur's dialectic of objective defilement and subjective sin, Dunning argues, is found in the phenomenology of guilt.[26] In guilt, consciousness apprehends itself as the source of its own pollution, a pollution that is now understood in moral rather than physical terms. The defiling object becomes the subjective self. Expiation – that is, reconciliation between subject and object – can only be accomplished by the binding of the self by the self. The forces of evil that stain the soul must be enslaved, and the result is what Ricoeur calls the servile will.[27]

Before applying these concepts to the symbolism of cannibalism, I want to say something about variation in the nature of dialectical opposition, because such variation is also evident in the dialectical oppositions I propose. In a review of the nature of formal dialectical structure, Dunning defines four types of dialectical opposition: negation, reciprocation, paradox, and mediation. When the poles of the dialectic stand in a relationship of contradiction, the dialectic is one of negation. Either pole is defined by the negation of the other. Such oppositions, Dunning says, "appear in . . . the bipolarities of structuralist and semiotic analysis."[28] The second type of dialectic goes beyond mere contradiction, but does not really supersede it. In this dialectic there is a third moment in which a reciprocal relation between the opposite poles is affirmed, but in such a way as to preclude further development or a synthesis of the poles. The example of the dialectic of reciprocity Dunning gives is contractual relations. In the third dialectic, the dialectic of paradox, "a genuine unity is achieved, but one that accentuates rather than supersedes the contradiction between the two poles." A well-known example of such a dialectic is the Chalcedonian claim that Christ is one person in two distinct natures.[29]

Dunning calls the fourth type of dialectic "Hegel's dialectic of

35

mediation." Here the poles of opposition are in more than a reciprocal stalemate. Mediation is a union of the terms of opposition

in which a third step takes the opposites up into itself as aspects or mo-
ments within a new reality. In this process, each pole loses its negative
character in relation to the other, and is thereby fulfilled in its true nature
as positively related to the other. Most important, the new third [term]
can now embark upon its own course, for it is a new entity which will
in turn find itself in a new contradiction. Thus a dialectic of mediation
never stops, never allows any dichotomy to reign supreme; its unities
always lead to new, more complex, dualities, until the entire process of a
particular idea is complete . . . a dialectic of mediation will have a progressive, systematic character, for it aims at representing the totality of
this process.[30]

The dialectical structure of the symbols of cannibalism

The subject–object polarities motivating cannibal practice illustrate
the several types of dialectical opposition outlined above. With respect to the polarity of subject and object, an example is seen in
the notion that the bodily substances of the corpse consumed in
the cannibal meal are endowed with a significance that derives
from its status in life as the social other, either as enemy or revered
compatriot. The flesh or bone marrow is a tangible conduit of
social and psychological attributes that constitute the subject by
either affirming or negating the relationships that join or separate
the subject vis-à-vis the other. Thus, parts of the body may be
consumed to imbibe the characteristics or the fertile force of the
other; or, consumption may break down and destroy characteristics of the other in the self. In either case a self is made – either by
synthesizing the other as part of the self or by negating the other
in the self. The self-other polarity takes different forms depending
on the cultural patterning of cannibal practice.

The subject–object polarities that I abstract from the case studies
listed in Table 6 and describe in more detail in the following chapters are summarized below. I suggest that the oppositions created
by these polarities predicate or "give rise to" cannibal practice in
the same way that Ricoeur suggests that "symbols give rise to
thought" in his discussion of the symbolism of evil.[31] The deline-
ation of the following oppositions is based solely on the case studies listed in Table 6.

The first polarity predicates cannibalism by a physical theory of being in which social personhood is constituted by the ebb and flow of psychobiological substances in and out of the body during the life cycle. The key ontological symbol in these cases is the female body.[32] The source of biological life is believed to reside in the female body, and, because biology is inseparable from the social, until differentiated by food rules, the female body is also the source of social life. Human life, social regeneration, and the perpetuity of the ancestral repository of life force are regarded as being dependent on the organized flow of substances that originate with the parental contribution to the fetus and end with their being deposited in the bodies of the living through acts of mortuary cannibalism while the bones are recycled to the ancestral repository of life force.

The primary opposition observable in this polarity is between biology and culture. Marriott refers to this opposition in his discussion of the characterization of persons in South Asia. He points out that persons are not thought to be "individual," that is, "indivisible bounded units," such as the units we identify with personhood in Western thought. Instead persons are thought to be "dividual," or divisible from a primordial, monistic origin: "To exist, dividual Persons absorb heterogeneous material influences." They also transmit from themselves particles of their own coded substances that reproduce in others something of the nature of the persons in whom they have originated. Transfers of bodily substance-codes occur in many different kinds of transactions, including parentage, marriage, trade, and interpersonal contact. These substances can also be transmitted through food exchanges.[33]

The dialectic of biology and culture is similar to the dialectic of subject and object in Ricoeur's discussion of defilement. The bodily substances conveyed by means of food through eating in the dialectic of culture and biology provide an externalized map for the internal experience of good and evil. This is similar to Ricoeur's stage of defilement because self-consciousness is located in an external object. The negative encoding of female bodily substances (such as menstrual blood and fertile fluids) differentiate male from female. Self-consciousness and the consciousness of the social other are experienced in terms of the subject's dread of pollution by the bodily substances of others. The dread of pollution differentiates social categories in the formulation of food rules regarding who should eat what cooked or grown by whom. Purification involves removing negatively encoded bodily substances. The dialectic displayed here is clearly one of contradiction and negation.

Ethnographic examples of the first subject–object opposition are found in the next two chapters. The Hua and Bimin-Kuskusmin notions of being illustrate how the maternal body and its physiological processes provide metaphoric aids for the organization of social and psychological life. The maternal body is the unitary symbol from which the oppositions of social life are separated. Social and individual consciousness depend on ritually forcing the seeds of biological life into their dialectical opposites. Ontology is literally merged with physiology. Dividing socially encoded attributes from the physiologically encoded primordial unity is the focus of Bimin-Kuskusmin ritual and Hua food rules. Like the fetus that depends on intrauterine feeding, social reproduction depends on the transfer of the ancestral repository of life force from one generation to the next in mortuary cannibalism.

The material reality underlying the association of the female body with the source of life and pollution is suggested by the perception on the part of men that the female body is faster growing and more fertile than the male body. The faster-growing female body may be a product of a diet high in carbohydrates and low in protein.[34] The political reality at issue is the dominance–subordinance relationship between affinally related groups and male resistance to the perception of female biological power. Men control women in their effort to forge a male gender identity by eliminating the primordial maternal substances with which they were born. In-marrying wives are feared because they carry substances associated with men from enemy groups. Such divisions and oppositions are reflected and physically reproduced in mortuary cannibalism.

The second polarity opposes and merges humans and animals and human and animal flesh. This polarity projects a we/they dichotomy in which humans are both distinguished from, yet related to, animals. Animals are the reflexive other in the predication of humanness. There is a reciprocal relationship between the eater and the eaten. Just as animals are hunted, so are humans; whoever wants to get food must become food. The dialectic of animal and human is found in Algonkian, Beaver, and Kwakiutl beliefs about the origin of cannibalism. The poles of the dialectic are related not so

much through negation (as was true of the first opposition described) as through reciprocity between the poles.[35] What animals
give to humans (namely, their flesh) humans should return to animals. Since animals are the source of life for humans, animals
represent a powerful force that must be assuaged in ritual practice
at the same time that the force is incorporated for social ends. The
dialectic of animal and human is encompassed by a vaster dialectic
of the one and the many. Animals and humans are part of an ultimate source of being in which they are indistinguishable until differentiated by the masks of biological life. The participation in the
same source of being predicates the reciprocal relationship between animals and humans in biological and social life. The merging of animal and human, represented at the level of the broader
cosmology, is seen in the relationship between the animal and human poles in an individual's lifetime. At puberty, individuals must
acquire an animal-spirit-friend who confers power on the individual. The incorporation of the animal-spirit-friend produces a third
term in which the human being becomes one with two natures. If
humans do not respect the other-than-human power of their com-
patriots, the latter are in danger of being dominated by their
animal-spirit power and cannibalizing other humans. Such a conceptual schema enforces contractual relationships between humans.

Several examples of this dialectic are presented. One is the Windigo monster of the Algonkians of North America, in which the
individual is transformed into a superhuman, man-eating giant
possessed of a heart of ice owing to a breakdown in reciprocal
relationships, as may happen during winter famines. Another example comes from the Beaver of North America. Their Wechuge
monster dominates the individual whose animal-spirit-friend has
been improperly treated by another (usually an outsider). The
monster first consumes the individual whose animal-spirit-friend
has received this treatment and then turns to consuming others. In
both of these examples the individual is infected by an outer
power. Both the infection and the symbolism of reconciliation,
which requires ridding the individual of the dangerous power, re-
mind us of defilement. The third example, from the Kwakiutl,
illustrates the polarization of and the reciprocity between animal
and human in the socialization process as well as a final synthesis
of the animal-human poles, which occurs in conjunction with

39

adult maturation and the internalization of responsibility. (See the discussion of sin and guilt in the section "Transformations in the chartering of cannibal practice.")

The material reality associated with this polarity is, first, the reliance upon animals for food (a reliance that predated the Kwakiutl dependence on fish) and, second, the extreme circumstances of the winter months when hunger is a reality. Winter is the time when concern with cannibalism is exhibited in these three societies. These cases also indicate that the concern with cannibalism is closely tied to a breakdown in social relations and in the reciprocal patterns that normally characterize the exchange of food. In each of these cases, cannibalism symbolizes both power and evil. Cannibalism is part of the construction of social and individual power as well as the agent for the destruction of the social order in the consumption of the social body.

In another example of the dialectic of reciprocity we find *chaos opposed to order, individual desire to social expectations, id to superego.* This dialectic is similar to the dialectic of animal and human. The difference is that the object is now defined not so much in terms of animals or animal-spirit-power as it is in terms of the dictates of the dream-soul. The dream-soul, however, as the case of the Iroquois will show, is ultimately derived from the vision-quest in the same way that the animal-spirit-friend is acquired. This dialectic formulates the nature of internal and external destructive forces in such a way that it enables people to regulate destructive aggression and dominate chaos at the same time that they derive power from both. This polarity is evident in the Iroquoian response to dreams that express an overwhelming need to satisfy the unconscious – to feed it, nurture it, and give in to its demands in exchange for the use of its power. The dialectic of chaos and order is also seen in Aztec and Fijian cannibalism. In these societies, however, the dialectic does not predicate individual consciousness in terms of subject and object, but in terms of a mythical charter for society in which chaos is the condition anterior to order and must be repeated in the regular construction of order. (The mythical chartering of cannibal practice is discussed later in this chapter.)

The material reality associated with these cases (at least during the time that the information on them was recorded) concerns the circumstances that made death a primary concern as well as the primary medium for expressing psychological states and phrasing social relations. Why the Fijians made death a way of life is not clear from the available material. Perhaps the competition with Europeans enhanced the competition among island groups. As for the Iroquois (especially the Huron) and the Aztec, the magnitude of the sacrificial and torture complex was known to have increased sharply in response to drought, famine, and the competition among Indian groups in the face of the European expansion. In all three cases, however, cannibalism was an ancient part of the ritual repertoire.

The ritual order of the Navajo is marked by the absence of symbols reflecting physiological functioning. *The core opposition observable in Navajo ontology is between the wind-soul and the individual.* This wind-soul is similar to the dream-soul just mentioned but is defined differently. For example, the Navajo do not project bodily processes onto the cosmos; rather, they project cosmic processes onto the body. Their metaphysical definition of the interaction between the individual and universal forces is seen in their thought and ceremony. In this case, the absence of ritual cannibalism is traceable to the symbolic opposition of wind-soul and human behavior and the logic that relates them in the predication of physical and social being. The Navajo construction of being differs from that of the groups just discussed in that it emphasizes synthesizing rather than negating or dominating antithetical forces. Navajo ritual emphasizes the integration rather than the celebration of opposing forces. This emphasis can be compared to the Kwakiutl ritual of the Cannibal Dance in which the cannibalistic desires of humans are celebrated before they are tamed and integrated into the personality. I suggest that the absence of ritual cannibalism among the Navajo is traceable to their key symbols of being as well as to their cultural elaboration of the dialectic of mediation, which in both ritual and mythical thought is reflected in action stressing accommodation and integration.

The mythical chartering and transformation of cannibal practice

The preceding section concentrated on the *key symbols* and oppositions generating cannibal practice. It is important to note that these symbols may be taken up in the language of myth, which in some cases charters cannibal practice and in others transforms it. Ricoeur presents four myths of evil that he says display three fundamental characteristics: They confer concrete universality upon human experience by means of archetypal personages; they contain a narrative of an ideal history oriented from a beginning toward an end; and they describe a transition from an essential nature to an alienated history.[36] He compares the myths of evil to the primary symbols of evil, pointing out that whereas the primary symbols of evil place fault in a totality of meaning that "is not perceived, not experienced, but signified, aimed at, conjured up," in the drama of myth the "experience of fault [is placed] into relation with the totality of meaning." Thus, the language of the confession of sins "is only a fragment of a vaster language that indicates mythically the origin and the end of fault, and the totality in which it arose."[37] Elsewhere Ricoeur emphasizes that in myth humans explore their "relationship to the world, to other beings, and to being as well."[38] In addition to reflecting existential realities, he notes further, myths record conflicts and are outlines of their solution.[39] These several functions of myth are crucial to certain aspects of the analysis presented in this book.

According to Dunning, the dialectical structure implicit in Ricoeur's discussion of the four myths of evil corresponds to the oppositions established in his discussion of the primary symbols of evil. The focus of the dialectic, however, is on creation and salvation. The first of the four myths Ricoeur discusses is the myth of primordial chaos (as exemplified in the Babylonian flood myth in the Gilgamesh epic and the Sumero-Akkadian theogonic myth), which merges creation and salvation just as subject and object were merged in defilement. Evil is not the result of human actions or motivations but a fact of the nature of existence. Evil is the chaos that is forever encroaching upon order: "Chaos is anterior to order and the principle of evil is primordial, coextensive with the generation of the divine."[40] Redemption from evil is not a "history of salvation distinct from the drama of creation."[41] Salvation is accomplished by the creation of order out of chaos, a deed performed continually both by the gods and by humans in their ritual activities. In this view, violence and the struggle for power are part of the scheme of things. In ritual, the original disorder depicted in myth is reproduced as a means of regenerating the social order. It is only by "disorder that disorder is overcome: [I]t is by violence that the youngest of the gods establishes order. Thus the principle of evil is twice designated: as the chaos anterior to order, and as the struggle by which chaos is overcome. . . . [B]y War and Murder . . . the original Enemy is finally vanquished."[42] Humans bear no subjective responsibility for evil; theirs is an objective responsibility carried out in the action of ritual.

The Iroquoian creation myth, which is also about the beginning of good and evil, presents a model of and for the Iroquoian response to inner experience. The myth begins with the merging of good and evil in a unitary symbol (again the female body) and ends with their splitting and the establishment of guidelines for the regulation of evil. Evil is regulated by giving in to its mythical manifestation just as dreams are given in to, that is, in a controlled manner. This solution is necessary because power to control adversity is perceived as emanating from the embodiment of evil. In Iroquoian myth, ritual, and dream theory disorder is overcome by acting on its demands in a controlled ritual setting.

The Fijian myth entitled "How the Fijians First Became Cannibals," is, according to Sahlins, a myth about the origin of culture. Structurally this myth also corresponds to Ricoeur's myth of primordial chaos. The merging of opposites in this myth is seen in the symbol of the primal horde controlled by the primal father. The play of unrestricted sexual and cannibalistic passion both within and outside the boundaries of the primal horde represents the chaos that the myth dramatizes. The hero comes as a terrible outside cannibal to a place where endocannibalism and incest reign. The chaos represented by these evils is that they imply the mutual extinction of the primal father and the stranger-hero, the source of fecundity. Redemption from chaos is accomplished by the social contract with its substitutive satisfactions and its resolution of the power struggle between the native chief and the hero. The social contract does not abolish such evils as endocannibalism; it simply regulates it by substituting endo- for exocannibalism.

Aztec cosmogony and associated ritual also merge good and evil in the figure of the primal mother. The origin myth of the Aztec is structurally analogous to Ricoeur's myth of primordial chaos. The Aztec sacrificial rites repeat the legendary sacrifices that brought this world into its present form from a state of chaos. In these rites, human hunger achieves cosmic status as hungry gods are fed the hearts of sacrificial victims and the blood of human sacrifice is splashed on idols to nourish them. Here we see that the vital essence encoded by human flesh and blood is exchanged between humans and the divine.

The Navajo and Kwakiutl paradigmatic myths of creation are reminiscent of the myth of the exiled soul saved through knowledge described by Ricoeur. These myths differ from the Aztec and Fijian myths in their recognition of fault and evil as a violated relationship. Here the drama of creation is distinguished from the history of salvation. Creation is objective and the order of salvation is subjective in that the rites of reconciliation attempt to achieve certain states in the subject. For the Navajo, the goal of ritual action is to bring the subject back into harmony with creation and with the universe; for the Kwakiutl, the goal is to transform inner bodily instincts that are destructive of social bonding. The Kwakiutl view cannibalism as an instinct harbored by humans; for them it is a major metaphor connoting the positive and negative dimensions of power. In the Cannibal Dance, cannibalism is expressed and then controlled in communal performance. This ritual provides an example of a people taking responsibility for their own actions by admitting them. Finally, there are a group of myths discussed in Chapter 9 that charter the end of cannibal practice.

The role of desire, identification, and emotional ambivalence in cannibal practice

In this and the next section I turn to the psychological mechanisms by which cannibal practice is predicated and changed. Jung defines a symbol as "the psychological mechanism that transforms energy."[43] By energy he means psychic energy or libido, a concept he defines in broader terms than did Freud, to mean "the intensity of a psychic process, its psychological value," "which is able to communicate itself to any field of activity whatsoever, be it power, hunger, hatred, sexuality, or religion, without ever being a specific instinct."[44] The ontological symbols and mythic images discussed earlier – for example, the primal mother, the primal horde led by the primal father, the cosmic one from which all being is derived, the androgynous ancestral figure – transform psychic intensities into specific content. These are key ontological symbols because they summarize and collapse culturally constituted dimensions of being. The dialectic established between the self and the other in the fragmentation of these symbols formulate the self through the processes of identification and individuation in the development of self-consciousness.

Ricoeur compares the psychoanalytic concept of identification with the Hegelian dialectic of the development of self-consciousness. "What psychoanalysis recognizes under the name of identification," Ricoeur says, "is simply the shadow, projected onto the plane of an economics of instincts, of a process of consciousness to consciousness."[45] Between the analytic relationship and the latter process

there is a remarkable structural homology. The entire analytic relation can be reinterpreted as a dialectic of consciousness, rising from life to self-consciousness, from the satisfaction of desire to the recognition of the other consciousness. As the decisive episode of the transference teaches us, insight or the process of becoming conscious not only entails another consciousness, the analyst's, but contains a phase of struggle reminiscent of the struggle for recognition. The process is an unequal relation in which the patient, like the slave or bondsman of the Hegelian dialectic, sees the other consciousness by turns as the essential and as the unessential; the patient likewise has his truth at first in the other, before becoming the master through a work comparable to the work of the slave, the work of the analysis. One of the signs that the analysis is ended is precisely the attainment of the equality of the two consciousnesses. Then the patient is no longer alienated, no longer another: he has become a self, he has become himself.[46]

Cannibalism is part of the drama of becoming a self and like the dramas uncovered by psychoanalysis, the drama of cannibalism begins with the mother, or some other entity symbolizing the whole, and follows a path that leads from the satisfaction of desire to the recognition of another consciousness through which the self comes to know the self. The stage of satisfaction (in which desire rules) and the stage of recognition (in which self-consciousness first becomes established) are early stages in the Hegelian dialectic of the achieving of consciousness. These stages, which are analogous to early stages in psychosexual development posited by Freud, are reminiscent of certain patterns seen in rituals of cannibalism. The first stage Hegel calls the "pure ego." According to Ricoeur, "the pure ego is the naïve self-consciousness that thinks it immediately attains itself *in the suppression or sublation of the object,*

45

in the direct consumption of the object" (emphasis mine).[47] In Hegel's words, self-consciousness in this stage

> is certain of itself only through sublating this other, which is presented to self-consciousness as an independent life; self-consciousness is *desire*. Convinced of the nothingness of this other, it affirms this nothingness to be *for itself* the truth of this other, negates the independent object, and thereby acquires the certainty of its own self, as *true* certainty, a certainty which it has become aware of in *objective form*.[48]

Called the stage of desire, the suppression of the object in the predication of the self is reminiscent of the first subject-object polarity described earlier, in which self-consciousness is experienced in terms of the subject's dread of pollution by the bodily substances of others. Individual and social identity is predicated by removing negatively encoded physical substances and consuming positively encoded substances including the vital essence carried by the corpse of the newly dead. This image of the flow of biological substances among individuals, which includes the flow of vital essence carried by human flesh from one generation to the next, is suggestive of intrauterine feeding. This and the powers attached to maternal fertile substances, which are more feared than any other substance, projects an image of a dialectic of a weak ego and an overpowerful maternal figure.

Examples of these images are the Hua primal body; the primal mother of the Gimi, the Bimin-Kuskusmin, Iroquois, and Aztec; the cannibal monster of the Kwakiutl; and the mythic primal family of the Fijians. These metaphors join all opposites and satisfy all needs; they represent the mythical image of the wellspring of society. Associated with these mythical images in each case is a force that breaks the image apart by violating its self-sustaining integrity. The force may be hunger, a sense of cosmic depletion, incest, grief, or rage – something that disrupts the unity and establishes in action the dialectical process by which subject and object are ritually opposed in the predication of self and society. In each case the image of the self-sustaining wholeness is opposed by a view of the self in infantile terms – an opposition reminiscent of the patient who at the beginning of analysis is merged with the analyst and has no identity of his or her own.

Neumann, a Jungian, claims that images of merging with the mother produce an ontology that focuses the "systole" and "diastole" of human existence in the functions of the digestive tract.[49] Neumann distinguishes two primal mother paradigms. The first is called the "maternal uroboros" and the second is the "great mother." The maternal uroboros symbolizes the merging of psychological processes with physical and alimentary incorporation by the maternal figure.[50] It corresponds with Freud's oral, "cannibalistic" phase in the psychosexual stages of development, in which sexual activity is not separated from the ingestion of food. This symbol is analogous to the female body in my discussion of the opposition of biology and culture. Although the maternal uroboros has no human form, the great mother symbol has human form but may retain the uroboric character in which all opposites are joined.[51]

The maternal uroboros is present in the Hua mythic symbol of the primal body and the Kwakiutl mythic and ritual symbol of the cannibal monster. Examples of the great mother are seen in the Gimi parthenogenetic female, the Bimin-Kuskusmin androgynous ancestress, the Iroquois mother of the good and evil twins, and the Aztec dual deity. In each example, destructive psychic energy is expressed in ritual acts centering on differentiating physically embodied psychological states from a primordial unity. I suggest that these are acts of individuation, of separating the energy of the nascent ego from the inchoateness of unchanneled psychic energy.[52]

If oral incorporation and the connection with the maternal are major themes, so are the themes associated with male sexual and physical aggression. Rituals described in conjunction with Goodenough Islander, Aztec, Fijian, and Iroquoian cannibalism pit men against one another in sadomasochistic roles in which the victim plays the passive role and the warrior the active. Here the satisfaction of desire is seen in the killing, mutilation, dismemberment, or burning of the victim before an audience of men in order to alleviate the warriors' rage and to feed the voracious appetites of the gods or offer procreative energy to the gods. Often these acts center on the phallus, the bodily manifestation of male energy and procreation. The Fijian war club is the mark of the phallus and the manslayer its living embodiment. A man whose club was still unstained with blood at death was doomed to pound human excrement with his dishonored weapon in the afterworld. Watched by senior men, Iroquoian warriors burned victims in their "fundament" with a firebrand in an atmosphere of unrestricted sensuous sadism. The epithet applied to the victim of the Aztec gladiatorial sacrifice was the name of a god that may have meant "he with a phallus." After the victim's heart was torn from his body, his skin was donned by men who took the name of the god impersonated by the victim. Identification in this case is between warrior, victim, and the god to whom the victim's heart is dedicated. The instrument of aggression here appears to be the phallus, and castration, projected onto the victim, is the means for controlling aggression and channeling its energy.

The phallicism of such warfare rituals merges body, mind, and emotions. According to Neumann, this kind of phallicism characterizes the deities who are companions of the great mother.[53] Being merged with the physical, phallic masculinity represents uroboric merging with the maternal uroboros and as such represents the infantile male ego not fully separated from the overpowering pull of the satisfaction of all desire experienced in the early stages of psychosexual development.

In rituals of phallic masculinity, individuation is achieved first in the identification between captor and captive and then in the ritual carving of the victim's body, which, Neumann suggests, symbolically disassociates the ego from its uroboric union with the mother. Self-consciousness occurs by virtue of the captive's submission and the captor's mastery, a process similar to the second stage in Hegel's dialectic of achieving self-consciousness, the dialectic of lordship and bondage. Analyzing this dialectic, Findlay says,

Self-consciousness exists in and for itself inasmuch, and only inasmuch, as it exists in and for itself for another, i.e. inasmuch as it is *acknowledged*. . . . Self-consciousness lives outside of itself in another self-consciousness, in which it at once loses and also finds itself. . . . Self-consciousness is intrinsically set to eliminate this alien self-hood, but, in being so set, it is both set to eliminate the other in order to achieve its own self-certainty, and also to eliminate itself in the process, since it is itself that other. This dual elimination involves, however, a return to self, since what is eliminated is its own other-being, while at the same time permits the other to be other, since it removes its *own* being from the other. The process just outlined . . . is not, however, carried out solely by one consciousness on the other, but by both consciousnesses on each other . . . each in fact demands that the other should treat it just as it treats the other.[54]

Applying this logic to Iroquoian torture, which provides a pro-totypical example of many torture rites, we see that the captor is recognized by the victim as his master. The victim who is brave and courageous in torture is recognized by the master, who marks the courage of the victim by consuming his flesh or drinking his blood. The captor actually enslaves himself, because he makes himself dependent on the victim for his own existence as master. Additionally, he knows that the victim's kinsmen will retaliate and that he, too, may be reduced to victim. The dialectic of captive and victim is one in which both poles of the opposition define the other in terms of their mutual negation. Thus, the victim may cry out during torture: "Ah! You will kill me, you will burn me. But also you must know that I have killed and burned many of your people. If you eat me, I have the consolation of having also eaten several of your nation. Do then what you will; I have uncles, I have nephews, brothers and cousins, who will well avenge my death, and who will make you suffer more torments than you know how to invent against me."[55] In death the victim is defined as a great man, a kind of lordship that transcends that of the torturers who consume the victim's flesh in recognition of his bravery. This switching of roles is complete when the torturers (or their com-patriots) become the victims in the next round of torture rituals. The process of reciprocal vengeance is a way of life for men whose gender identity is formulated in terms of lordship and bondage.

Torture rituals bring to mind Freud's discussion of the role of aggression in predicating social interaction. Because the inclina-tion to aggression is primal – "an original, self-subsisting instinc-tual disposition in man" – Freud says that this instinct is given a social outlet in the form of hostility toward outsiders.[56] "It is al-ways possible to bind together a considerable number of people in love, so long as there are other people left over to receive the man-ifestations of their aggressiveness."[57] Freud postulated that the phenomenon of life reflects the concurrent or mutually opposing action of two instincts: Eros and the death instinct. Eros is the instinct that binds people together; the death instinct, from which aggression is derived, tears them apart.[58] Freud claimed that emo-tional ambivalence – "the simultaneous existence of love and hate towards the same object" due to the concurrent action of the two instincts – is a fundamental phenomenon of emotional life and "lies at the root of many important cultural institutions."[59]

Following Freud, Sagan suggests that emotional ambivalence plays the key role in acts of cannibalism. He says that cannibalism "deals with the basic ambivalent nature of all aggression, and of oral aggression in particular. It does so first, by directing aggression outward away from the tribe and the family and, second, by containing within it some aspect of that affection present in all aggression."[60] Mortuary cannibalism also exhibits emotional ambivalence:

> The undeveloped imagination of the cannibal does not deal very adequately with metaphorical usage. He is compelled to take the urge for oral incorporation literally. He eats the person who, by dying, has abandoned him. This act of literal oral incorporation has an affectionate and an aggressive dimension. As with all of us, the aggressive aspects of the situation are not conscious with the cannibal; he gives voice only to the affectionate feelings involved in this action.[61]

Emotional ambivalence is evident in many of the rituals described in the following chapters. For example, sexual desire, love, hate, and aggression are explicitly linked in the orgiastic, sometimes caressing, torture and sensuous cutting up of the Iroquoian torture victim, who is adopted as a parent or child. However, as should now be clear, emotional ambivalence does not motivate cannibalism as much as the underlying ontology that makes eating human flesh a channel for the predication of social and individual identity as well as the means for controlling innate aggression.

The body in cannibalism can be likened to the alchemist's *vas* in which certain ingredients were mixed to achieve desired states in the experimenter. Sagan's approach does not help explicate the rigid social rules applied in mortuary cannibalism and followed in torture rituals. The careful staging of the torture, which includes a set role that is willingly followed by the captive, suggests that more than the ambivalent nature of all aggression is being expressed. The social rules observed in these cases suggest that what is at stake is the simultaneous expression and repression of basic instincts as cultural and social forms are generated and reproduced. Although provocative and useful for illuminating some of the dimensions of desire in the expression of cannibalism, Sagan's ar-

gument is ultimately limited by the emphasis on emotional ambivalence.

Transformations in the chartering of cannibal practice

Once constituted, the key symbols and mythic images of an
ethno-ontology are usually retained in the course of history. However, in response to particular economic, social, or ecological exigencies, the practice of cannibalism predicated by these symbols
may be *projected, substituted, or synthesized* in the interest of the social order. This suggestion is prompted by the observation that the
key symbols of cannibalism are often retained even when the actual practice is abolished or projected outwardly.

Projection of primal cannibalistic urges is evident in the Aztec,
Fijian, and Iroquoian images of divine hunger. Such a projection
provides a means for ritually regulating, hence controlling, endo-
cannibalistic urges that might destroy a social group. In projection, it is the external "other" – enemies or the gods – who is the
cannibal, not the internal "we." In ritual expression, the internal
"we" indulge in cannibalism to communicate with and feed the
gods in pursuit of group goals that use the body as a model for the
destruction of evil and the construction of good.

Projection of cannibalistic urges is also evident when evil is projected outwardly on the ethnic landscape. Those who are beyond
social boundaries, that is, men and women of enemy groups, are
cannibals and must be tortured and eaten to compensate for the
similar fate of one's own or to gain ascendency in the struggle to
channel fertility through the generations. This form of projection
predicates dominance-subordinance relationships between groups
in which one group's power and dominance are affirmed by consuming and digesting the power harbored by the flesh of the
enemy. This pattern also illustrates the projection of the theory of
the flow of substances to the group level. Vital essence is exchanged between groups in the torture and cannibalization of the
enemy, as seen in Iroquoian torture rituals and in other rituals described in the following chapters.

If the key symbols of cannibalism constitute a theory of being,
as I suggested earlier, it is important to ask how this theory is
exploited when external events threaten a group's survival. The
chronic warfare in which the Iroquois were involved during the

seventeenth century, for example, became a fight for survival in which the dialectic of chaos and order, individual desires, and social expectations were enacted on the bodies of captives. The endemic capture of victims for torture and cannibalism or adoption, as already mentioned, suggests an attempt to define self and regenerate society by dominating the social other during a period of increasing social anomie.

In addition to *projection,* we can see the processes of *substitution* or the *synthesis* of cannibalistic urges in several case studies. Substitution is evident in the Melpa fear of cannibalism, which can be interpreted as an exploitation of the primary symbols of being by men who resolve the contradiction between mortuary cannibalism and expanding exchange ties by substituting pig for human flesh.[62] The prohibition against cannibalism is consistent with the Melpa stress on proliferating exchange ties, and on facing outward to an expanding network. The Melpa fear cannibalism because it represents greed for consumption and interferes with the ethic of pig production for exchange.[63] The Melpa equation of human and pig flesh in mortuary rites reverts to the externalization of consciousness, but there is a structural transformation in the substitution of pig for human flesh. This substitution is accompanied by a birth rite that breaks the connection between mother and child and substitutes a connection between the child and the clan territory. This is accomplished by burying the child's navel string and its mother's placenta together in a spot where a cordyline plant or a banana tree is planted to symbolize the growth of the child. "The navel string," Strathern says, "which once connected the child to the mother in her womb, now connects it to the earth, and this link is represented by the cordyline."[64] Bloch and Parry suggest that this rite replaces women by clan territory.[65] I suggest that this rite breaks the dialectic that merges mother and child by synthesizing the poles of social and biological opposition in the symbol of the cordyline plant, which represents a polar term in a new opposition posing one clan territory against another in a dialectic of exchange. Strathern's discussion suggests further that the transformation from the physical expression of cannibalism to its internalization as a symbol of negated human relations may be part of a historical process connected with the greater intensification of agriculture, at least among the Melpa.[66]

The Melpa system of substitution and of preserving outwardly oriented social relationships includes some aspects of the second primary symbol in Ricoeur's typology of evil. In sin, evil goes beyond objective pollution and involves the transgression of some objective demand. Here the focus is not so much on harmful substances as on violated relationships. The concern now is with the ethics of social relationships rather than with the flow of power between subject and object. Evil is connected not so much with an externalized object as it is with the violation of reciprocity. Evil does not infect the individual, as in the symbolism of defilement; rather, evil negates social relationships. The Melpa locate evil within the individual by representing cannibalism as greed for consumption and other forms of antisocial behavior.

Finally, the process of *synthesis* (or mediation) is seen in the case of the Kwakiutl Cannibal Dance in which cannibalistic urges are treated as a power that must be integrated into the personality of the individual. By integrating these urges, the individual synthesizes (in the Hegelian sense of the concept *Aufheben,* meaning that both terms are taken up into a third term and preserved in the new whole) the animal-human opposition within the personality. The process of synthesis is reminiscent of the third symbol in Ricoeur's typology, guilt. Here consciousness realizes that the defiling object is the subjective self. In this stage the object of consciousness and the subject of consciousness are seen to be the same self. This stage represents the reconciliation and synthesis within the self of the primary symbols of evil. Thus, guilt takes "both defilement and sin up into itself."[67]

Another example of guilt is suggested by the Navajo conception of individual fault in sickness. The symbols of defilement and sin are evident in the Navajo notion that the sick individual has been infected by a harmful wind-soul or by the witchcraft of someone else, which causes the individual to experience a ruptured relationship with cosmic forces. Reconciliation with these forces is not accomplished by external acts of expiation (as Ricoeur argues is true of sin-consciousness), but by working on the internal state of the patient. The rituals that restore wholeness to the patient do so by introjecting cosmic wholeness onto the patient through the sandpainting that physically and spatially reintegrates the individual in the universe. Although the sandpainting retains the element of the physical and the external, only the meaning, not the substance, is internalized by the patient. Kwakiutl and Navajo ritual

53

acts move the initiate or the patient from a state of inferiority vis-à-vis the ritual other to a state of accommodation and integration. In these cases the development of self-consciousness reaches a state of equality vis-à-vis the other, and we see the "attainment of the equality of the two consciousnesses," which characterizes the end of a successful analysis when "the patient is no longer alienated, no longer another: he has become a self, he has become himself."[68]

The Navajo myth of emergence, in particular, represents a dynamic progression of recurring syntheses in which the ego moves from a position of inferiority and slavehood to one of equality and mutuality vis-à-vis the other. In this progression, the social usefulness of domination and aggression is transformed, and family or sexual ties are the basis for social bonding. Such a transformation is also suggested in the Trobriand myths analyzed in Chapter 9. These cases illustrate the operation of Eros separated from the derivatives of the death instinct. Here the reconciliation of emotional ambivalence is not the basis for the development of culture. The social contract is modeled on Eros and is expressed, in the case of the Navajo, in the tie between mother and child, or, in the case of the Trobriands, in the tie between potential marriage partners trying to attract one another.

Conclusion

In this chapter I have outlined the analytic framework that structures my reading of the case studies presented in the following chapters. Cannibalism can be analytically distinguished from the act itself and the key symbols and oppositions that formulate its expression in a ritual context. As a cultural system, ritual cannibalism is part of a system of symbols that predicates individual and social consciousness and regulates as it formulates inchoate human desire. The ritual symbols of cannibalism enact in the flesh a model *of* and *for* reality at the same time that grief, rage, or anxieties about social and cosmic continuity are allayed by offering the corporeal in the interest of establishing the eternal. Underlying the specific performance of cannibal ritual is a generic human concern for perpetuating life beyond the limits of individual life histories.

In the following chapters I describe a variety of rituals and beliefs involving cannibalism. The rites are conducted in explicit recognition of their social import: Human fertility is assured and thereby the continuation of social life; or, hungry gods are fed as a condition of continued social and cosmic existence; or men display masculinity and achieve the perquisites of adult warrior status; or a group displays its ferocity and hence its dominance to other groups; or, the categories of social exchange are activated and reaffirmed, and, so on. The basic psychological mechanism that seems to be involved here is individuating by projecting inner feelings onto outer persons where the feelings can be clarified and given social form. Although the effects of hunger are sometimes explicitly recognized as motivating forces, these effects are usually secondary to concerns about the replacement of personnel or about transmitting psychobiological substances from the dead to the living or from humans to the gods.

As for the relationship between cannibalism and hunger or other sources of stress, many societies can be observed in which hunger is severe or there is occasional famine but cannibalism is absent (see discussion in Chapters 9 and 10). In my argument, ontological considerations take precedence over the utilitarian concerns given priority in the materialist point of view. I suggest that we must first look at the key symbols that predicate being. These symbols are paradigm forming in that they develop according to the postulates by which self is related to the other. The postulates predicating psychobiological being by means of the exchange of physiologically encoded substances lead to cannibalism as do postulates that merge animal with human flesh or those that predicate human reality in terms of the expression of human desire. Postulates that construct biological reality in terms of metaphysical entities or in terms of a reciprocal relationship between subject and object are not likely to be associated with cannibalism, as cannibalism in these cases would not be appropriate for social and individual regeneration. Additionally, an ethos that emphasizes accommodation and integration with cosmic or social forces, as opposed to the domination and control of those forces, finds in cannibalism a ready symbol of evil.

The symbols that give rise to a cannibalistic consciousness

3 · The mysteries of the body: Hua and Gimi mortuary cannibalism

The inside of the body is the temple, the place where the awesome powers reside; internal body states are imagined in intense detail. . . . Any body is awesome, but the female body, possessor of the mystery of fertility and nurture, is the most awesome. In this religion of the body the female body plays the star role.[1]

The logic of Hua mortuary cannibalism is the main subject of this chapter. This logic provides the basis for my analysis of Gimi mortuary cannibalism and Melpa mortuary practices in which pig flesh is substituted for human flesh. These examples establish the relevance of maternal and intrauterine imagery for comprehending the meaning of cannibal practice. I suggest that the primordial pull of the maternal, the unitary symbol from which all opposites emanate, establishes the moods and motivations that make Hua and Gimi cannibalism inevitable. For both groups, cannibalism is part of a system of symbols by means of which individual and social identity are defined and biological and social reproduction ensured.

The concerns evident in Hua ontology may be tied to protein deficiency and the delayed rates of growth, relative to females, that this deficiency produces in males. The indivisibility of mother and child is also evident in Gimi ontology; however, male control of pig flesh extricates men from the cycle of cannibalism displayed by women alone. Both societies are located in the sparsely populated fringe region of the New Guinea Highlands where large herds of domestic pigs are absent. Both societies also exhibit the marriage exchange system that Strathern (see Chapter 1) associates with the practice of cannibalism. Strathern's comparison of the Melpa, who do not practice cannibalism, with the Gimi illustrates other concomitants of cannibalism. For example, Melpa birth rituals break the connection between mother and child in establishing a ritual identity between the individual and the clan territory, while dividing from the female remains a central ritual preoccupation throughout the Hua and Gimi male life cycle.

Two patterns in this material constitute the social order. In the first, the physical is the idiom for the social. The encoding of psychological characteristics and social bonding via the exchange of substances and food helps make sense of the practice of mortuary cannibalism. In this schema social relationships are regulated through the regulation of food consumption so as to control the exchange of positive and negative substances between humans. In the second pattern, the exchange of goods is the idiom for the social. Psychological and social characteristics are encoded and regulated by reference to rules of consumption and exchange of goods. In this schema mortuary cannibalism negates the rules of consumption and exchange. In either case, the patterning of exchange – exchange of substances in the first pattern and of goods in the second – provides the major idiom for regulating and defining social relationships.

Hua cannibalism: The body as a model for the social

"[T]he ultimate reality [for the Hua,]" Meigs says, "is not society but the mysteries of the body."[2] Hua "[s]ocial interdependence and cohesion are expressed through the reality and the metaphor of cannibalism."[3] Some 3,100 Hua, divided into various intermarrying social groups, live at an altitude of 6,050 feet in the Eastern Highlands Province of Papua, New Guinea. Today they are slash-and-burn agriculturalists. The sweet potato introduced some 350 years ago accounts for 90 percent of the dietary intake. The Hua have pig herds and although they consume large quantities of pork during exchange ceremonies, pork is a minor part of the diet. Despite the inadequate amount of protein in their diet, signs of malnutrition are relatively minor and infrequent. As is typical of a population with an imperfect diet, the Hua, particularly males, exhibit a slow rate of growth, delayed attainment of maturity, and marked decreases in body weight with aging. Despite the slow rate of growth, occasional occurrences of Kwashiorkor (which the Hua interpret as pregnancy when it occurs in men), and chronic respiratory disease, the Hua are described by their major ethnographer, Anna Meigs, as "not only extremely fit but very healthy."[4]

Meigs's ethnography offers an excellent description of the predication of the social via the physical. The Hua have been in contact with Europeans since 1954, when a government patrol post was established nearby. Much of Meigs's ethnographic account of the Hua draws on informants' memories of past belief and practice since many aspects of traditional culture, including cannibalism, were abandoned owing to the impact of Australian pacification. She conducted fieldwork in two Hua villages for periods of nine months each between 1971 and 1975. She went to the Hua expecting to work on divorce but changed her topic when she discovered that informants wanted to talk about food restrictions. The symbolic evaluation of food was a major preoccupation of the Hua, and Meigs discovered that questions about food provided the most natural approach to more subtle discussions of social and biological issues. On the basis of her work with most of the adult population in the two villages, Meigs concludes "with confidence" that her data on food rules "represent a social consensus on a cultural passion."[5]

The Hua image of the inchoate subject is focused on the human body. According to their story of the origin of life, the opening of bodily orifices brings the human being to life. In the story, Roko, one of the original Hua ancestors, is seeking to catch birds whose feathers are used as valuables in bride prices. He is also collecting nuts and salt, other important exchange items. In his travels he comes upon a round house that has no door and no openings, but that shows signs of inner life because smoke is rising from the roof.

Roko went up to the house and poked a hole through the thatch, peeked in, and called out, "Are you in here?"

The creature inside replied only, "Muuuuu."

Roko then asked, "Where is your door?"

And the creature again responded only with, "Muuuuu."

Roko circled the house, again looking for a door, but was unable to find one. He asked himself, "By what door does this creature come in and go out?"

Roko then went back to the hole he had poked through the thatch and called, "Hey, my cross-cousin, Kunei," to which again the creature responded only with a "Muuuuu."

At this Roko broke down the wall of the house and entered. And there he found an enormous creature. It had ears but these ears lacked openings. It had a mouth but it was sealed. It had eyes but they could not open. It had legs, and arms, and hands, but these had not been freed from the body.

Roko took a knife and cut open the mouth. And then he cut open the eyes [*fuke,* "caused them to burst"]. Then he cut free Kunei's legs and straightened them out for him.

Kunei then said, "My cross-cousin, what have you done to me?"

To which Roko replied, "I have made it happen to you. And now I will give you salt, and nuts, and ginger."

Kunei cooked these and ate them and his mind awakened.[6]

In this story the individual, Roko, is confronted with a glob of psychic energy that appears in the form of an undifferentiated human being locked in the house of his body. In this inchoate subject Roko first finds and then makes a self. The fact that the inchoate subject is a cross-cousin, the kin-type with whom ego can mate if of the opposite sex, or who will supply a mate, suggests that the inchoate subject of the story is the social "other." The glob of humanity, Kunei, resembles the Hua conception of the fetus prior to the formation of the head, orifices, and limbs. Kunei achieves biological and social identity through the opening of internal and external passages and through the act of exchange. The opening of Kunei's senses and of an entrance into the house containing him constitutes a primordial metaphor whereby consciousness is initiated, the mind awakened. The opening of the house brings an end to the life that focuses solely inwardly. Psychological energy is let out and social energy allowed in with the opening of the house – a metaphor, perhaps, for ending incest and endogamy. The social energy is symbolized by the exchange items given to the occupant of the house once his body has been prepared to receive these items. First the mouth is opened, and this act enables the creature to speak. Once the eyes are opened and the legs are straightened the creature receives exchange items and ginger. Only after Kunei eats the ginger does his mind awaken. The Hua attribute psychological and physical power to particular foods. Ginger, for example, has the power to open passages, particularly the passage through the ear to the brain.[7]

The Hua believe that passages provide the conduit for a physical force, a vital essence, considered to be the source of life, fertility, and growth. The vitality, endurance, sexual potency, and fertility of any animate object – be it plant, animal or human – is attributed to the number and size of its passages. Anything that is fast growing and fertile is credited with many passages, whereas a slow rate of growth and infertility are the result of having fewer and smaller passages. Males claim that because the lower body openings of women are much larger than theirs, the rate of women's growth is faster and their vitality is greater.[8]

The central mysteries for the Hua are those of the body, of life and death, of procreation and birth. Growth and aging, death and illness, the contrast between fertile female bodies and hard male bodies are processes and conditions the Hua dwell upon and explain in terms of a principle of vital essence called *nu*. It is a truism among the Hua that women are *korogo*, soft, juicy, fast growing, and fertile. Women are like *pitpit*, a fast-growing, rapidly reproducing edible grass that has a soft, wet interior. Men are *hakeri'a*, hard, dry, slow growing, and infertile. They are like the *kimi*, black palm, an extremely slow-growing, hardwood tree used in making bows.[9] The states of *korogo* and *hakeri'a* depend on varying proportions of *nu* and its solid counterpart *haugepa* in the body. Meigs calls the Hua idea of *nu* an "overarching central metaphor. . . . a theory of broad scope that attempts to explain, if not the whole world, then at least the biological and social aspects of life."[10]

Substances thought of as *nu* include sexual fluids, feces and urine, breath and body odors, sweat, body oil, hair, saliva, fingernails, and one's own flesh and blood.[11] Any biological liquid is *nu*: water, blood, urine, sap, and fat. Hair is nourished by liquid *nu* in the scalp, just as plants are nourished by the moisture (*nu*) in the ground. Breath is "mouth steam," its relation to liquid *nu* being analogous to the relationship between steam and water.[12] No matter what its form, "*nu* is conceived as the source of life, vitality, and fertility."[13]

Whatever can be eaten or otherwise ingested is a source of *nu*. Food transfers *nu* directly by virtue of the homeopathic relationship it has to some other source of *nu*. For example, male initiates may not eat foods that are dark on the interior because this darkness is alleged to resemble the interior of the female body, a source of pollution for males. In addition to having a homeopathic property, food bears a contagious and consubstantial social value. All food carries some of the *nu* and therefore some of the power of the persons who cultivated or prepared it for eating. The eater absorbs *nu* through contagion. Thus, a mature male may not eat leafy green vegetables picked by his real or classificatory wife or first-born child. Food may not only carry *nu,* but may be congealed *nu.* Like blood, breath, hair, sweat, fingernails, feces, urine, foot-prints, and shadows, food is viewed as an effusion of the body, particularly of its labor. The consubstantial social value of food is evidenced by the prohibition against mature males eating pigs raised by, wild animals shot by, or certain garden products pro-duced by his real or classificatory wife, his first-born child, or his agemates.[14] These prohibitions mark ambivalent and potentially hostile social relationships that are objectified and thereby con-trolled through the rules for the proper ingestion of *nu.*

All aspects of the physical life cycle from birth to death are understood in terms of gradual gains and losses of *nu* and of shifts between *korogo* and *hakeri'a* states. The growth of children depends on the expenditure of *nu* by parents. The *nu* that brings the child into being and sustains him or her is drained from the parents' bodies. The growth of children is directly related to the parents' decline. Implicit in this conception of growth and development is the idea that human *nu* is not a renewable resource. It is not gen-erated by an individual's effort but received from other people who have received it themselves. It is a finite quantity available to the community as a whole, and individuals must be careful in its ex-penditure. Overexpenditure in sexual activities results in too many dependents and less energy with which to provide for them.[15]

The quantity of *nu* remains relatively fixed because it can be converted into transferable forms via the contagious and consub-stantial social value of food. Because life is perpetuated in a single closed system of *nu* transfer, survival means feeding on one an-other, on each other's flesh and blood, on the products of others' labor, even on exuviae. Most of the transactions of social life, in-cluding eating and sexual intercourse, involve the sharing of *nu* between otherwise discrete individuals. Thus, social interdepen-dence, cohesion, and continuity between the generations "are ex-pressed through the reality and the metaphor of cannibalism."[16] At death, the flesh and blood of the corpse and the products of the person's labor in life – garden produce and pigs – all have the power to increase the growth and vitality of certain others through eating. If a person fails to eat the corpse of his or her same-sex parent, it is feared that the crops, children and animals belonging to that person will be weakened, having foregone their rightful inheritance of vitality. By the same token, a boy whose growth is stunted or whose health is impaired drinks blood let from the veins of the men he calls father.[17]

Because *nu* is a dualistic substance having both positive and negative qualities and because it is passed between humans via contact with food, strict rules regulate its transfer from one person to another. The ambivalent and contagious aspect of *nu* makes it a powerful regulator of social relationships. Depending on whether the transfer of substances benefits the recipient, *nu* can be either good, *aune,* or harmful, *siro na* (polluting). The positive or negative value of *nu* depends on the nature of the social relationship that obtains between the donor and receiver of *nu* and their sex.[18] Friendly and hostile social relationships are expressed in terms of the opposition between the positive and negative manifestations of *nu.* "The basic rule of self-preservation is to avoid the ingestion of *siro na* [because it] withers, stunts, and kills, and to increase the consumption of *aune* [because it] strengthens and preserves."[19]

At its negative pole, *nu* is the physical manifestation of evil because it is associated with decay, rot, and death. Menstrual blood and parturitional fluids are the most dangerous and polluting of all substances and yet they are also the only means for the transmission of *nu* in its positive, life-generating aspect. The Hua believe that the fetus is created almost exclusively from menstrual blood and nourished by parturitional fluids.[20] Human fertility lies in the "dark, smelly, explicitly rotting interiors attributed to females' bodies."[21] A man can achieve and maintain his masculine identity only through purifying himself of the female substance he acquired from his mother and is exposed to in his wife.[22] In addition to recognizing the creative power of the female, the Hua attribute creative power to that which is rotten. Possums, the animal symbol for females, are believed to reproduce from leaves left to rot in the marsupial pouch. The continuity between the generations depends on consuming the decaying flesh of a departed relative. Social and biological reproduction are thus grounded in a metaphor that emphasizes the progression of life from death and from the female body.

The Hua fear contamination by the polluted *nu* of distrusted others. Pollution means contamination by the rot and decay associated with the negative properties of *nu*. Because men especially fear defilement, there is an esoteric and private level of Hua religious practice carried on by men alone. Since menstrual blood is the source of fetal life, men are born with female natural substances in their body that must be extruded at puberty if they are to be truly male. Men secretly reduce the amount of maternal essence in their bodies, which they were born with, at the same time they eat female foods to restore vital essence. Men guard the sacred flutes, the tangible symbol of fertility, which they say once belonged to women. This embarrassing and secret quest by men for access to and control of female physiological powers is a constant theme of ritual and taboo. It is this quest that results in the types of behavior we read as male dominance and female subordination.

It would be more within the Hua cultural context to interpret this quest as an attempt on the part of males to predicate a separate male identity by reducing their essential and natural femaleness. In short, the female body is the prime organizing metaphor for Hua gender identity. Whereas the female gender identity is part of a natural developmental process, the forging of the male gender identity involves the cultural making of an antithesis. All Hua are born in the image of the female: Men are made according to contrasting images.

On the surface, Hua men appear to be superior, powerful, and pure, whereas females are inferior, malevolent, weak, and polluted. This stereotypic portrait is based on the residential segregation of the sexes, the existence of men's cults, the males' fear of menstrual and parturitional fluids, the various rituals of the symbolic expulsion of female substances that men believe they were born with, and the rules of female avoidance in general. These rules are laid down in the rules of food prohibition. Any discussion with a Hua person about why he or she avoids a food invariably leads to a disquisition on the nature of sexual differences. Most foods refer to sexual states, and indigenous explanations of food rules are rife with sexual references. Foods provide the Hua with an objective correlative not only of good and evil but also of male and female.[23]

Thus, the Hua wrestle not only with the problem of evil and of identity, but also with the problem of gender: How are androgynous males to become fully and only males? If we can understand how the Hua approach these problems, we will begin to uncover the reasons for their cannibalism and sexual asymmetry. The theory of *nu* connects these problems. The theory of *nu* as it applies in everyday life is analogous to a theory of life and death, of male and female. Cannibalism plays an important role in this theory as a conduit of vital essence from one generation to the next. The transfer of bodily essence between the generations is accompanied by the transfer of physical property in the form of gardens and pigs. Thus, cannibalism is essential for social reproduction as well as for the biological reproduction of the generations. The thinking that motivates Hua cannibalism is reducible to hunger for vital essence and social continuity. Cannibalism is part of a primordial system of life metaphors that takes the body as its central model. In this mental schema cannibalism is evil only when it is unregulated by *nu* rules.

I suggest the regulation of the transfer of *nu* reconciles emotional ambivalence and stimulates social bonding within the Hua community and across the generations. The Hua recognize that there is emotional ambivalence between certain categories of kin. Close relatives – those who we would say might be drawn into incest or oedipal combat – and distant relatives – those who might be drawn into intergroup hostility – are kept apart by the rules regulating the transfer of *nu*.[24] The major social distinction made by the Hua is between their consanguines, who are *bgotva' auva* ("one skin") and their affines, who are *kta vede* ("heavy or difficult people"). Relations of distrust exist mainly between affines because, like other New Guinea Highland people, wives often come from groups with whom the husband's group does not enjoy a secure and stable relationship. Generally a person may eat foods freely from consanguines, but not from affines. The exceptions are those classes of kin toward whom ego must practice avoidance and observe food prohibitions. These are the eldest child, the agemate of a man, a fellow graduate of the initiation ceremony, or a cowife if a woman, and wife or potential wife.[25]

Constraints on *nu* transfer as well as other taboos against bodily contact between parent and eldest child suggest considerable ambivalence between these kin types. The Hua describe the eldest child as the one on which the parents waste their strength, because it is into the body of this child that most of their *nu* is drained. Like the first fruit of a plant, the eldest child is believed to be the largest, strongest, and most vital, having been produced at the time of the parents' greatest strength. In addition, the eldest male child is feared as being eager to usurp the father in physical and social power. A man does not carry his male eldest child on his shoulders lest he be prematurely "put down" by him.[26]

Another exceptionally dangerous alter whose *nu* pollutes and must therefore be avoided is the wife, or any woman of the class from which a wife as a rule would be chosen. A man cannot eat the food a wife has prepared or produced, nor can he allow her shadow or her body over his, nor can he permit her any of the proscribed forms of body contact. These rules apply in the early days of the marriage when the new wife is considered to be still loyal to her consanguines rather than to her affines. In any dispute between her husband and her brother, she may side with her brothers and provide them with her husband's *nu* to be used in sorcery against him. The wife on the other hand, is not enjoined to fear her husband and his relatives. Although she is a threat to them, they are not a threat to her.[27]

Nu is also dangerous when it comes from sources genealogically too close or too far. Ego must eat food related to consanguines of a middle distance. No one may eat meat acquired by or the prize garden food grown by someone who is consubstantial with the self, meaning that it is one's own or acquired by one's child or grandchild. To eat one's own food or the food of one's offspring would be to consume one's self. Physical degeneration would set in because, as the Hua say, "My *nu* will turn around and put me down."[28]

It is dangerous to eat food that comes from too great a genealogical distance because it involves the ingestion of an untested and potentially hostile *nu*. The marriage rules follow the same principle. The preferred spouse lies within the middle genealogical distance. To marry with one who is too close genealogically is like eating one's self. A marriage with a stranger community holds the same dangers as eating their food. These eating and marriage rules, Meigs says, "reflect the social dangers of community withdrawal and introversion on the one hand and indiscriminate community expansion and extroversion on the other."[29]

Nu flows properly from the senior to the junior generation. The senior generation can give blood from its veins, the produce from its garden, animals it has raised or shot, its flesh after death to members of the junior generation but the junior may not make the same gifts to the senior. To eat the *nu* of the junior generation is morally contemptible and dangerous and will result in respiratory illness, debilitation, and possibly death.[30] According to Meigs, restrictions on the transfer of *nu* between the generations encourage exchange and the formation of extrafamilial ties as well as ease the conflict over reciprocity inherent in the parent-child relationship. The message of this rule is that there can be no reciprocity in the nurture relationship, that *nu* transfers from the senior to the junior generation are one-way gifts. To desire reciprocity from the junior generation is contemptible.[31] The rules regulating the transfer of *nu* from the senior to the junior generation are most evident in Hua mortuary cannibalism.

To conclude, the Hua conception of life as a limited good, seen in the idea that human *nu* is not a renewable resource and their identification of the human body with the source of *nu* explicate their mortuary cannibalism.[32] Human *nu* is a limited good that cannot be generated by the individual's effort. It can only be received from other people who have, in turn, received it themselves.[33] The Hua perception of the quantity of energy as finite is implicit in their idea that the individuals of today are less powerful and well built than their ancestors. Balding, a sign of an inadequate supply of *nu,* is said to occur in ever younger men. The *nu* that exists today continues to do so only by virtue of its convertibility into transferable forms. The leakage from such a system, which inevitably occurs, forces the Hua into an interdependent, closed system of *nu* transfer. Survival depends on observing the rules of this transfer. The losses in one's own energy system must be made up in gains from others.[34] Hence death is the bearer of new life, and life inevitably ends in depletion and death as individuals pass their vital essence on to others.

The coercive power of the theory of *nu* is based on fear of contamination by the polluted *nu* of distrusted others. The separation of specific types of people enforced by fear of contamination suggests that Hua fears are complex and that they are found not only in the tidal pull of female reproductive powers but also in oedipal tensions, rivalry between agemates, tensions between groups, death in the community, and in the usurpation by children of parental vital essence. The fear here is that one will be swallowed up in the primitivity symbolized by the rot and decay associated with the negative qualities of *nu* if the rules regarding the transfer of food between certain social categories go unobserved. There is also the fear of total extinction if the rules regarding the transfer and conservation of energy should go unheeded.

The symbol of the maternal in Hua cannibalism

The Hua exhibit a fear of life and a fear of death. Rank defines fear of life as a reaction to the trauma of separation caused by loss of connection with a greater whole experienced by separation from the mother.[35] The theory of *nu* has its psychological basis in its association with the female body. As already mentioned, menstrual blood is the most awesome physical representation of good and evil. Menstrual blood is at once the most dangerous of all substances and the only means by which *nu* is transmitted in its life-generating aspect. The fetus, the inchoate image of the source of life, is created almost entirely from menstrual blood. All blood is considered to be female.[36]

Because they spend their early years almost exclusively with their mothers, the forging of individuality is particularly difficult and problematic for Hua men. Separation from the mother is marked by the painful purging of maternal substance and other practices designed to remake men physically. Fear of death, according to Rank, is "fear of the loss of this dearly bought individuality . . . of being dissolved again into the whole."[37] Having achieved a masculine identity, Hua men spend a good deal of their ritual time maintaining this identity at the same time that they secretly seek to balance the masculine with the feminine they have rejected by eating female foods in the men's house out of the sight of women.

The maternal imago acts as a root paradigm organizing Hua predicating metaphors. The maternal forms the nucleus of an autonomous complex that directs much of Hua behavior in connection with the body, food, birth, initiation, and death. An autonomous complex, according to Jung, is an image of certain psychic situations that has a strong emotional charge, a powerful inner coherence, its own wholeness, and a relatively high degree of autonomy in that it is under control of the ego only to a limited extent.[38]

The Hua image of the maternal underlying the theory of *nu* can be likened to the symbol of the maternal–alimentary uroboros described by Neumann. According to Neumann, the alimentary uroboros symbolizes the earliest stage in the development of social consciousness. In this stage the individual and the group, the ego and the unconscious, body and psyche, and male and female are merged. There is an unconscious "psychization" of the body and a preponderance of metabolic symbolism.[39] Inside is projected outside, and the outside awakens the inside. Consciousness is realized through eating. The body (equated with consciousness) assimilates unconscious content through eating. Conscious realization, Neumann says, "is 'acted out' in the elementary scheme of nutritive assimilation, and the ritual act of concrete eating is the first form of assimilation. . . . Over this whole sphere of symbolism looms the maternal uroboros in its mother–child aspect, where need is hunger and satisfaction means satiety."[40]

The maternal uroboros can be likened to the Hua image of the inchoate subject Kunei and to the Hua theory of *nu,* which combines all opposites in the maternal body. The story of Kunei suggests that social consciousness is physiologically encoded. In the story, the opening of the passages of the body turned in on itself initiates social exchange. Uroboric imagery is also implied by the Hua theory of entropy – which holds that the vital essence encoded by natural substances is slowly leaking from the self-subsisting social body and forcing humans into a closed system of *nu* transfer from one generation to the next. This conception of a closed system of transfer of vital essence explains Hua mortuary cannibalism. The cultural focus on turning within that these symbols represent is also evident in the domain of social exchange.

Both in the realm of marriage and in exchange practices the Hua exhibit the "turning back" characteristic described by Strathern in his analysis of the social concomitants of cannibalism in the highlands (see discussion in Chapter 1). The marriage system preferred by the Hua links two groups of Hua villages. One group, smaller in number than the other, is referred to as the "people [who] live inside the Hua people."[41] Although the Hua have pig herds, they do not exhibit the elaborate network of exchange documented for the Melpa. Nor do pigs figure as prominently in Hua mortuary rituals as they do among the Melpa. Melpa mortuary rites transfer the spirit of the corpse into the world of the ghosts by means of a pig sacrifice designed to ensure the goodwill of the new ghost and the community of ghosts. Here we find the element of exchange of vital essence from the community of the living to the community of the dead via the eating of pig flesh. The eating of pig flesh coincides with the release of the deceased's soul. The pigs, Strathern concludes, are substitutes for the person's body: "[T]he pork is eaten *instead of* the deceased." The funerary pig sacrifices are presented to the ghosts "in order to persuade them to accept a new ghost, and to the deceased's maternal kin, in substitution for the flesh which will rot and return to the earth." The bones of the corpse are kept by the paternal kin and placed in special houses.[42] Thus, through the medium of pig flesh the deceased's spirit is replaced; what the Hua accomplish through mortuary cannibalism the Melpa accomplish through pig sacrifices.

The Gimi, culturally similar neighbors of the Hua, claim that their mortuary ceremonies were like those of the Melpa before women invented cannibalism.[43] Cannibalism by women of male corpses is supposed to release men's souls in the same way that consumption of the sacrificed pigs releases the spirit of the Melpa corpse. Closer examination of the Gimi in comparison with the Hua shows that Gimi cannibal ritual also reflects maternal symbolism.

The primal mother and the substitution of pig for human flesh: Gimi mortuary cannibalism

The Gimi are a group of about 10,000 who live in an isolated region of the Eastern Highlands province of Papua New Guinea. Ideally, the men and boys of a Gimi hamlet, which may number from 200 to 400 adults, are patrilineally related and sleep together in one or two large oval men's houses. Married women usually live virilocally in smaller round dwellings at the compound's edge.[44] The rigid separation of the sexes is also evident in Gimi cannibalism.

In her analysis of cannibalism among the Fore, who are neighbors of the Gimi, Lindenbaum notes that recent population increases and conversion to the sweet potato led to the progressive removal of forest and animal life and the keeping of domestic pig herds to compensate for the loss of wild protein. "As the forests protein sources became depleted, Fore men met their needs by claiming prior right in pork, while women adopted human flesh as their supplemental *habus,* a Melanesian pidgin term meaning "meat" or "small game."[45] Gimi males have also avoided human flesh, at least since the early 1950s, and monopolized pig flesh. Gillison's analysis of Gimi concepts of sex and gender in the light of Gimi mortuary ceremonies suggests that men were able to monopolize pig flesh, at the same time that they made women the prime producers, by exploiting women's need to nurture and by equating pig flesh with the male flesh devoured by women in mortuary ceremonies – the only time when women ate pig flesh.

Like Attis, Adonis, Tammuz, and Osiris, Gimi males are not merely born of a mother; they are loved, buried (although not slain), bewailed by, eaten, and reborn through women. Before it was abandoned in the early 1960s, cannibalism among the Gimi "was looked upon as a practice that women invented and in which they were especially prone to engage. Adult males who ate human flesh were [called] . . . 'nothing men,' . . . [and were considered] men of low status who, by eating the dead, made themselves weak like women." Furthermore, it was thought that "eating human meat drained a man of his strength so that he was . . . helpless before his enemies on the battlefield."[46]

The alimentary maternal uroboros is evident in the gestation of all Gimi life. Women breast-feed pigs and babies and sleep embracing both. All nurtured life depends upon the exclusive attachment of and symbolic incorporation by female caretakers. In order to grow and prosper, all new life must achieve a state of union with the female. Women sing endearing songs to the plants and pigs they nurture. A newly planted tuber of sweet potato is encouraged to "enlarge like the echidna, sleeping inside its warm nest, lodged within the dense and entangled roots of the huge fig tree." This incantation is said to symbolize "the silent growth of the human foetus encompassed by its mother."[47]

The Gimi image of the maternal combines features of the uroboric Great Mother. As described by Neumann, this is an androgynous, self-sustaining, female figure who combines good and evil.[48] The androgynous nature of the Gimi image of the maternal is represented by the belief that women once owned the flutes, the symbol of phallic power, which were stolen from them by men. As owners of these flutes, women are considered to have once been parthenogenetic and self-sustaining. The good and evil nature of Gimi women lies in their nurturing power, which is perceived as

73

both fostering growth and inhibiting separate development. "Because it is founded upon attachment," Gillison points out, "women's nurturance tends to 'turn back on itself,' . . .[by promoting and then inhibiting] the development of separate entities (cultivated goods and human beings) which men can detach from women."[49] Thus, the female may permanently retain by reabsorption.

The Gimi myth of the flutes, which men steal from women, "serves as a premise around which the culture is organized."[50] The stealing of the flutes, Gillison says, mirrors men's greatest fear: "that they would remain, like the foetus, merged with the female and indistinguishable from her, or that they would live, like the newborn, as her phallic appendage."[51] Much else in Gimi thinking reflects this fear of the destructive powers of the female and the fragility of the masculine gender. Menstrual blood kills: Contact with menstrual blood can cause a man to die; it is called "dead womb blood."[52] During initiation men induce vomiting as a means to rid their bodies of polluting mothers' breast milk and all mothers' food. By expelling maternal food, men dissociate themselves from the maternal and the female. Similarly, by disgorging food from their bodies men disidentify from the female state of having food inside.[53]

Women's eating of the male corpse reestablishes maternal androgyny – reminiscent of the uroboric character of the Great Mother – which the ownership by men of the flutes denies to women. When a man dies, men carry his body inside his mother's or wife's house and lay him down. In the small hut women relatives crowd around him and exhibit an orgy of grief: They lift and caress his limbs, press their mouths onto his face and chest, beat their breasts, throw themselves onto the floor, and wail for long periods of the day and night. After about four or five days, the male relatives of the corpse move him on a litter to his garden and place him on a wooden platform built high off the ground for temporary burial. There the men leave the body to decompose among the man's garden produce so that his vital juices will fertilize the garden. But the women, unable to contain their sorrow, secretly drag the corpse off the funeral bed. They dismember the corpse in the garden, carry the sections of the body inside the men's house, where ordinarily no woman is ever allowed entrance, and remain secluded there for days while they further divide up, eat, and digest the flesh.[54] According to Gillison, in the men's house the women are treated as men by being allowed to sleep there and to see the flutes. Symbolically "the women have penes – invisibly, inside them. Momentarily, in 'ritual time,' the women become what they have eaten."[55] Androgyny and self-sufficiency is thus restored to women.

As the women finish their cannibalistic meal inside the men's house they are called outside by name by the brothers and sons of the dead man and given sections of pork that match the parts of the man they are said to have eaten. Each woman is asked to name the part that she has eaten. As the parts of the body are named, the corresponding parts of the pigs are distributed.[56]

During the period of her fieldwork Gillison observed the distribution of pig meat in a mortuary ceremony. The dead man was buried in the garden and, after the women gathered in the men's house, his sons and brothers distributed among them the cooked sections of pigs. The pigs were cut into four categories of meat: the whole skin, the bones with some meat, the meat, and the innards. The skin was distributed to mourners who came from other villages. The rest was given to female villagers, Gillison suggests, just as it was once offered to cannibals in exchange for the deceased's man's digested spirit.[57] This practice of presenting pigs to maternal kin is similar to the Melpa practice of slaughtering pigs for presentation to the ghosts and to the deceased's maternal kin, "in substitution," Strathern says, "for the flesh which will rot and return to the earth."[58] According to Gillison, referring to Gimi women's cannibalism, "men's gift of pork precipitated women's departure from the men's house because it replaced their human meal and induced them to leave behind the residue, the bones."[59] This association of pig flesh with the flesh of male corpses eaten in the men's house, I suggest, also represents a substitution of pig for human flesh – a substitution that is based on the equation of pigs and men in women's physical nurturing of both. The equation of pigs and men is further suggested by the fact that as Gimi women are not allowed in the men's house except on mortuary occasions they are also not allowed to eat pig flesh except in the men's house on these occasions.

Like the Melpa, the Gimi entrust the bones to the paternal kin.

About a year after the presentation of the pig flesh, the man's bones are taken to cordyline trees planted at the borders of his garden and to caves, hollow trees, and other sequestered places in the clan hunting ground, considered an exclusively male realm. The bones are deposited in uterine crevices in trees that are thought of as male, and there the man is reborn into the forest spirit world. By being deposited in these crevices, the bones are believed to induce plant and animal fertility by the spirit within them. Later, by reentering the female body in sexual intercourse, the spirit will fertilize a woman and human life will be regenerated. Thus the women's cannibalism is the first stage in a process of regenerating the dead – the means by which the continuity of existence is maintained through the transference of human vitality from the dead to the living.[60] The inclusion of pigs in the cycle reflects women's role vis-à-vis pigs.

There is an orgiastic component to women's cannibalism, which deserves comment in the light of Neumann's depiction of the orgiastic nature of the Great Mother figure. The Attis, Adonis, Tammuz, and Osiris figures of Near Eastern mythology are their mothers' lovers. These son-lovers are not their mothers' equals; they succumb to her in death and are devoured. The masculine principle does not balance the maternal-female principle; "it is still youthful and vernal, the merest beginning of an independent movement away from the place of origin and the infantile relation."[61] The Great Mother is primarily concerned with the son's phallus, which in her uroboric form is part of her being.[62]

In playlets performed during marriage celebrations and initiations, women mimic their version of the cannibalistic feasting of the past with a dummy corpse. The whole affair is portrayed as an orgy in which wives and mothers dance through the crowd and force the male players surrounding the dummy to back away. Shouting with joy and wailing and beating their breasts in sorrow the women "dismember" the dummy and fight greedily over the parts to be eaten.[63]

Removing bamboo knives from their waistbands, the women "cut" the body, flinging "innards" (dried wild banana leaves) into the air as they fight greedily over choice parts. "I'll eat the penis. The head is mine! I put them aside for me!" shouts one woman. "I put aside that leg!" shouts another. "Give me! Give me! Give me!" the women all cry, as the audience laughs in appreciation of their poignant self caricature.[64]

The women claim that their cannibalism enables men to achieve eternal life. Older women remember that human flesh had a uniquely delectable sweetness, but they assert that their main desire was to prevent the ravages of decomposition. They say to the body: "Come to me so you shall not rot on the ground. Let your body dissolve inside me!" The rotting flesh contains vital essence. Until disintegration is complete, the rotting flesh retains vestiges of the deceased's awareness. Women say, "We would not have left a man to rot! We took pity on him and pushed him into our bamboo [cooking vessels] and ate him!" If the women did not do this then the man would disintegrate totally and his vital essence would be lost to society. The cannibalism is necessary for the rebirth of the man's vital essence. For by eating his flesh, women prepare his bones (the symbol of a man's essence) to return to the forest spirit world to fertilize nature.[65]

Gillison suggests that in their cannibalistic act women once again incorporate the penis that they lost in myth to men in the form of bamboo flutes stolen from them by men. Just as women steal the corpse in cannibal ritual, men stole from women the flutes that symbolize male fertility. Thus, both sexes struggle to gain control of phallic power and with this power to reconstitute the primordial androgynous state. This struggle produces the Gimi brand of sexual antagonism, which, as Gillison describes it, "is a conflict over who controls the *indivisible* power to reproduce the world, a power which resides in the body because 'the important aspects of the cosmos are inside man's body, not outside it.' "[66]

By exchanging pig flesh with the women, I suggest, men not only identify the male with pig flesh, they also manage to break the orgiastic reincorporation of the male by the female and thereby regenerate the opposition of male and female. As mentioned, men exchange pig flesh for the release by women of their orgiastic and all-consuming hold on one of their brothers. The myth of the theft of the flutes and the secreting of these flutes in the men's house also perpetuates the poles of the gender dialectic, forever in danger of collapsing into one another. These acts, symbolic and real, are impelled by the belief in and fear of the inertia of the uroboric state in which the satiation of the female may cause her to retain the male in her body. As long as he is trapped inside the female body, the male becomes indistinguishable from her and unable to join the world of the spirits from which Gimi society is regenerated.

In that case human life would regress back to the uroboric state where all is one in the female body: Males have no identity and psychic energy no impulsion. Thus the focus of Gimi ritual life is the splitting apart and keeping apart of gender categories while ensuring that life is regenerated from the indivisible source for all life represented by the Gimi version of the primal mother paradigm.

Conclusion: Comparison of the Hua and Gimi with the Melpa

From the Hua and Gimi come examples of how the maternal body and its physiological processes provide metaphoric aids for the organization of social and psychological life. At the center of the Hua conception of their identity and of biological and social reproduction is the theory of a natural substance that has its primal source in the female body. The thinking that motivates Hua cannibalism is reducible to hunger for vital essence. Survival for the Hua means feeding on one another, on the flesh and blood of others, and on the products of their labor. Like the fetus whose life depends on intrauterine feeding, the life of society depends on the transfer of vital essence between individuals. The losses in one's own energy system are made up by gains from others. As Meigs says, Hua "[s]ocial interdependence and cohesion are expressed through the reality and the metaphor of cannibalism."[67]

Hua religion centers on the body. "[T]he body, sacred temple of all power," Meigs says, "is approached directly, its contents assessed and monitored, its intake and output carefully regulated."[68] The Hua story of the origin of life presented at the beginning of this chapter depicts the body as the focal metaphor for subjective and social consciousness. Kunei, the inchoate subject, is awakened by his exchange partner, who opens a passage into the house that contains his physical body (a metaphor, perhaps, for the social body) and then opens his bodily orifices. Consciousness is established in the inchoate subject by eating ginger and the other exchange items given him by Roko. Eating, however, entails more than the birth of subjective consciousness; it also involves the awakening of social consciousness. The act of giving these items of exchange initiates an exchange relationship, which, no doubt, will include the exchange of wives (since Roko is also seeking bird feathers to amass bride wealth in the story). Thus, the story tells of the establishment of two kinds of relationship – one between the individual and his physical environment, the other between him and his social environment.

The theme of exchange also figures prominently in Gimi mortuary cannibalism and in Strathern's analysis of the social concomitants of cannibalism in the highlands. By giving women pigs, Gimi men release the spirit of the corpse consumed by the women and, perhaps, ensure that the women will nurture the pig herds just as they nurture plants and humans. Strathern notes that the ecological variation associated with the practice of cannibalism in the highlands is matched by social variation, found in the marriage exchange system, male initiation ceremonies, and in the substitution of pigs for persons. The marriage exchange system of the Melpa is open; that is, there are rules against marrying kin, against repeating marriages between small groups, and against direct sister-exchange.[69] As noted earlier, the preferred marriage pattern of both the Gimi and the Hua follows a more endogamous structure.

On the surface, it would seem that the Melpa gender ideology differs radically from that of the Hua and Gimi. The Melpa do not have male initiation ceremonies nor is there any need for a ritual focusing on the separation of males from females. Marilyn Strathern points out that Melpa gender identity is a given and there is "no suggestion, for example, that men's organs came first from women. Sex is 'innate' and immutable. Maleness and femaleness are in this sense non-manipulable. On this axiomatic base women are excluded from the mystical domain."[70]

The Melpa gender ideology, however, can be viewed as a transformation of an ideology that postulated an original indivisible unity of males and females and that included a focus on the exchange of physically encoded vital substances. Strathern describes the common elements underlying the sexual ideologies of the Melpa and Gimi. These elements are not dissimilar from those described for the Hua.

In sexual intercourse, the sexes "eat" each other. . . . females consume male semen, but do so in order to achieve reproduction through a combination of semen and their own blood. Menstrual blood is dangerous because it is "dead" and rotten; so it can threaten men with death rather than promising them children. Loss of semen also means depletion and thus decrepitude for males. Women lose their "grease" in breast-milk fed to children. The overall process of reproduction, symbolised in the passage of semen from male to female, and the passage of milk from female to child, is associated with the death of the body, overcome only by the survival of the spirit of life-force, identified ideologically with the paternal or male side. In this way, women and death become closely linked.[71]

I agree with Strathern that such ideas can be seen as a cultural substratum or baseline. The Hua, Gimi, and Melpa differ in the cultural means of creating the divisibility of male from female. Hua and Gimi initiation rituals and food regulations accomplish what Melpa birth rituals divide at birth. The Melpa individual is rooted in a particular locality from the time of the cordyline ritual, performed soon after a child's birth. In this ritual

the child's navel-string and the mother's placenta are buried together, and a cordyline or a banana tree is planted on the spot. The father is supposed to do the planting and to construct a fence around the cordyline. . . . As the plant grows, so the child will grow. . . . The navel-string, which once connected the child to the mother in her womb, now connects it to the earth, and this link is represented by the cordyline, which in several Melanesian cultures is a plant that marks the boundary between life and death.[72]

Thus, there is the suggestion that the core symbols predicating Hua and Gimi cannibalism are transformed by the Melpa in the rite that breaks the connection between mother and child in order to introduce a new term in the individual's social identity, that of his identification with a clan territory. As the cordyline tree stands for the growth of the person, pig flesh and wealth stand for the vital essence of the person. The substitution of wealth for the person, Strathern claims, "makes cannibalism both unnecessary and unacceptable and thus ensures that it [cannibalism] is classified directly with witchcraft."[73] The act of cannibalism is thus robbed of the positive, reproductive aspects found in Hua and Gimi mortuary rites.

The act of cannibalism, however, retains its destructive connotations in Melpa thinking (as it does in Hua thinking when cannibalism is unregulated by *nu* rules, or in Gimi thinking when cannibalism is the indulgence of greedy, orgiastic women). The Melpa believe that cannibalism is a primal appetite, an instinct, or desire for power, which takes, consumes, kills, and does not obey the laws of reciprocity.[74] Rumors of cannibalism break out whenever there is a sense that the internal consumption of goods transgresses acceptable limits and the rules of reciprocity have broken down. Such rumors externalize the fear of big-men that increased consumption patterns (associated with goods introduced by Europeans) will lead to internal self-destruction in the breaking down of basic rules regulating exchange. In-married women are usually suspected of being the secret cannibals, because consumption is associated with the female gender, whereas exchange is in the hands of men. The fear, then, is not just of social self-destruction, but of potentially uncontrollable female consumption patterns if rules of reciprocity, regulated by men, break down.[75]

When there is an inward-turning focus on the body as the source and generation of life and this focus is mirrored in social relationships, ritual cannibalism is a likely concomitant of rituals of social reproduction. Strathern's discussion of the Melpa shows that the terms of such an ideology may be transformed. Melpa notions about the growth of the body are transformed from the fertilizing quality of the female body to the growth capacities of the cordyline tree and to pig flesh as a substitute for human flesh. Were the Melpa forced to turn back on themselves, were they faced with a depletion in the traditional goods animating their elaborate system of exchange, the growth aspects of the maternal body and the exchange value of human flesh might play the role now played by cordyline trees and pigs. In other words, the ecological concomitant of cannibalism may not be depletion of protein resources, but depletion of physical objects that are adequate enough in value to substitute for the psychobiological aspects of personhood. Where nothing of value is available the body is resurrected; or, as I have suggested elsewhere, a focus on the body sometimes reflects a ritual response to physically threatened social boundaries.[76]

It is important to note that each of the three cases of cannibalism considered in this chapter is associated with fears of social breakdown. The Hua fear the slow depletion of vital essence from the Hua social body and eat human flesh to preserve this essence as part of their mortuary rites. Gimi female mortuary cannibalism, feared by men, represents the self-destructive nature of a standoff in the war between the sexes for phallic self-sufficiency. Melpa cannibalism (it is not clear whether secret cannibalism is actually practiced) represents a metaphor for internal self-destruction from uncontrolled consumption patterns. The common element is fear

– fear of total extinction if the rules regulating relations between the sexes or channeling exchange – be it of wealth or vital essence – should break down. What people do and think about the body in times of social stress confirms the potency of the image of society, as Mary Douglas suggests, "to stir men to action."[77] The evidence presented in this chapter illustrates how the body affords a cognitively accessible forum for the projection and ritual resolution of concerns vis-à-vis social and physical well-being.

4 · The androgynous first being: Bimin-Kuskusmin cannibalism

Bimin-Kuskusmin reject the view that any parts of human bodies can become "food" (*yemen*) in any ordinary sense. They do acknowledge, however, that the restricted consumption of certain parts of certain persons by particular social others in special contexts and in a prescribed manner is of major ritual importance. And the complex symbolism that marks these contexts, beliefs, and acts is densely articulated with other realms of Bimin-Kuskusmin cultural construction and social action.[1]

About 1,000 Bimin-Kuskusmin live in rugged mountainous terrain in West Sepik Province of Papua New Guinea. They have known about Europeans since 1912 but did not experience direct contact until 1957. When Fitz John Porter Poole studied them from 1971 to 1973, such contact was still quite limited. Most of the population had not seen a European and the influx of Western technology was not in evidence beyond the use of steel tools.[2]

The Bimin-Kuskusmin exhibit many of the features associated with Hua and Gimi cannibalism. Pig herds are tiny by New Guinea Highland standards and are replenished by capturing feral pigs.[3] The marriage pattern "turns back" as most (80 percent) marriages are within the tribe. The remaining marriages are almost always contracted with Oksapmin groups who threaten Bimin-Kuskusmin political and economic integrity.[4] These alien wives physically epitomize the Bimin-Kuskusmin conception of evil. The Bimin-Kuskusmin also have a monistic view of reality. Their primordial ancestor is a hermaphroditic being in whom the senses, gender, and good and evil are merged. This monistic conception is repeated in the Bimin-Kuskusmin theory of fetal development and the growth of the individual. Social and individual consciousness depends on ritually forcing the seeds of social and biological life into their dialectical opposites. The primary rituals accomplishing these ends are life-long male initiation ceremonies, mortuary rituals involving cannibalism of the corpse, and a periodic fertility ritual, the Great Pandanus Rite, which involves the cannibalism of the corpse of an enemy.

Despite the limited contact with Europeans in this area it was well known that government officials had forbidden cannibalism and that missionaries regularly preached against it. During the two years of his fieldwork, Poole observed acts of mortuary cannibalism on eleven occasions but notes that such acts were commonly treated with reticence and ambivalence perhaps because of European influence. In addition, he reconstructed the details of the Great Pandanus Rite, which he did not observe. The only tangible evidence of the existence of this rite was contained in the skeletal and other *sacrae,* said to be a part of the ritual, which Poole was shown at the site of its last performance.[5]

Bimin-Kuskusmin cannibalism, according to Poole, provides an idiom of expression that they employ in many contexts to address both themselves and others about who they are as a people.[6] Cannibal acts performed in mortuary ceremonies and in the Great Pandanus Rite of fertility are regulated by complex theories of natural substances. These acts reflect, orchestrate, and recreate the various dimensions of social personhood. Like that of the Hua and the Gimi, Bimin-Kuskusmin ontology is merged with physiology. Procreative substances (semen, female fertile fluids, and menstrual blood) form the basic elements from which the psychobiological nature of the person is built.[7] Dividing socially encoded attributes from the biological unity of male and female substances that construct the fetus is the focus of Bimin-Kuskusmin rituals. Thus, to understand the movement of Bimin-Kuskusmin cannibal ritual we must delve first into their psychobiological conception of personhood.

The primordial symbols of Bimin-Kuskusmin ontology

Hermaphroditic ancestors represent the Bimin-Kuskusmin image of their mythic origins and divine afterlife. These ancestors first reproduced by bodily fission. They were siblings who mated with one another and with their offspring to produce the totemic ancestors of the original clans. Both possessed a penis-clitoris and breasts. The more female of the pair, Afek, gave birth through a vagina in each buttock. The ancestors of the Bimin ritual moiety came from the right buttock and those of the Kuskusmin came from the left buttock. Yomnok, the more male of the pair, gave birth through the single aperture of the penis-clitoris. The ancestors that issued from this birth were parallel lines of nonhuman creatures (all possessing critical aspects of personhood) who symbolically represent the agnatic unity of the Bimin-Kuskusmin.[8]

The mythic origin of life is reflected in the fetal androgyny of prenatal development. Fetal androgyny is due to the fact that both parents contribute male and female natural substances in conception. Agnatic blood, semen, female fertile fluids, and menstrual blood provide the biological components from which the fetus develops. During menstruation a gelatinous, whitish mass (*yemor*) forms in the uterus that consists of female fertile fluids, menstrual blood, and the agnatic blood of several lineage categories. Agnatic blood is effective in the formation of females and males but is thought to originate in males. The agnatic blood transmitted by a woman to her offspring includes the blood of her own lineage and of the lineages of her mother as well as of her parents' mothers. Through multiple acts of sexual intercourse deemed necessary for conception to occur, the male transmits semen that is infused with the agnatic blood of his lineage and that of his parents' mother.[9]

The male procreative contribution envelops the reddish "skin" formed of menstrual blood, which, in turn, covers the whitish *yemor* mass. The orientation of a hole in the male procreative contribution determines the biological sex of the individual: If pointed toward the vagina, the gender is female; if toward the interior of the womb, the gender is male. This orientation can change during the pregnancy and its ultimate position is determined just before birth.[10] The androgyny of the fetus until late in fetal development is also seen in the fact that boys are given female names early in life and are said to be essentially female until they have been made into males through the successive stages and ordeals of the male initiation cycle.

The Bimin-Kuskusmin monistic view of mythic and biological beginnings can be likened to the symbol of the uroboric Great Mother, who contains all opposites. This symbol is fragmented, Neumann says, "[w]hen the ego begins to emerge from its identity with the uroboros, and the embryonic connection with the womb ceases."[11] The fragmentation of the maternal imago splits "the bi-valent content into a dialectic of contrary qualities."[12] Pleasure is separated from pain, male from female, and good from evil. Such a dialectic of contrary qualities is present in the Bimin-Kuskusmin conception of good–evil and male–female, and in their definition of the ethnic other.

The splitting of good and evil and the projection of evil is evident in the Bimin-Kuskusmin map of their social universe. At the center of this map are the normative and regulated images of humanity and at its periphery the antitheses of these images. This arrangement calls to mind Freud's contention that culture begins with the prohibition or regulation of destructive instinctual wishes – "incest, cannibalism, and lust for killing."[13] Rather than repressing these instincts, however, the Bimin-Kuskusmin project them in their unregulated form to the periphery of their universe and enact them in their regulated form in cannibal ritual.

The Bimin-Kuskusmin classify themselves as "true men" because their acts of cannibalism are regulated by strict rules. The antithesis of true men is found at the periphery of society and beyond in the form of "animal-man beings." These are fantasy creatures – deformed, asocial monsters who display an insatiable desire for human flesh and who hide in the forest to capture members of the opposite sex in order to eat their genitalia. Their ever-present lust for blood is satisfied by torturing and eating alive unwary travelers. The lust may be based on meat hunger, for, in the absence of hunting and trapping implements, human meat is all that is available. No bodily parts go untouched; brains and gall bladders, considered the most repugnant of bodily parts by ordinary human beings, are especially prized. Tales like this of the animal-man beings are told at night to educate unruly children.[14]

If in the outer zone of their universe libidinal bonding is absent and destructive aggression rules, in the next zone there is also little evidence of a balance between the life and death instincts. In this zone, however, creatures who are identified as humans appear to have a human subsistence technology as it is said that these people cook animal and vegetable foods in earth ovens. These foods are combined with human flesh in feasts enjoyed by men, women, and children. Settlements are described as being littered with dismembered human remains. All parts of the victim are eaten with the exception of the gall bladder because it fouls the taste of human flesh.[15]

The humans of this zone do not observe any of the rules regulating Bimin-Kuskusmin cannibalism. They take no account of ethnic status, eating both the bodies of enemies and the bodies of their own kin killed in disputes. Considerations of gender, kinship, ritual status, and bodily substance are of no consequence in consuming human flesh. These people engage in warfare in an incessant search for human food. The Bimin-Kuskusmin fear these people in a more tangible way than they do the animal-man beings of fantasy as they believe that some of their people have been actually killed by the "human creatures."[16]

The nearest zone to the Bimin-Kuskusmin encompass those groups with whom they interact on a more or less regular basis and who form a buffer zone between them and the first two groups. Called "human men," these are the people of the ethnic groups with whom the Bimin-Kuskusmin trade, form alliances, fight, intermarry, and forge ritual relations. Among these groups some Bimin-Kuskusmin may have friends, kin, or affines with whom they can seek refuge in times of war, famine, drought, or personal difficulties. The source of the dreaded *tamam* witchcraft is imputed to these groups and it is from these groups that the Bimin-Kuskusmin seek victims for the Great Pandanus Rite held once in a generation.[17]

The innermost category of humankind is represented by the Bimin-Kuskusmin. Here cannibalism follows strict rules. People who do not observe these rules are less than human. The insane, the possessed, the starving, as well as tricksters, witches, sorcerers, women, and children are believed to ignore or deliberately violate the rules of cannibalism. The inclusion of women and children in this group demonstrates the Bimin-Kuskusmin belief that cannibalism is a natural evil basic to the character of all humans that must be regulated and transformed by the moral and jural rules of society. Since these rules are inculcated as part of the male initiation ceremony, women (with the exception of the female ritual elder who is instructed in male secrets) and children are denied the benefits of social regulation granted to initiated males and are consequently more susceptible to the kind of behavior found beyond the buffer zone of humanity. Women may become witches who devour male substance; children may attack and consume the womb and later the nipple.[18]

Thus, the Bimin-Kuskusmin map of their social universe and their fantasies regarding the behavior of the uninitiated tell us something about the role of desire in the construction of the social order. In this case, at least, desire is manifested by some (women, children, enemies) and controlled in others (initiated males). Desire is encoded in terms of incest, murder, and cannibalism, particularly cannibalistic impulses of women and oral aggression of children. Whereas these desires are controlled in the painfully learned lessons of personal denial taught in the male initiation cycle, they are projected in the Great Pandanus Rite onto the body of the victim, where they are physically deconstructed in acts of ritual anthropophagy (see discussion of Great Pandanus Rite later in the chapter).

Gender opposition in Bimin-Kuskusmin ontology and sociology

To understand the biological and social splitting of masculine and feminine from the androgynous beginning, it is useful to delve further into the symbolic construction of Bimin-Kuskusmin society and of the biological constitution of the individual. Bimin-Kuskusmin social structure is conceived in a male (agnatic) idiom. The major social groups are traced through shared "agnatic blood" in the procreative transmissions of men (for patrilines) and of men and women (for kindreds).[19] Agnatic blood links the individual most strongly and significantly to male kin but also to female kin through the mother, who transmits a weaker form of agnatic blood to her offspring. The importance of agnatic blood is evident in the symbolic and corporeal effects attributed to agnatic blood transmitted at conception. Agnatic blood contributed by both parents is present in corporeal and symbolic form in the veins and arteries and heart of the child. Thus, agnatic blood represents the physical bond linking certain relatives. Female substance, especially menstrual blood, weakens agnatic blood, which is strengthened by male ritual and by consumption of male foods.

Menstrual blood is the antithesis of agnatic blood. Men have no biological connection with the production of menstrual blood. The menstrual blood of the mother passes to all offspring. In daughters it is the cause of their menstruation and forms the placenta at conception and diminishes at menopause. The blood of the mother is also transmitted to sons and is strengthened by the ingestion of breast milk. During the male initiation cycle, menstrual blood is extruded from boys' bodies, particularly from the ritually important area of the head. Ritual bleeding, symbolic extrusion of breast milk, and abstinence from female foods remove and reduce dangerous and debilitating female natural substances in the initiates.[20]

Menstrual blood is a dualistic substance. Although essential to natural female fertility, it is inimical to the growth of all but weak, soft female substances. It is strengthened by other female substances and linked to the effluvia of illness, wounds, decay, and death. It carries the capacity for witchcraft, mystical malevolence, and certain illnesses. It is black in color, unlike agnatic blood, which is red, especially in its *finiik* aspect. Contact with menstrual blood is debilitating to men and women, for it weakens the agnatic *finiik* spirit and other aspects of male substance. However, the power of menstrual blood in relation to female fertility causes men to seek ritual control of it as a means for controlling agnatic fertility.[21]

The male analogue of menstrual blood is found in the dualistic conceptualization of the spirit *kusem* which is transmitted by semen. The *finiik* aspect of *kusem* is strengthened by agnatic blood, semen, and male foods and ritual. It represents the social and moral dimensions of personhood. It stores collective knowledge and experience and is like conscience and intellect. Unacceptable behavior such as that exhibited by the feared *tamam* (witch) is a sign that the *finiik* is weak and the other aspect of *kusem, khaapkhabuurien,* is dominant. *Finiik* is strengthened in all ritual enhancement of masculinity, whereas its antithesis, *khaapkhabuurien,* gains vigor from female substance, especially menstrual blood. *Khaapkhabuurien* represents the unpredictable and idiosyncratic aspects of personality that differentiate individuals from one another. In this sense, it contrasts with the moral and jural dimensions of *finiik.* All humans possess *finiik* and *khaapkhabuurien.* However, *finiik* is strongest in initiated men and the androgynous female ritual leader, the *waneng aiyem ser,* because of the prolonged initiation endured by both, their frequent consumption of male foods, and their ritual efforts to remove antithetical female substances. *Finiik* links all ancestors, from the original androgynous ancestors to the most recently deceased elder or child, to the living.[22] Thus, *finiik* and the agnatic blood that strengthens it can be called the natural substance of social bonding.

Khaapkhabuurien strengthened by menstrual blood is the natural substance of destructive aggression and represents the polar negation of *finiik* and agnatic blood. Unmodulated behavior, as exemplified in the "man of perpetual anger," the "promiscuous woman," or the "female witch," is taken as a sign that the *finiik* is weak and that the *khaapkhabuurien* is becoming dominant. The erratic behavior of anyone may be viewed as a temporary imbalance in the two aspects of *kusem*. In general, however, *khaapkhabuurien* is held responsible for the somewhat more unruly behavior in women than in men. This is because in women the *finiik* is weakened and the *khaapkhabuurien* is strengthened by menstrual blood.[23]

Despite the ambivalent constellation of the masculine gender due to the dual spirit *kusem,* ultimately women are conceived as inherently the most potentially dangerous. This is because of marriage patterns bringing nonagnatic women into the kinship group and sending agnatic women out in marriage. The dreaded phenomenon of *tamam* witchcraft is said to have originated among Oksapmin women to the north and to have entered the Bimin-Kuskusmin community through intermarriage. Although more than 80 percent of all marriages are intratribal, a sufficient number of marriages are contracted with Oksapmin to perpetuate the dread of *tamam* witchcraft.[24]

The *tamam* witch represents the image of the polluted and the dangerous in men and women. She has hidden magical power and transforms male fertility and menstrual pollution into power that works toward destructive ends. She gobbles up male substance in excessive intercourse and cannibalistic incorporation of male substance. She menstruates incessantly and becomes fat with male procreative elements that she transforms into female substance without bearing children. She can harm both men and women.[25] She is truly the image of the terrible mother.

The transmission of *tamam* capability is the inverse of the transmission of agnatic blood. Agnatic blood transmitted through a female link flows in increasingly weakened form for three descending generations. The *tamam* capacity when transmitted through a male link also flows in increasingly weakened form for three generations. When transmitted through successive female, uterine links, it continues undiminished over the generations just as agnatic blood continues in undiminished form when transmitted through male, agnatic links.[26]

The persona of the *waneng aiyem ser,* the epitome of the nonpolluting agnatic female, is the polar opposite of the *tamam* witch, who is the epitome of the asocial, nonagnatic polluting woman. A woman who becomes a *waneng aiyem ser* is postmenopausal and relinquishes all ties with her affinal kin as she is ritually initiated among agnatic kin. She comes from her married home back to her natal home and remains there. As a mother she is noted for having transformed female fertility and menstrual capacity into children, especially sons, and as a ritual leader she transforms female fertility without menstrual pollution into male ritual power. During her initiation she is bled at the temples (the locus of male sacred knowledge) to remove menstrual blood from the female substance (flesh) adjacent to her skull (male). This ritual bleeding strengthens her skull for future placement in the clan cult house, and her *finiik* for formal participation and ancestorhood. In comparison with her *finiik,* she possesses weak *khaapkhabuurien.* Her navel, the locus of female knowledge, is covered with yellow mortuary mud so that she will acquire no further female knowledge, but may retain what she learned "when she was a woman." In her body "she represents an ideal agnatic female of fertile powers (male) and without menstrual flow (female)."[27] She dramatizes matters of birth, genesis, decay, and death; fertility and pollution; male and female. She is the "image of the hermaphroditic ancestors Afek and Yomnok, with whom she is identified."[28]

Thus, defilement and purity map gender-consciousness and group-consciousness for the Bimin-Kuskusmin. Natural substances provide an externalized map for the internal experience of good and evil and for the conception of ethnic identity in a multiethnic space. Superimposed on the antithesis of good and evil is a dialectic of the purified agnatic in-group and the contaminating affinal out-group. Evil is projected not just onto the objective world outside the subject, but also onto the world beyond the Bimin-Kuskusmin ethnic boundary. The women who marry into the Bimin-Kuskusmin world from the outer world bring the projection back to its origin; foreign wives represent the material metaphor for the withdrawal of projected evil.

The antithesis of the images of the witch and the female ritual leader deflects the symbolism of evil from the plane of the subjective and the body to that of the intersubjective and the social. This projection solves the Bimin-Kuskusmin version of the problem of incest. The Bimin-Kuskusmin believe that menstrual blood is mixed with agnatic blood. The flow of menstrual blood thus includes the letting of agnatic blood, which at all costs must be avoided on ancestral land for fear of provoking the wrath of the ancestors. Women cannot menstruate on their clan's land nor can agnatic men fight on this land. Agnatic females must therefore marry out and nonagnatic females marry in. Those wives who are brought from alien groups, as sometimes happens, endanger agnatic purity and introduce evil. Thus the problem of incest places the Bimin-Kuskusmin in a double bind: Agnatic purity cannot be bought at the expense of debilitating incestuous practices, but it may be endangered by the contaminating influences of foreign blood and witchcraft.[29] The solution is found in the purifying practices of male initiation rites and in the cannibalism of the mortuary and great pandanus rites.

The problem death poses for the Bimin-Kuskusmin is that they must ensure that it is a good death, one that returns them to the ancestral underworld of Afek and Yomnok. This can only happen if the proper burial customs are observed. These customs purify the body of polluting female substances and prepare it for reentry into the ancestral world, where all inhabitants are represented as fully initiated *finiik* of the Bimin-Kuskusmin. As already mentioned, *finiik* is responsible for the moral and ordered behavior of initiated men and *waneng aiyem ser*. As a consequence of prolonged initiation, frequent consumption of ritual taro, and the ritual removal of antithetical female substances, *finiik* is strong in them. *Finiik* is the "essential, noncorporeal substance that links all ancestors, from Afek and Yomnok to the most recently deceased elder or child, to the living in terms of clan, moiety, and sometimes age group identity."[30] All the human inhabitants of the ancestral underworld must be fully initiated *finiik* of the Bimin-Kuskusmin. Thus, anyone at death who has not been initiated must be initiated after death at one of the mythological passages to the ancestral realm. In the ancestral underworld male and female *finiik* possess roughly similar ritual powers because they have become equivalent in exclusively male substance (that is, *finiik* spirit).[31]

Having been born female it would seem that the Bimin-Kuskusmin spend their immortality as male. At death the paramount female ritual leader approximates an almost male identity and other females are endowed with male substance. Mortuary practices in effect transform females into androgynous beings, a transformation that was wrought in males by the male initiation ceremony. Thus, in death the Bimin-Kuskusmin return to the androgynous state of their biological and mythical beginnings.

Mortuary rituals are devoted to reconstellating the individual in the image of the great androgynous ancestors who represent the imagined whole of ancestral times when outside influences did not contaminate the body and society by introducing evil and death. Mortuary cannibalism recycles the ritually efficacious and reproductive power of the dead to appropriate categories of kin. Its stress is mostly on binding vital essence to particular groups of related individuals. The Great Pandanus Rite, on the other hand, is a communitywide ritual that ideally involves all adult, fully initiated men and women. This ritual models the psychobiological and social influences that can destroy society and those that create cooperation and solidarity. In both types of ritual the predication of the individual and social personae via the physical is dramatically evident.

Constellation of the natural and social selves: The Great Pandanus Rite

According to Poole's reconstruction based on interviews with ritual elders, the Great Pandanus Rite is held about once in every generation in a sacred grove of giant pandanus trees near the western end of the northern Bimin-Kuskusmin valley. The ritual consists of two separate performances, each lasting about ten days and ideally involving the entire adult community. The first performance held at the beginning of a major semiannual harvest of nut pandanus revolved around the fertility and growth of the *kauun* nut pandanus – a female food – and required an adult male victim who was captured in a raid on the Oksapmin to the north (the source of *tamam* witches). The second performance, held at the end of the other major semiannual harvest of nut pandanus, was concerned with the fertility and growth of the *bokhuur* nut pandanus – a male food – and required an adult female victim also acquired from the Oksapmin.[32] Ritual cannibalism by men and women was essential to achieving the goals of the ceremony, which had to do with both human and plant fertility. These goals were also contingent on the sacrifice and consumption of male and female anatomical parts of cassowaries and wild boars, creatures often used to represent human beings in ritual performances (just as pigs are used in Melpa funerary rites). Each eating act was marked by the dialectical opposition of male and female, defilement and purity, and good and evil.

Taken as a whole, I suggest the rite represents a model of the divisibility of the social and the asocial in interpersonal behavior and a model for the destruction of the asocial and the construction of the social. The adult male victim in the first enactment of the rite and the adult female victim in the second enactment represent a living artifact of emotional ambivalence in their physical embodiment of good and evil, and of purity and defilement. The torture, killing, and butchering of the victims disassembles the constellation of personhood into its culturally defined components. The consumption and digestion of those parts of the victim associated with the negative provide a model for reducing these attributes in the individual. Consumption of other parts of the victim associated with positive aspects of the self physically enhances these states in the individual. These cannibalistic acts were seen as essential for successful achievement of the rite's goals. An analysis of some of the aspects of the ritual demonstrates how the symbols and acts of ritual killing, butchering, and eating summarize the social and regulate the antisocial.

The first performance of the Great Pandanus Rite begins with the physical reconstitution of mythic beginnings. A massive log is lashed between the upper trunks of two female pandanus trees. Hung at the end of each log are the skulls of male victims from previous performances, which are decorated in the manner of paramount male ritual elders at the conclusion of their mortuary rites. Cassowaries and wild boars are slaughtered for later consumption and a live male victim (for the first performance; a female victim for the second) is bound to the center of the great log on his back with his face upward, dressed in the regalia of the Bimin-Kuskusmin paramount ritual elder. These acts merge critical social and natural categories: pandanus trees, cassowaries and wild boars (ritual representatives of the androgynous ancestors in their plant and animal refractions), ritual elders, and human enemies. From this primordial unity the rite proceeds, first breaking into parts, through acts of eating and torture, and then reconstituting the parts according to mundane and ritual roles such as lineage agnate, ritual leader, sorcerer, trickster, and witch. At different points of the rite, the Bimin-Kuskusmin participants take on these roles in ritual acts of anthropophagy.[33] In the process, Bimin-Kuskusmin ontology is dramatized in a grand and exciting metastatement of the group's social, physical, and psychological constitution. The acts of the ritual present exteriorized models of selves that are physically transformed through sacrifice, torture, bodily decoration, and cannibalism and upon which the eternal nature of the social self depends.

The physicality of the symbols of the psyche and of the ritual actions that fuse and break apart these symbols are reminiscent of Hallowell's point that what goes on outside the human skin can be as psychologically relevant as what goes on in the mind. The Great Pandanus Rite poses and solves the problem of evil externally to the individual and then incorporates the solution in the bodies of the men and women participants, reminding us of Murray's comment, made in another context, that "much of what is now inside the organism was once outside."[34]

In this and certain other respects the rite can be likened to the medieval alchemical experiments that also worked on an externalized psyche. The relationship between good and evil, spirit and matter, or spirit and instinct greatly concerned the alchemists. They encoded these relationships, as they did all psychological problems, in terms of the qualities and reactions of matter – which to them were chemical mysteries to be solved in carefully conducted experiments. The changes they engineered in these experiments were more than just the reactions of their substances. It seemed to them that the reaction that took place in the substances occurred simultaneously within the alchemist. The changes that the Bimin-Kuskusmin engineered in the body of their victim and then introjected in their own bodies were also thought to have a more wide-ranging application. The cannibalistic disassembling of the victim's body according to prescribed rules was essential for the fertility of humans and nature.

The rite begins with the recollection from the parts of their imagined universe key dimensions of the Bimin-Kuskusmin view

95

of reality. These dimensions are brought together in the lashing of the victim brought from enemy territory and the skulls of ritual elders to the pandanus trees of the opposite sex. In another context, that of the first of ten stages of male initiation, the female pandanus rite begins a boy's separation from his mother and the male pandanus rite ends the ceremony and marks the transformed boy's acceptance as a man by men.[35] In the context of the Great Pandanus Rite, the pandanus trees also preside over the task of separation and transformation. In the lashing of the skulls and then the victim to the pandanus trees, culture is joined with nature, good with evil, masculine with feminine, the primordial past with the living present, and the defiling with the pure. The remaining job of the rite is to break apart this initial symbol of totality into its various components so that these components can be mixed and transformed in the bodies of the living to fashion and ensure the intergenerational continuity of key social and ritual roles.

The human victim brought from a major enemy group represents the evil that has been projected and that the rite brings back to its uroboric beginning. By withdrawing the projection and bringing it back to their territory, the Bimin-Kuskusmin inadvertently recognize the problem of evil that exists within society and the individual. The importance of the primordial past in the progression of the rite is evident in the prominence given to the ritual elders and in the role played by the parts of cassowaries and wild boars saved for consumption as an antidote to the contamination of eating parts of the victim. The cassowary is associated in myth with the more female of the primordial ancestor, Afek, as is the female ritual elder. Yomnok, the more male ancestor, is represented by boar's blood and meat in male initiation ritual and by the male ritual elder.

The union of good and evil, the pure and the defiled, nature and culture, the past and the present, represented in the symbol of totality with which the rite begins suggests that all instincts are merged. In the interest of social and biological reproduction this symbol must be split apart. The splitting centers on the victim's body, which is dismantled from the log on which it was originally lashed, and after enduring death by slow torture, the victim is dismembered and the parts distributed. Some of the parts are re-attached to the pandanus tree, others are given to specified participants for consumption.

The division of the victim is similar to a process known in alchemy as the *divisio, separatio,* and *solutio.* A common goal of alchemical experiments was to make a noble being, also called the
"wonder-working Stone," which would consist of spirit and body
united in harmony, not continually opposed as they were in the
ordinary person.[36] Through their experiments the alchemists believed that the spirit could be redeemed from matter and be made
into a body that resisted the action of the instincts.[37] In making the
stone, they had to find a means of uniting opposed natures or
spirits conceived as pairs of opposites such as body and spirit, matter and form, or male and female. The union was represented as a
mystical marriage – *coniunctio* – taking place within the alchemical
vessel. Occasionally the union was conceived as a devouring of
one element by the other in the alchemical vessel.[38] This vessel is
the chamber in which the transformation took place that produced
the stone, or the purified self.[39] Purification meant changing the
black, the instincts or shadow, into the white in order to reach for
the gold, a symbol of the purified self.[40] The alchemist Dorn explicitly equates gold with fecundity when he likens the gold he
sought in his alchemical experiments to the male God's creative
seed in matter.[41]

The bodies of the Bimin-Kuskusmin victim and of those who
consume the victim represent vessels in which the goal of purification and transformation is biological and social reproduction.
The victim's body is purified through torture and sacrifice. The
rite identifies the evil in the victim by inserting arrows and bone
slivers into those parts of the body identified with major enemies
and witches. The torture and pain inflicted on the victim are essential to the reduction and transformation of the major enemy
and witchcraft status of the victim. The victim must show that he
or she is made of strong material by withstanding the torture. The
torturers help in this process by prolonging the victim's agony
while ensuring that he or she does not die prematurely.

Similarly, the alchemists considered it important to conduct
their transformation experiments in a container made of strong
material, lest the hot liquid boil over and the spirit escape. Anything lost in their chemical mixtures, they believed, would nullify
the process and the final product would be incomplete and imperfect. They warned against such an outcome, for the purpose was
to transform the spirit – thus, if any part of it escaped, the whole

undertaking would be ruined.[42] The idea was that evil must be transformed, not blown off or repressed. The contents to be transformed were seen to be the irrational, instinctual, and inhuman factors of the psyche.[43] The similarity between the logic of the Great Pandanus Rite and that of the alchemical philosophy motivating Dorn's experiments is striking. Dorn divided the body into three parts: the animus (male), which Von Franz calls the ego intention or will; the anima (female), a neutral force that is the impulse of life and that has and receives sensations; and the body, which desires whatever is corrupt but which cannot move without the help of the anima.[44] It was Dorn's idea that these parts were chaotically mixed in humans and that humans would remain exteriorized and in an abyss of darkness (meaning evil) if these parts were not separated and reunited according to his formula. He said that "first one has to unite animus and anima; when that has been accepted by the body then from three you can make a harmonious oneness, but it can only be done if you first make this *distractio* or *separatio*."[45] He likened *distractio* to a

voluntary death reached by making animus and anima one and by making them subdue the body which has to be forced to give up his petulance, his agitation and his constant worry about worldly things and also his lack of moderation in his desires. . . . Just as wild animals become ferocious if they eat too much and get a cancerous tumor if they do not cleanse their bodies of all superfluous juices through the excrements, through defecation, so the philosophical medicine has to cleanse our bodies from everything which is superfluous and corrupt, and then it can cure the body.[46]

Dorn believed that the alchemist's personality had to undergo such a transformation so that it would become magically potent and be able to transform the materials of the alchemical experiment. The alchemical experiments he conducted follow a similar logic. They consisted of two basic steps: "[F]irst comes the solution, the dissolution of the body; and second the coagulation or condensation of the spirit, after which the hidden gold appears which has to be coagulated into a new body, and that would be the gold."[47]

Throughout the Great Pandanus Rite there is considerable evidence of a concern with reducing and transforming destructive energy in the interest of the intergenerational continuity of natural substances encoding ritual and procreative strength (the analogue of the alchemist's gold). There is also evidence of the process of *coniunctio* in each act of reduction and transformation. After the victim is dead, for example, the head (considered a male substance) is severed and tied to one of the pandanus trees to rot. The other pandanus tree receives the victim's female bodily parts. This separation of the victim's body into male and female parts, which are then linked to the two trees of the opposite sex of the victim, represents the separation of the masculine and feminine from the totality constellated at the beginning of the rite and then joined to the opposite sex in nature in the interest of fertility. In almost every ritual act both the antithesis and the union of male and female are reiterated.

The remaining acts are concerned with reducing the asocial in the victim in order to transform the victim into a deceased Bimin-Kuskusmin ritual elder so that the victim's ritual power will enhance the fertility of humans and pandanus trees. In the elaborate and detailed acts reducing the major enemy and witchcraft status of the victim, the polar opposites in Bimin-Kuskusmin social roles are brought continually into play. Witches, sorcerers, and tricksters (both male and female) play their part and strut their finery. In every instance the acts of reducing and transforming have their parallel in mortuary cannibalism, which is also devoted to perpetuating reproductive and ritual strength. The goal is repeatedly one of redeeming virtue from evil and eating it. The Bimin-Kuskusmin appear committed to the idea that, if destructive energy is not transformed, fertility will be blocked. Perhaps they fear that in the absence of a concerted effort to solve the problem of evil through cultural means they will be like the animal-man beings at the fringes of their universe.

Conclusion

Bimin-Kuskusmin endocannibalism is part of an overall schema controlling the flow from one generation to the next of predicating natural substances between and within "dividual" persons, that is persons thought to be divisible from a primordial, monistic origin (see the discussion of Marriott's concept of "dividual persons" in Chapter 2). Evil is encoded at the physical level by harmful substances emanating from the maternal body, and, at the social level by the social counterparts of these substances. Subjective and social awareness is expressed in terms of the dialectic of agnatic purity and defiling affinal substances introduced by in-marrying wives.

The Great Pandanus Rite, the context for exocannibalism, is a model *of* Bimin-Kuskusmin ontology and a model *for* resolving the inherent antitheses these people perceive in their world. Taken from their main enemies, the Oksapmin, the victims supply a tangible symbol of the evil that is ritually destroyed in the interest of social and natural fertility. Reaction to a perception of external social threats in all likelihood motivates the rite's performance but not its ontological basis. Although the Bimin-Kuskusmin were once the dominant partners in trade with the Oksapmin, since the arrival of the Europeans the Bimin-Kuskusmin have become so dependent on the Oksapmin that their very identity is threatened. The political, economic, and ritual ascendancy of the Oksapmin is reflected in the Bimin-Kuskusmin perception that Oksapmin witches are attacking them with increasing malevolence. "It is in this context," Lindenbaum notes, "that Bimin-Kuskusmin ritually transform the identity of Oksapmin victims through cannibalistic acts that obliterate destructive male and female substances and enhance the reproductive powers of Bimin-Kuskusmin and their pandanus trees."[48] The destruction of the enemy and witchcraft status of the victim in the Great Pandanus Rite and the reconstruction of Bimin-Kuskusmin social categories in this rite mirror the fears of a threatened people and their hope that by taking action they can control the forces that threaten their social being.

Finally, the evidence for any relationship between Bimin-Kuskusmin cannibalism and hunger or protein deficiency is extremely meager. Poole notes that initiated men "provide considerable meat sporadically" and that adult women "are permitted to hunt some large game on occasions, but are denied access to male implements of the hunt and use crude clubs and small (female) stone axes."[49] A symbolic association between the availability of meat and cannibalism appears in the fantasy of the animal-man beings who are said to satisfy their meat hunger in cannibalism because human flesh is all that is available in the absence of hunting and trapping implements. A different kind of symbolic association appears in the equation of cassowaries and wild boars with human beings in the Great Pandanus Rite. Ritual cannibalism and the consumption of parts of wild boars and cassowaries were essential to achieving the fertility goals of the Great Pandanus Rite. One might add that perhaps the fertility of cassowaries and wild boars was also at stake. Such speculation should not, however, detract from the more obvious necessity of the Great Pandanus Rite for regenerating and reproducing ontological and social categories.

5 · Cannibal monsters and animal friends

It is very natural that in a country which really produces isolated instances of such horrors [cannibalism], and with a nation so devoted to fancies and dreams, superstition should be mixed up in the matter, and that at last, through this superstition, wonderful stories of windigos should be produced, as among us, in the middle ages, the belief in witches produces witches. . . . in the same way fear has caused some gloomy-minded people to be regarded as windigos; and, worst of all, this fear and the general opinion have so worked upon some minds, that they believe themselves to be really windigos, and must act in that way. . . . It is just like the "Sorrows of Werther." First, there is a Werther in real life, whom the poets render celebrated, and at last the nation is innoculated with Werthers.[1]

In this chapter I discuss the meaning of three cultural images of the cannibal monster: the Windigo of the Algonkian Indians of northeastern North America; the Wechuge of boreal forest Athapaskans (North America); and the Man Eater of the Kwakiutl Indians of the Northwest Coast of North America. Fear of the cannibal monster in the form of animal-man beings or the *tamam* witch was encountered in Chapter 4. This fear, dressed in various cultural clothes, is probably a cultural universal, appearing in all societies in response to concerns about the antisocial power of hunger. As Chapter 4 demonstrated, the cannibal monster may be a creature who must be conquered before social life is possible or a creature whose existence in the realm of the wild provides the screen against which social humanity is defined in contrastive images.

The cannibal monsters discussed in this chapter are not projections to the realm of the wild but representations of the monster

102

who, under certain conditions, rises within the individual and destroys others. The primary opposition of the ethno-ontologies discussed in this chapter is not between self separated from maternal substances and the other defined in terms of physical substances, or between male and female. The primary opposition is between self as human individual and the other as animal, or, between human persons and other-than-human persons. These oppositions are merged in a unitary conceptualization of original being from which they must be divided by means of mythical or ritual acts of transformation. In the division of these oppositions, animal and human are defined in terms of the other: Animals are like humans and humans are like animals. Humans harbor animal power and animals are humans in animal dress. Other-than-human persons display animal and human characteristics.

Paralleling the opposition of animal and human is an opposition between individual power or desire and social cooperation. Individual power is derived from one's animal refraction mediated by a spirit helper who can take on animal or human form. Human emotions are phrased in terms of the power gained from animal or spirit helpers and the objective correlatives of subjective states are seen in the personified acts of animal-spirit-helpers or other-than-human persons. Thus, whereas Chapter 4 focused on the objectification of emotions in bodily and food substances, this chapter focuses on the reification of emotions in the guise of animals or other-than-human persons.

In two of the cases considered here, the relationship of eater and eaten between animals and humans is conceived in reciprocal terms. Humans expect that animals may turn into cannibal eaters of humans. Because of this expectation – that what they do unto animals could easily be done unto them – humans endow animals or their spirit masters with superior powers and treat them with respect so that animals will not retaliate and eat humans. This means, in the case of the Athapaskan Beaver Indians, that humans must respect the powers granted to other humans by animal spirits lest this power consume the individual and cause him or her to consume others. In the other case, out of respect for the animals they eat and knowledge of the demonically hegemonic power of hunger, the Kwakiutl ritually tame the cannibalistic urges of humans in a drama that teaches animals and humans alike the social value and power of taming these urges. In the first case to be considered, that of the Algonkians, the primary relationship that sustains men in their quest for food is the power a man gains through dreams from a spirit-animal helper. Dreams have the power to transform individuals as well as confer power upon them. Under certain circumstances an individual can be transformed into a cannibal monster with an addiction to human flesh.

The Windigo monster

As early as the seventeenth century the cannibalistic madness (as it was called) that later came to be known as "Windigo psychosis" was observed among the Algonkians, northern neighbors of the Iroquois. The earliest reports of the madness are found in the Jesuit Relations (see Chapter 6). Le Jeune's Relation of 1635 relates a tale of the cannibalism that took place during a famine that struck two winters in succession. A man said that his wife and sister-in-law contemplated killing their brother for fear that the brother would kill and eat them during their sleep. Murdering the brother was necessary because, as explained to the Jesuit, "[he] is half-mad; he does not eat, he has some evil design; we wish to prevent him."[2] Elsewhere in the Jesuit Relations an account is given of the cannibalistic madness of Cree deputies of the Jesuits during the winter of 1660–1. These men are described as being seized with an unknown ailment that combined lunacy, hypochondria, and frenzy

which affects their imaginations and causes them a more than canine hunger. This makes them so ravenous for human flesh that they pounce upon women, children, and even upon men, like veritable werewolves, and devour them voraciously, without being able to appease or glut their appetite – ever seeking fresh prey, and the more greedily the more they eat. This ailment attacked our deputies and [the Jesuits report] . . . as death is the sole remedy among those simple people for checking such acts of murder, they were slain in order to stay the course of their madness.[3]

In twentieth century reports, the Windigo monster, as the person seized with aberrant cannibalistic desires came to be called, is usually imaged as a superhuman, man-eating giant possessed of a heart of ice. Human beings could be transformed into these monsters through dreams, by sorcerers, or through famine and starvation. Some Indians believed that this monster represented all those who had died of starvation. Famine, once a constant reality among the Indians of this area, had been known to drive individuals to eat members of their own family. The Indians regarded such an act as revolting and reprehensible, but understandable. They believed that once an individual had tasted human flesh, he or she developed an insatiable desire for it and in this state became a Windigo. When a person refused to eat ordinary food or was chronically nauseated, he or she was suspected of being a Windigo. The afflicted individual might make the same inference and ask to be killed at once.[4]

Food animals were sparse in the coniferous forest of Northeastern Canada. Although fishing contributed to the food supply of some groups, fishing was not central to the food economy. According to Teicher,

the lonely and remote woodlands stretched unbrokenly, providing a rigorous and relatively resourceless physical environment in which eking out the necessities of life was a ceaseless struggle. Practically nothing could be grown and so the food quest was concentrated largely on hunting and trapping local fauna. There was a stern and merciless quality to the frozen land, making famine a constant companion. Death by starvation threatened ominously and was certainly not infrequent. In a sense, cold and hunger were the harsh geographical contributions to a cultural matrix in which food quest inevitably assumed a dominant position.[5]

The necessities dictated by the food quest meant that human beings lived in small family groups (usually a hunter, his wife, and children) forever moving in search of food except during the summer season when food was more abundant and groups merged. However, during most of the year isolation was the rule. To survive in these conditions individuals had to accept separateness, aloneness, and self-sufficiency. The hunter was trained to starve and to rely for assistance and companionship only on his spirit helper. Dreaming was the means by which the individual communicated with spirit helpers. The ability to dream was cultivated from early childhood. The desire to dream something unusual was developed in children in order to prepare them for the important dreams sought on attaining maturity – the dream in which the spirit helper was revealed.[6] The uncertain food supply resulting in frequent famine conditions exacerbated individualism and the fear of cannibalism. "The fear of death by starvation and the possibility that eating human flesh might be the only means of survival," Teicher says, "was a ubiquitous concern among the Indians of

105

Northeastern Canada, to the point where cannibalism was a highly significant cultural theme."[7]

It is not surprising that the soul of the individual was the center of attention in these lonely, difficult circumstances. The monster with a "heart of ice" conveys the image of an individual who has mastered dangerous forces at the expense of his own humanity. The heart of ice may also refer to the fact that most reports of Windigo behavior in both myth and reality are associated with the winter period when food is scarce. One story about the Windigo says, for example, that "the frost was his manitou," meaning that the frost gave him his other-than-human status.[8]

There are two categories of "person" in Ojibwa ontology: human beings and other-than-human persons. Persons of both categories interact "in a 'society' that is cosmic in scope."[9] Social relations among human beings belong to the sphere of waking life, while social interaction with other-than-human persons is experienced primarily by the self in dreams. Between the experiences of dreams and those of waking life there is "no sharply defined differentiation between subjectivity and objectivity."[10] The other-than-human persons may be personified natural objects or animals. These "persons" are "thought of as persons; they may be addressed as such, and interaction with them is cast in a personal mode."[11] For example, in myth the movements of the Sun are those of a person. When Sun appears in a dream he addresses the dreamer by the same term used by old men to young persons, "my grandchild." Another typical category of other-than-human persons are the owners or masters of species of plants and animals. All of these beings share in a common essence. The metaphysical core of the Ojibwa conception of being, Hallowell says, is the superficiality of outward appearance. For example, the Thunderbirds, who live in the land above the dwelling place of humans,

like other entities of the other-than-human category, have . . . the same basic, enduring essence as do human persons. It is this vital core that is constant in both categories of persons. Human persons, too, have a constant and enduring essence . . . and a bodily form . . . which, under most circumstances is an identifying characteristic. But in neither category of the person class is the inner essence accessible to *visual* perception under any conditions. What can be perceived visually is only the aspect of being that has form. . . . metamorphosis, under certain conditions, is also possible for human beings. Change in outward appearance is potentially inherent in individuals belonging to both categories of persons.[12]

Living and dead human beings may assume the form of animals and animals may be human beings. Metamorphosis and power, "malign or benevolent, human or demonic, . . . underlie the entire Indian mythology, and make sensible the otherwise childish stories of culture heroes, animal husbands, friendly thunders, and malicious serpents."[13] Metamorphosis is an earmark of power because within the category of persons there is a gradation of power, with other-than-human persons occupying the top rank in the power hierarchy. Although human beings do not differ from them in kind, they do in power. The other-than-human beings can assume a variety of forms, but in the case of human beings, the capacity for metamorphosis is "associated with unusual power, for good or evil. And power of this degree can only be acquired by human beings through the help of other-than-human persons. Sorcerers can transform themselves only because they have acquired a high order of power from this source."[14]

The Windigo is the epitome of evil in the Ojibwa mind. In their folktales and in the telling of actual instances of so-called Windigo psychosis it is said that an individual is transformed into a Windigo by the circumstances of famine, the acts of a sorcerer, or by the power of a dream. There are many tales about the actions of Windigo. The following tale illustrates some of the themes common to these tales.

This Indian had a family of four. He and his wife and his eldest son turned into devils and what they eat were Indians. They ate up the rest of the family first and then they went around eating others. They became Windigoes. Another Indian had two sons, a wife and a daughter, and they knew that someone was coming to kill them, so they are trying to run away. They traveled and traveled and had nothing to eat, but still they knew the enemy was following them, and they went on till they couldn't go any further, they were so tired and they hardly had flesh left on them as they hadn't ate anything for some time, so they just built a little camp and were going to let the enemy kill them. They all laid down and they soon heard someone coming who came in and looked at them and saw how thin they were, and went out again and came back with a big moose and cooked it for them, and went out and got another big moose and got a lot of wood for them and then went away. This Windigo was all right in the summer, he lived the same as others, but in the winter he killed and ate Indians. So when winter came this Indian knew that the Windigo was coming again, so he takes the insides out of a big moose, and they went over by a lake and got inside this moose and let the snow cover them. This Indian who was a devil (or Windigo) was coming and knew they were under the snow. He had a pointed stick and was feeling around for them. He had almost found them when this Indian saw the stick and pulled it away from him. So then the Windigo gave up trying to kill them. So when summer came this devil came and lived with them and wanted to marry the daughter very much, so this Indian lets him marry her, and as winter came when they would be sleeping at night he'd bite the daughter and she would shout and they knew that he was going to eat her, so they killed him while he slept.[15]

The story begins with human beings, members of one family, being transformed into other-than-humans in the form of devils. This is one response to hunger; another response is reflected in the plight of the second family, who travel to escape the ravages of hunger, personified in the form of Windigos. Not having anything to eat, this family prepares for death. However, they are saved by the superior power of the Windigo, who gives them moose meat to fatten them up. The theme of being fattened by the Windigo or of the Windigo eating fat humans is a common one in the Windigo folktales. Those who are fat are marked for eating by the Windigo. Since most of the tales are told in the context of the winter hunger, the implication of this theme is that those who hoard food and become fat instead of sharing will be those who fall prey to the Windigo threat. The rest of the tale goes on to relate the seasonal aspect of the Windigo phenomenon. The Windigo is quiescent in the summer, killing and eating humans only in the winter. The tale ends with the equation of cannibalism and sex. During the summer the Windigo marries the daughter. During the winter, he bites her when they are sleeping at night. This act suggests that sexuality becomes transformed into cannibalism and so the Windigo is killed.

The implicit connection between cannibalism and sexuality in some cases is also suggested by several descriptions Teicher gives of Windigo psychosis. These case studies include descriptions of incestuous-like behavior in which a mother and son, for example, kill and eat the father. Another case, which Hallowell describes "as an instance in which cannibalistic desires . . . may possibly have been the culturally determined disguise of unconsciously activated incestuous desires," involves a young man who is seized with "a strong inclination to eat his Sister."[16] A similar case describes a father and daughter who killed and ate six of their own family.[17]

In addition to providing a channel for extreme behavior, in relation to either sex or eating, Windigo beliefs model environmental extremities that are feared. Hallowell describes a case in which fearful natural forces were personified, and their causes understood, in terms of the Windigo monster.

One midwinter night at Poplar River, when a terrific gale was blowing, word got around that a *windigo* would likely pass that way. All the Indians on the north side of the river left their homes at once and congregated in a house across the river. In order to protect themselves they engaged one of the leading shamans to conjure all through the night in order to divert the *windigo* from his reputed path. The Indians firmly believed that the cannibal passed without harming them and part of the evidence they adduced was the fury of the wind, which was interpreted as a sign of his presence.[18]

Such an interpretation of the "fury of the wind" is in keeping with the Ojibwa attribution of metamorphosis and power to the other-than-human beings.

A number of anthropologists have attempted to explain the Algonkian belief in cannibal monsters and the associated Windigo disorder. Teicher stresses that periodic famine alone cannot explain the cultural emphasis on cannibalism, because bordering societies, such as the Eskimo and Athapaskan Indians, also experienced periodic food scarcity, and, although there were occasional reports of cannibalism from these areas, the widespread and constant concern with cannibalism was not evident.[19]

Fogelson suggests that physiological reactions, "produced by drastic dietary change, chronic or periodic mineral or vitamin deficiency, or, . . . consumption of toxic food substances," may be responsible. He also suggests the possibility of genetic factors that could easily become manifest in this area where small breeding populations are the norm. However, the data to test such hypotheses are not available and Fogelson concentrates his analysis on the psychosocial determinants of Windigo.[20]

Writing in 1860, Kohl hypothesized that isolated occurrences of famine cannibalism in conjunction with cultural fantasies about cannibalism produced the image of the Windigo monster, an image that was then applied to any asocial act. This image became a self-fulfilling prophecy for individuals who acted abnormally. As Fogelson says, summarizing Kohl: "The man who is out of step with his fellows becomes feared by society. Fairly soon he internalizes the society's image of him, and the process of becoming a Windigo is accelerated."[21] Kohl's analysis foreshadowed the later anthropological analyses of Hallowell on the role of cultural factors in perception and Teicher's thesis that Windigo belief determines Windigo behavior.[22] Thus, from behavior exhibited in the plight of famine an image like the Windigo disorder is constituted; the image then guides and defines antisocial behavior. Such a conclusion is supported by the work of Fogelson, who shows that a variety of mental disturbances ranging from mild episodes of anxiety neurosis to full-blown psychoses are encompassed by the term *Windigo*.[23]

Referring to the work of Sagan and his own on the Arapesh image of the unthinkability of cannibalism, Tuzin suggests that images of the cannibal monster could be based on a deeper kind of knowledge found in the oral-aggressive fantasies of early childhood operating in conjunction with "certain neurological associations detectable between eating and emotionality."[24] Tuzin recognizes that intense fear of cannibalism may also be related to a historical experience of famine conditions in which parents have eaten children.[25] This kind of experience, I suggest, would undoubtedly elicit the deeper knowledge of a child's utter vulnerability and subordination to parents in such conditions. Thus, the image of the cannibalistic monster could also arise from fear of the cannibalistic parent.[26]

Analyzing cultural factors in Windigo behavior, Hay finds two features unique to the Northern Algonkians that produce Windigo behavior: "The first of these is the extraordinary importance attached to following one's dreams without consulting others. The second feature is the absence of alternative patterns for displacing cannibal desires from members of the band or for expressing them symbolically."[27]

The Algonkian belief in the necessity of obeying unconscious promptings meant that individuals who dreamed of eating human flesh would be likely to yield to these desires. Unlike the Iroquois, who, as demonstrated in Chapter 6, discussed their dreams in public and subjected inner promptings to social control, the Algonkians felt that their relationship with the other-than-human beings would be seriously compromised if dreams were publicly revealed. The privacy with which the dream was held meant that unconsciously motivated behavior was removed from social control.

Hay notes that the cures of the Windigo disorder were achieved in patients cared for by individuals who were unafraid of the patient and who thus enabled the patient to gain control over cannibalistic urges by helping to reduce the strength of the impulses to the point where the individual no longer needed to struggle against them.[28] The importance of peer group pressure is also suggested by the fact that the majority of those who became cannibals did so along with at least one other person. According to Hay, "the outcome of a case of incipient windigo psychosis depends on the degree of control of their own impulses exercised by the people who are close to the patient."[29] Noting that cannibalistic impulses are frequent among psychotic peoples in all societies, Hay concludes that the Windigo disorder is the direct expression of psychosis in the absence either of alternative patterns for expressing destructive wishes of the soul or of strong peer group models of self-control.[30]

The Wechuge cannibal figure

Based on fieldwork among the Athapaskan Beaver Indians, Ridington questions the diagnosis of Windigo behavior as psychotic. Ridington describes a form of cannibal belief and behavior that is similar to the Algonkian Windigo, which, he says, is "central to a sense of cultural and individual strength rather than weakness." The Beaver cannibal figure, called Wechuge, is feared "because he has become 'too powerful,' not because he is in some sense psychotic."[31] Ridington's close reading of the ethnographic context of cannibal beliefs offers additional insight into the ontological dimensions and the sociological import of the cannibal monster.

Ridington notes that Athapaskan and Algonkian behavioral adaptations to the boreal forest are similar. Both believe in giant man-eating monsters. Beaver myth cycles tell of a time when giant animals hunted and ate people. Metamorphosis and power were also central to the Beaver ontology. Animals hunted people and the giant people-eaters conferred supernatural power to the child on his or her vision quest. This power enables a person to be successful in finding animals for food. The idea of metamorphosis,

111

that animals are sentient volitional creatures like humans, makes the "idea of Person-like animals who eat animal-like people . . . a logical transformation of the economic fact that people must eat animals in order to live."[32]

In Beaver tales, Wechuge is portrayed as a human who behaves like one of the man-eating animals of mythic times, hunting people by taking advantage of their desires and weaknesses.[33] A real person who becomes Wechuge thus behaves like the giant animal that is the source of his supernatural power. Ridington knows of only one instance of "more or less authenticated cannibalism," which occurred sometime in the late nineteenth century. In several other instances he knew individuals who were said to have begun the transformation to Wechuge and who were cured.[34]

"To become Wechuge," Ridington says, "is to become 'too strong.'" A person becomes Wechuge by virtue of the supernatural power acquired from his or her animal friend. Older people are generally thought to have more power than younger people. The key to avoiding the Wechuge phenomenon seems to be respecting "[t]he space around a powerful person. . . . so as not to violate one of the personal taboos that go with his power."[35] The taboos in question relate to the action of the giant animals that hunted people in mythic times. If the taboo that has been imposed on a powerful individual is violated, that person begins the transformation to Wechuge.

For example, when a white woman tried to take a picture of an old man using a flash, she was told that the old man did not like the flash. When the white woman persisted, the old man covered himself with a sleeping robe in the back of the tent. To all those present, his action demonstrated his power, for "[t]o have been exposed to the flash would have made him 'too strong.'"[36]

It would have risked bringing down to earth the power of Giant Eagle whose flashing eyes still penetrate from heaven to earth in time of storm. The power would have compelled the man to become the Person-eating-monster and the man would have lost his own will and judgement to that of the all consuming monster inherent within himself by virtue of his encounter with it during the experience of visionary transformation as a child.[37]

If a person who begins the transformation to Wechuge is not cured by enticing the power of the giant-man-eating-animal-spirit to leave his body and return to its place within the medicine bundle, "he will begin to eat his own lips, which will turn to ice within him."[38] The final stage in the transformation occurs when the individual turns toward humans rather than animals for food. Because the social space of the medicine bundle has been consumed by virtue of the violation of respectful taboos, the power inherent in the bundle turns to the consumption of humans. Thus, when the rules of social life are transgressed, biological life is destroyed.

Ridington concludes that the Wechuge phenomenon is not a psychosis but a social sickness that can only be cured "by the benevolent application of supernatural power from within the group." The ice of the Wechuge who cannot be cured is overcome only by his death "and the application of fire, the symbol of camp life, to the remains."[39] Thus, the Wechuge phenomenon is the antithesis of social life. It is a sickness that is associated with the influx of strangers and the mixing of people who do not know the taboos respecting a person's medicine bundle. Ridington points out that the only person said to have become Wechuge did so at a time of maximum social upheaval. The other cases in which an individual was threatened with the Wechuge transformation were precipitated by an individual who was outside the social circle. Like *ta-mam* witchcraft, which was associated with alien wives, Wechuge models outside threats to internal social cohesion. Ridington suggests that the longer period of disruptive influence from contact with Europeans experienced by the Algonkians as compared with the experience of the Beaver Indians together with the pressures that caused considerable mixing among Algonkian groups explains the larger number of Windigo relative to Wechuge incidents.[40]

The Kwakiutl Man Eater

Reid compares the Beaver cannibal complex with that of the Kwakiutl and concludes that the two contain the same symbolic elements: "giant animals that hunt and eat men, acquisition of power in a quest, identification with a man-eating monster that leads to cannibalistic behaviour, curing of cannibalistic behaviour etc."[41] The differences lie in the Kwakiutl acceptance into the personality of the cannibal monster by an initiation process during

113

which the individual is first born of the cannibal monster and then tamed so that the monster's power is integrated in the personality.

Although the Kwakiutl of the Northwest Coast of North America are coast dwellers who have relied on runs of anadromous fish as a basic resource of their diet for roughly 5,000 years, Reid says that the mental world of the Kwakiutl, like that of the Beaver, revolves around hunting and one of its key elements is "the idea that animals might hunt and eat men."[42] The Kwakiutl descended from inland hunters thought to have come from the same region as the Athapaskans. Their history of hunting, Reid says, "must have formed their philosophic conceptions and expressive culture long before they came to the coast."[43]

The concept of metamorphosis is central in Kwakiutl thought as is the reciprocal relationship between man and animals, individual desire and social necessity. Humans and animals participate in the same original being. They are, as Walens says, "serial incarnations of the same souls, each dying so that the other may be reborn." Animals are the reflexive other in the predication of humanness: Animal behavior provides the external basis for the structuring of human behavior, and the structure of human society provides a metaphor for the structure of animal societies.[44]

Reciprocity between man and animals is vital for social and biological life and the regeneration of both. An example of the dependence of humans on animals is seen not only in food-getting activities but also in mortuary beliefs. In the societies described in Chapters 3 and 4, humans depended on mortuary cannibalism for the release of vital essence from the newly dead. The Kwakiutl also depend on mortuary cannibalism – in this case, by ravens – to accomplish similar goals. In dismembering the corpse, ravens are believed to cause its true death, which releases its soul. In digesting the flesh, ravens transform it from secular to sacred matter. Thus, ravens bring about the transfiguration of human flesh, without which no human could die.[45]

There is a special life-giving relationship between humans and salmon. Humans and salmon are the mirror images of one another and the two are intertwined in a web of resurrection-oriented rituals. The animals that eat salmon are therefore also linked in a relationship of eater and eaten with humans. Walens explains the logic of these relationships:

114

[A]ll animals that eat salmon must perform the rituals that make the salmon want to die, the rituals that promise them resurrection. But even more important, since salmon are humans, and humans eat salmon, by analogy humans eat humans – and are thus cannibals. Furthermore, crest animals that eat salmon are themselves de facto man eaters. In point of fact, most crest animals actually do eat humans, either live humans (killer whales, wolves, and bears) or dead humans (eagles and ravens). Thus, because these animals are all direct links in the cycle of resurrection for both humans and salmon, they are themselves by definition humans. Like all animals, they are considered to be humans who have donned magical masks and blankets (skins), which transform them into the animals seen in daily life. All those animals whose food is in some way related to that of humans are a part of the same system of transubstantiation and metempsychosis as are humans and salmon, and thus must be dealt with in a manner consistent with the highly sacred character of man's role in the chain of being.[46]

In Kwakiutl myths and rituals, game animals of the summer reappear as man eaters in the winter.[47] Reciprocity between eater and eaten is a moral law that permeates mythology and ritual: "[H]e who wants to get food must become food."[48] In winter initiation rituals, the initiates voluntarily offer to be eaten by animal spirits. In being eaten by these spirits, the initiates become the Man Eater, gaining its power, which would be turned to eating humans if the power was not tamed and the initiate was not socialized to live with his newly acquired power in human society.

The Kwakiutl Man Eater is the figure that corresponds to the Beaver Wechuge. The two figures are similar in that the individual acquires power from them. The difference is that, once incorporated into the personality, the Man Eater must be tamed. As Reid says about the Man Eater,

[t]he spirit represents (or "images") a split of the self. He is the projection of those aspects the self cannot cope with – the forbidden drives and antisocial aspects of the self which the child has been taught to reject in the course of socialization. He is revolting because he represents the most deeply repressed desires of the individual, his "ugly" face.[49]

Whereas the power of Wechuge is tempered by observing taboos respecting the individual's private source of power, the antisocial power of the Kwakiutl Man Eater is tamed by being integrated in the personality of the socialized individual. By integrating individual desire in the winter initiation ritual, the Kwakiutl give equal importance to the individual and the social. The same attitude is seen (although differently phrased) in the respect that the Beaver accord the individual in order to preserve social cohesion.

Individual desire is represented in Kwakiutl myth and ritual by the overwhelming power of primal hunger, which represents a force that must be transformed or tamed for the social good. The moral regulations guiding Kwakiutl behavior are present in many myths. Walens discusses one of these myths, which he says encapsulates

the basic moral charter of Kwakiutl culture. Just as Freud postulated in *Totem and Taboo* that morality arose out of a single Oedipal instant in early human history, so the Kwakiutl believe that morality arose from the actions of . . . Transformer, the being who transforms the world from its past, amoral, hunger-dominated condition to its present, moral, hunger-controlling state.[50]

The act that initiates the Transformer's ordering of the human and animal world is the refusal on the part of his father and stepmother to share food with their children in a time of hunger. Transformer takes revenge by transforming his father into Heron and his stepmother into Woodpecker. He then leaves to "set things right in the world."[51]

In this and subsequent acts, Transformer creates transformation (the process by which things and people can be changed and death can be transformed to life) and he creates differentiation (the process by which things acquire identity through naming). Thus, Transformer is the Creator.[52] With the power he has acquired by punishing and transforming his father and stepmother, Transformer alters the world outside his family. He begins by acquiring power over hunger through the acquisition of a *sisiutl* belt, which he wins by killing a *sisiutl,* one of the most terrifying of beings – a giant two-headed serpent with a face in the middle of its body. Snakes are frightening creatures that can enter the human body through the anus and devour their insides. By killing the snake, transforming its skin and wearing it as a belt, Transformer becomes the master of *sisiutl* and acquires its power, which is related to the potency of the penis. These acts, Walens says, mean that all-pervasive hunger and death are transformed through the actions of men into the power of fertility and rebirth.[53] "Morality comes

from the conquering, not the ignoring, of evil thoughts and desires."[54]

The power of primal hunger and the need to control it is also
acted out in the Cannibal Dance of the Winter, an initiation rite.
Here cannibalism is presented as the ultimate manifestation of all
the forces that can destroy society. The Cannibal Dance, Walens
says, "is the keystone to the entire interaction between mankind
and the supernatural, between the bestial and humane facets of
human nature, and between the cosmic forces of creation and those
of destruction. It both represents and is the moment of the utter
taming of those forces that would send the world into the chaos
of uncontrollable rapaciousness."[55]

Consumed by the Man Eater, the initiate becomes the Cannibal
Dancer, who trembles, gnashes his teeth, cries and moans as he
displays his irresistible hunger for human flesh. He attacks all who
are near him and bites flesh from the bodies of the living until he
is chased off by the opposing power of the Bear Dancers. Not even
the power of sacred songs or the temptation of incest with a sister
quells his desire for human flesh. A corpse is brought into the
room and he begins to devour it; his hunger, however, is only
appeased not negated. Only the pull of the primal mother manages
to conquer his appetite.

In the final dance, the negation of his voracity occurs only when the other
dancers press a smoldering blood-soaked menstrual napkin into the Cannibal's face. Once the sacred smoke enters his body, he is satiated, for his
primal desire has been satisfied by the primal food of menstrual blood.
At this point, the Cannibal is thought to lose all knowledge of human
behavior; he must be taught all the basics of human life as if he were a
new-born infant: speech, walking, sleeping, eating, and drinking. All are
taught to him in a ritual process lasting months, before he can again enter
the world of other human beings. However, upon reentering society, he
is magically more elevated than any other person, because he has conquered the destructive force of primal voraciousness.[56]

Thus, in the paradigmatic myth of creation chaos is transformed
by the male who conquers the symbol of phallic power and transforms it to work for human fertility. In the paradigmatic ritual of
the Cannibal Dance, chaos, represented by the appetite of the Cannibal Dancer, is conquered by reciprocal interaction between the
spirit and the human world. The dance symbolizes a transition
from the spirit world of uncontrolled hunger to the human world

117

of control. The dance is a ritual mechanism for channeling powerful forces into society and transforming those forces for social purposes. The transition is effected by an exchange between the two worlds in which humans give their flesh to the spirit world when the Cannibal Dancer bites their flesh and devours the flesh of the corpse. In return, humans are given the tamable spirit of the Cannibal Dancer who is born as a fetus into the human world. By agreeing to feed the Cannibal Dancer on her blood (symbolized by the menstrual pad), the human mother contracts to bear and feed the fetus in her body. The ensuing acts of socialization transform what was once a spirit being with the uncontrolled energy of the spirit world into a controlled human being.

Walens concludes that the winter ceremonials of the Cannibal Dance

prove that no matter how terrible the power of hunger, no matter how many fearsome guises it assumes, no matter how many masks it wears, and no matter how many voices it speaks with, morality will be the ultimate victor. So long as humans have the knowledge to use food correctly, they need never fear hunger nor its awful accompaniment, death.[57]

By their controlled activities, their covenant to feed those for whom they are responsible, human beings kill not because they are hungry, but because it is their responsibility to kill, to eat, and to be the vehicle of rebirth for those with whom they have a covenant.[58]

The puzzle presented by the Kwakiutl concern with hunger and eating – a concern that makes metaphors of assimilation a "model for both action and ontology," which pervade "Kwakiutl ideas of sociality, of human nature, of animal behavior, and of religion."[59] – is that there is little evidence of food scarcity. The facts of Kwakiutl food economy simply do not justify interpreting their preoccupation with hunger and eating as an expression of anxiety conditioned by sheer want. Writing about the Skagit, also of the Northwest Coast, Snyder stresses the discrepancy between anxieties about food and cannibalism expressed in Skagit stories and in reality. She suggests that food anxiety originated not from food scarcity in the present but from hunger endured to make contact with the supernatural.[60] However, in an intriguing footnote, she adds that the need to contact the supernatural for food together with the philosophy and social behavior concerning food "suggests that there may have been in the distant past of the Skagit an adjustment of a world-view oriented to a real lack of food to accommodate new conditions of plenty, and new sorts of social relationships conditioned by plenty."[61]

Summarizing Kwakiutl culture as reflected in mythology, Boas points out that tales referring to the time before salmon existed and before the world was regulated as it is now contain many references to starvation and hunger "due to continued bad weather . . . , because the salmon had not been brought into our world . . . , because there were no tides." In these stories it is also reported that the wolves had no food in midwinter. Stories of starvation are more numerous among the inland tribes than among the island tribes. The causes of hunger in these tales are the failure of hunters to kill goats, the absence of salmon trap, and the failure to catch fish.[62]

Walens notes that food was plentiful, but that access to food was limited because resources were controlled by a small percentage of titled nobility. Considerable anxiety was attached to the food quest, however, because of worries about whether fish would bite and whether there would be enough food to last the winter. In addition, anxiety accompanied the activities of the food quest: A canoe could tip over as a 400-pound halibut was pulled into it; a man could fall from the fishing weir and be drowned; sharks or killer whales could overturn the canoe; a storm could arise, or enemy warriors could attack; or a sea monster could surface, bringing instant death to all who saw it.[63]

Walens does not link the realities motivating food anxiety to the importance of hunger and food in Kwakiutl ontology and cosmology. He does, however, suggest that increased potlatching activity during the nineteenth century was due to the fact that between 1830 and 1900 the Kwakiutl population declined by almost 90 percent.[64] In their potlatches the Kwakiutl destroyed coppers, which are metaphors for human beings. In keeping with its human identity, the destruction of a copper mimicked the destruction of the human body: "[T]he first piece removed is the head, after which the body is cut up." Such acts released the soul and allowed it to return to other realms and replenish the numbers in that realm – the eventual result would be the replenishment of human beings on earth through reincarnation. Killing the copper by dismembering it enabled humans to buy the pieces of copper, often for more

119

than they were originally worth; in this way the number of souls the copper represented was increased. Riveting the pieces together reincarnated the copper as a living being, and the souls it contained remained in the world of humans. The man who bought a copper's pieces and reassembled them showed his commitment to maintaining world order and asserted his ability to create life, Walens says, because "he [gave] to the copper the same life that the copper will give to the beings to which it is finally sent."[65]

The population decline that the Kwakiutl sought to control ritually by means of increased potlatching made death a primary subject of interest, the primary focus of rituals, and the primary condition of Kwakiutl existence. Walens suggests that during this period, potlatching increased because "[i]t was the responsibility of righteous men, who believed that the souls of the dying Kwakiutl were being taken to vivify the bodies of an ever increasing number of white men, to take those souls from storage and to be extravagant in their distribution so that there should be enough to reincarnate all those Kwakiutl who had died and not come back to life."[66] In this atmosphere, fantasies about the Man Eater, the being who hunts and consumes humans, would serve as a metaphor for consumption by external sources, just as the Wechuge became the metaphor for the violation of personal space when strangers came together, or the Windigo became the metaphor for consuming natural or human forces. Although hunger might not have been the force threatening Kwakiutl social life, threats from other sources undoubtedly increased the attention paid to rituals that provided models of and for the regeneration of life from the hungry jaws of death.

Conclusion

The maternal symbolism described for the New Guinea cases and the animal symbolism described in this chapter are reminiscent of ancient fertility figurines depicting swollen women and the animal drawings on cave walls dwarfing human stick figures. If we accept Ricoeur's maxim "symbols give rise to thought," we can suggest that such primordial symbols predicated human consciousness in the symbolization of the human dependence on and merging with the visible sources of life: animals or the maternal body. The discussion in this and the last chapter suggests further that social relationships may be patterned on the positive and negative symbolic oppositions established in the fragmentation of these monistic symbols. The cultural patterning of social reproduction in these cases may include actual cannibalism or fears of cannibalism. For example, anxiety about the depletion of vital essence that flows between humans and the biological other motivates Hua and Bimin-Kuskusmin mortuary cannibalism discussed in Chapters 3 and 4.

The case studies presented in this chapter provide examples of how the behavior and interdependence of humans and animals generate the basic elements that reflexively define animal and human being. Like the maternal body of the Hua, animals have a dual nature: Animals are at once the givers and takers of life (just as the Hua maternal body was conceived as the source of life and death). Humans are simultaneously animal (by virtue of the spirit power the individual acquires) and social (by virtue of the contract humans make with animals and other humans to kill animals and share food according to certain rules).

Emotional ambivalence, encoded by positive and negative bodily substances in the New Guinea cases, is encoded by the positive and negative forces generated by the animal power focused in individuals and utilized positively for the social good or negatively in antisocial patterns of consumption. The transition from the inchoate in human behavior (described in the Hua story of Roko and Kunei) to the conscious and the social is made in the acquisition and transformation of animal-spirit-power, in the case of the Algonkians and the Beaver, and in the acquisition and taming of this power in the case of the Kwakiutl. The Hua process of transformation (seen in the Hua story) included the exchange and eating of food, while the transformations described in this chapter involve, first, the acquisition of power from the animal-spirit-other and, second, the social use of this power by sharing the food acquired with it. Thus, as was true of the Hua, the elementary structures of consciousness are based on the establishment of a reciprocal relationship between the individual and his or her physical and social environment.

Cannibalism represents a symbol of life-giving power and destructive human desire in the cases described in this chapter. The negative and positive connotations of cannibalism are enacted in the Kwakiutl Cannibal Dance in which the social person is constructed by integrating the positive aspects of the Man Eater and taming the negative. This ritual can be compared with the Great Pandanus Rite, which, as I suggested in Chapter 4, is in part a rite of individuation. The difference lies in the fact that attributes of the person are actually eaten in the latter case, whereas in the former attributes of the person tend to be enacted and staged for an audience by reference to the role of the Man Eater.

The negative connotations of cannibalism receive greater stress in the cases of this chapter and are comparable to the Melpa representation of cannibalism as a primal appetite, an instinct, or desire for power, which takes, consumes, kills, and does not obey the laws of reciprocity. The negative connotations of Algonkian, Beaver, and Kwakiutl cannibalism are also associated with fears of social breakdown. The response in each of these cases provides a forum for responding to those fears by asserting moral control. Although there is a clear connection between the Windigo cannibal monster and famine, such a connection cannot be made in the case of the Beaver and the Kwakiutl. Like the *tamam* witch and animal-man-beings of Chapter 4, the Beaver Wechuge and the Kwakiutl Man Eater represent uncontrolled desire and antisocial behavior. We must ask about the forces that produce such behavior. The Kwakiutl myth relates hunger to uncontrolled desire and the antisocial behavior of parents. The Beaver blame social relationships, especially the mixing of strangers who may not understand the special taboos each individual must observe vis-à-vis the giant-man-eating-spirits from whom the individual acquires his medicine power. Thus, the cannibal monster is a product of a variety of broken relationships. Reactions to the cannibal monster become the means for responding to the effects of environmental extremity or intergroup antagonisms.

The mythical chartering and transformation of cannibal practice

6 · The faces of the soul's desires: Iroquoian torture and cannibalism in the seventeenth century

[T]his "contempt" for the body [as shown in eighteenth century public tortures and executions in Europe] is certainly related to a general attitude to death; and, in such an attitude, one can detect . . . a demographical, in a sense biological, situation: the ravages of disease and hunger, the periodic massacres of the epidemics, the formidable child mortality rate, the precariousness of bioeconomic balances – all this made death familiar and gave rise to rituals intended to integrate it, to make it acceptable and to give a meaning to its permanent aggression.[1]

Many early commentators on the Indians of eastern North America described the emotional satisfaction evident in the prolonged tortures inflicted upon war captives, which in many cases ended with the death of the victim and consumption of parts of the body. The motive for cannibalism was to appease the appetite of the war god who demanded that captives be taken and eaten. The motive for torture was to avenge the death of a family member lost in war. It was customary to adopt war captives. Some were allowed to live and assume the rights and duties of the family members lost in war; others were tortured to death and eaten. In a fundamental sense, it did not matter whether the victim was allowed to live or was tortured to death, because in either case the victim was physically incorporated into the community.

The Iroquois were reported to be eating war victims as late as 1756. Along with cannibalism, there is evidence of heart sacrifice. The heart was fed to the young men of the tribe, probably to imbibe the strength of a victim who had stoically endured prolonged torture. The victim's blood would be drunk for the same reason.[2] The body was cut up and distributed to the chief and common people for feasting. In many respects rituals of torture

125

and cannibalism fulfilled the socioemotional function of mortuary feasts, providing a social occasion for relieving the melancholia of loss.

Incidents of torture and cannibalism are vividly described by the Jesuits who lived among the Iroquois as missionaries and who recorded their impressions in letters and reports sent to their superior in France. In the first half of the seventeenth century, the Iroquoian-speaking Huron lived at the southern end of Georgian Bay in what is now the Province of Ontario, Canada. In 1649 the Huron were driven from their homeland by the Iroquois.[3] The Iroquois were culturally similar neighbors of the Huron and their traditional enemies. The most extensive data on both groups are contained in *The Jesuit Relations,* a careful compilation of the Jesuit experience among the northeastern American Indians. In these writings the Jesuits display their devotion to scholarship, particularly in their treatment of sources. Elizabeth Tooker, who compiled an ethnography of the Huron from 1619 to 1649 utilizing *The Jesuit Relations* as one of her sources, says: "They [the Jesuits] often carefully noted the source of each item of information, and whether it was actually observed or was hearsay."[4]

An example of this carefulness is found in an account of how the Iroquois tortured and cannibalized a Jesuit priest in a Huron village. The details of the torture were obtained from Christian Hurons who were present in the village where the priest was captured and tortured by the Iroquois on the same day. These details were corroborated by examining the tortured priest's remains, which were obtained the day after the departure of the Iroquois from the Huron village. According to the Huron's account, the Iroquois stripped the flesh from the priest's legs, thighs, and arms and roasted and ate it. When the priest was about to die, an opening was made in the upper part of his chest, his heart taken out, roasted, and eaten. Other Indians drank his blood, saying that the priest had been very courageous to endure so much pain and that by drinking his blood they would become courageous like him.[5]

About these and other details of the torture, the writer says: "I do not doubt that all which I have just related is true, and I would seal it with my blood; for I have seen the same treatment given to Iroquois prisoners whom the Huron savages had taken in war, with the exception of the boiling water, which I have not seen poured on any one." Regarding his examination of the remains of the body and that of a second priest, the author continues:

I am about to describe to you truly what I saw of the Martyrdom and of the Blessed deaths of Father Jean de Breboeuf and of Father Gabriel L'alemant. On the next morning, when we had assurance of the departure of the enemy, we went to the spot to seek for the remains of their bodies, to the place where their lives had been taken. We found them both, but a little apart from each other. They were brought to our cabin, and laid uncovered upon the bark of trees, – where I examined them at leisure, for more than two hours, to see if what the savages had told us of their martyrdom and death were true. I examined first the Body of Father de Breboeuf, which was pitiful to see, as well as that of Father L'alemant. Father de Breboeuf had his legs, thighs, and arms stripped of flesh to the very bone; I saw and touched a large number of blisters, which he had on several places on his body, from the boiling water which these barbarians had poured over him in mockery of Holy Baptism. I saw and touched the wound from a belt of bark, full of pitch and resin, which roasted his whole body. I saw and touched the marks of burns from the Collar of hatchets placed on his shoulders and stomach. I saw and touched his two lips, which they had cut off because he constantly spoke of God while they made him suffer.

I saw and touched all parts of his body, which had received more than two hundred blows from a stick. I saw and touched the top of his scalped head; I saw and touched the opening which these barbarians had made to tear out his heart.

In fine, I saw and touched all the wounds of his body, as the savages had told and declared to us.[6]

Apparently, the Iroquois were indiscriminant in their search for torture victims to appease their war god and their own rage at the mounting losses they experienced in the chronic warfare of the seventeenth century. Europeans as well as enemy Indians were acceptable as victims.

This chapter traces the dialectic of ego-id, active-passive, violent infant and omnipotent parent observable in the cannibalism and torture rites of the Huron and Iroquois. Where food, eating, and characteristics of animals provided the objective correlatives of human subjective states in the cases discussed in Chapters 3–5, the desires and their expression predicated Huronian and Iroquoian personhood. Unlike the Hua and Bimin-Kuskusmin, whose subjective states are encoded by characteristics imputed to food and bodily substances, Iroquoian subjective states are encoded by the wishes of the soul revealed to the individual in dreams. The Iroquois believed that if they did not act on the wishes of the soul they would die. The uninhibited expression of passion and sadism in the torture rites was part of the acting out of such inner wishes directed by a dreamer or a mourning relative. As in the Hua and Bimin-Kuskusmin, the body figured centrally in Iroquoian ontology. However, while the Hua and Bimin-Kuskusmin body is the reservoir of life-giving as well as defiling *natural substances,* the Iroquoian body harbors the positive and negative *spiritual forces* that animate individual and social power. An analysis of these forces as they are expressed in myth, dream theory, and torture rituals illuminates the logic of Iroquoian cannibalism.

The displacement of desire and the projection of cannibalism

If an Iroquoian dreamed of antisocial desires directed inwardly toward members of the social group, the desire was acted upon in some symbolic form, which as Wallace says, "had a prophylactic effect."[7] Dreams directing hostility at members of other nations were satisfied either in pantomime or real life. Additionally, Hay says, the Iroquoian practice of torturing and eating captured enemies "provided an opportunity for displacement of the impulse to eat members of one's own group onto outsiders."[8]

The importance the Iroquois attached to controlling cannibalistic urges toward one of their own is seen in the story of the foundation of the League of the Iroquois, a union of five Iroquoian nations formed to end the constant warfare among them that had made them vulnerable to attacks from other Indian groups. Deganawidah, the mythical figure who sets out to bring peace to the nation, established a code stressing righteousness, health, and power. Righteousness meant justice practiced between nations; health meant soundness of mind and body; and power meant authority, "the authority of law and custom, backed by such force as is necessary to make justice prevail." In order to bring this message of peace into the world, however, Deganawidah first made a journey "to bring such evils [as cannibalism] to an end, so that all men may go about from place to place without fear."[9]

The fear of cannibalism may have been related to the practice of endocannibalism in response to famine conditions. There are numerous references in *The Jesuit Relations* to cannibalism in connection with prolonged famine among the Huron and the Iroquois. Bressani's Relation of 1653 describes famine conditions that forced the Huron to eat their dead.[10] The Relation of 1649–50 mentions that the people of one Huron mission were too weak to cultivate the land during one year and had to live in the woods on roots, wild fruits, and a few fish. The writers of this Relation say that although the Huron felt no compunction about eating their enemies, necessity forced them to eat their dead: "[F]amished teeth ceased to discern the nature of that they ate. Mothers fed upon their children; brothers on their brothers; while children recognized no longer, in a corpse, him whom, while he lived, they had called their Father."[11] In a letter written in the Huron country dated March 13, 1650, Ragueneau writes to the father general about the scourges of famine, plague, and warfare:

For, in truth, our Hurons are distressed not only by war, but by a deadly famine and a contagious plague; all are miserably perishing together. Everywhere, corpses have been dug out of the graves; and, now carried away by hunger, the people have repeatedly offered, as food, those who were lately the dear pledges of love, – not only brothers to brothers, but even children to their mothers, and the parents to their own children.[12]

In fantasy, also, famine was associated with cannibalism. For example, in 1636 the Good Twin of the Iroquoian creation myth was reported to have been seen carrying the signs of a very bad year. These signs were a poor ear of corn he carried in his hand and a man's leg that he was seen tearing with sharp teeth.[13]

I suggest that cannibalistic urges were as salient for the Iroquois as they were for the Algonkians and that during the period after the formation of the League these urges were displaced in the warfare complex of the Iroquois.[14] Although the Iroquois were more sedentary and cultivated corn, life for men was much the same as it was for the Algonkians. Iroquoian women were the farmers; men hunted, trapped, and engaged in warfare. Boys were expected to acquire spirit helpers in much the same manner as described for the Algonkians. These guardian spirits, as they were called, took the place of the parents upon whom the boy depended and from whom he had to separate emotionally in order to become a whole man.[15] The belief that the most powerful of these spirits, Aireskoi, desired human flesh, suggests that in addition to the urges that were displaced onto the bodies of war victims, cannibalistic urges of parents were projected to the realm of the supernatural.

The Huron deity Jouskeha and the Huron-Iroquois deity Aireskoi were personifications of the Sun.[16] Aireskoi was called the "Master of life" just as the Algonkians considered animals to be "master of the game."[17] Invoked on many occasions, Aireskoi was offered sacrifices, including human flesh. During the torture of a female captive, an old man prayed to Aireskoi saying: "Aireskoi, we sacrifice to thee this victim, that thou mayst satisfy thyself with her flesh and give us victory over our enemies."[18] The Jesuit captive who describes the torture of this woman also observed a bear sacrifice offered to Aireskoi in atonement for not eating the bodies of captives. According to this priest the following prayer was offered:

Aireskoi, thou dost right to punish us, and to give us no more captives [referring to the fact that they had not taken an Algonkian captive that year] because we have sinned by not eating the bodies of those whom thou last gavest us; but we promise thee to eat the first ones whom thou shalt give us, as we now do with these two Bears.[19]

The Iroquoian creation myth as a paradigm for focusing desire

The Iroquoian creation myth, which is also about the beginning of good and evil, presents a model of and for the Iroquoian response to inner experience. The myth begins with the merging of good and evil and ends with their splitting and the establishment of guidelines for the regulation of evil. Evil is regulated by giving in to its mythical manifestation just as dreams are given in to, that is, in a controlled manner. This solution is necessary because power to control adversity is perceived as emanating from the embodiment of evil.

Such an approach to evil is structurally similar to the constellation of evil described for the Hua and the Bimin-Kuskusmin. The Hua, it will be remembered, merged good and evil in female fertile substances and constructed strict rules regulating the flow of these substances between individuals so that the power of the substances would continue to operate while its good and evil manifestations were separated. The Bimin-Kuskusmin Great Pandanus Rite begins with the merging of good and evil, which are subsequently

130

separated in the rituals of torture and cannibalism. At the level of myth, the Iroquoian creation myth represents a similar evolution from an initial unity to the dialectical splitting of socially encoded contraries.

The Iroquoian conception of creation exists in numerous texts and summaries that differ only in minor details. The Huron legends of the seventeenth century are not as extensive and detailed as the version recorded later among the Seneca, one of the member nations of the League of the Iroquois.[20] Tooker says that the Huron creation myths recounted by the French are incidents from the Iroquoian origin myth.[21] The version paraphrased and discussed here is from Wallace's presentation of the Seneca version recorded in the nineteenth century.[22]

In the beginning there was a world above in the sky. This world was good: There was no sickness, no need to work, and it was never too cold or hot. In this world there was a great tree that shed light half the time and half the time kept dark. There was a family with five sons. The youngest son loved a young woman so much that he became weak. He told his parents to tell the woman of his love and his weakness and that if she married him he would become strong again. The woman consented to become his wife but soon the youngest son became sick and weak again. He called his oldest brother and told him that he had received instructions in a dream that the tree must be plucked out by the roots by the four older brothers. In the dream, the tree spoke saying "There is another generation coming out of the living tree. It will sprout out of the ground beside that living tree which gives light and control over the land." The younger brother instructed the older brothers to do away with the old tree so that the young tree could grow and prosper.

The brothers went to the tree and saw that a young sapling was indeed growing on top of the ground. The younger brother then said he would go forward and take hold of the living tree and pull it down by hand, as the dream dictated. But the oldest brother said again, "Why do you think you will die if we do not pluck out the tree of light?" And the sick man said, "It is a true dream that has power by itself. It must be done; if not, I shall die for cause of disobedience."

After the brothers pulled the old tree down, an air came up through the hole in the earth, very tender, and they heard the sound

131

of the south wind, which is the air of life. And from this air the wife of the youngest brother conceived a child. After she had conceived, her husband pushed her through the hole to the earth below so that she would become the mother of earth-beings. On earth she is supported by a mud-turtle who supports the earth on his back. She gives birth to a daughter who becomes very fond of going to the water against her mother's wishes. When the girl is a young woman and begins her monthly periods, she disobeys her mother and goes into the water, where she conceives twins, called the Evil Twin and his brother the Good Spirit.

The twins dispute in their mother's womb over how they shall be born. The Good Twin was born in the right way but the Evil Twin came out under his mother's arm. The mother dies after she has instructed her own mother to bury her body so that "the sun will rise at my feet and go down toward my head and the moon likewise." She also says that from her body cornstalks will grow that will bear corn that will be good for seed. She says, "Keep it and plant it here, for generation after generation of my children will live here forever. One of my sons shall be called the Good Spirit, and he will place good things upon earth and will regulate it. And the other you shall call the Evil Spirit, and he will place all the evil things upon the earth."

The Good Spirit creates the sun, moon, and people. He also makes rivers and streams and improves the corn that grew from his mother's grave so that it is easier to grow. He also creates game animals. The Evil Spirit undoes the good his brother makes and in an attempt to equal his "creative elder twin," he creates evil things, like bats, frogs, owls, worms, snakes, and carnivorous monsters. Once he even stole the sun, and he and his grandmother ran away with it to keep it for themselves, but the Good Spirit brought it back.

When the work of creation is nearly completed, the Good and Evil Spirits meet and each claims to be responsible for the creation. They agree to settle the dispute by a contest of magical power. Each one would try to make the Rocky Mountains move. The Evil Spirit tried unsuccessfully. Then the Good Spirit made the giant turn around with his back to the mountains, and while the giant's back was turned, he moved the mountains close up behind him. When the giant turned around he bashed his nose against the side of the mountain.

Then the giant said, "You are the Creator. I submit and beg to be allowed to live." The Good Spirit granted the request, on condition that he would help the people and take them as his grandchildren. So the bargain was made: If the people would wear masks representing the giant, and would burn tobacco for him and give him a little cornmush, he would give them power, through the masks, to handle hot coals without being burned, to withstand the cold without shivering, and to drive away disease, witches, and high winds.

The manifest content of the creation myth presents an exemplary model for acting upon wishes revealed in dreams and for emulating the behavior of the gods in masked ceremonies. In the myth it is said that a true dream "has power by itself." If the wish of the dream is not done, the narrator says, "I shall die for cause of disobedience." The narrator is preoccupied with love for a young woman and becomes progressively weaker until his desire for her is fulfilled. Passions, represented by the Evil Spirit or Giant, are also fed at the same time they are controlled. In the bargain that the Giant makes with the Good Spirit, it is agreed that the people are to represent his passions by wearing the masks and feed his desires by burning tobacco and giving him cornmush. In return, he grants them power, through the masks, to handle adversity.

The dialectic of ego and id, active and passive, violent infant and omnipotent parent revealed in dreams and the masked ceremonies is evident in the creation myth. The narrative opens in a world where all opposites are united. The powers of love and hate are held in balance and both are thereby neutralized. Death and pain are nonexistent, life is abundant, there is no sickness, and no one has to work. In this paradise the focal symbol is the tree that unites light and dark, an image of the union of good and evil. This scene represents uroboric unity in which there is complete inertia because all energy is still.

The tree symbolizes the uroboric unity of mother and son. In his analysis of symbols of transformation Jung makes frequent reference to the role of the tree as a symbol of mother-son union. The tree, he says, personifies the mother on the one hand and the phallus of the son on the other.[23] The sapling growing by the tree suggests Neumann's image of the "infantile ego consciousness" still attached to the maternal uroboros, "not yet detached from it and only just beginning to differentiate itself from it."[24] The felling of the tree by the brothers is done "for the sake of the new creation of the world," an act that liberates the sapling "to grow on solid ground" and "live forever." The felling of the tree can thus be read as liberating the germ of the male ego from unity with the parthenogenetic mother, in the same way that the stealing of the flutes liberates the Gimi male from the parthenogenetic female.

The weak, undifferentiated ego of the son is indicated by his inability to act upon his desire for the young woman and his need to send parental figures to get her. His weakness is again exhibited when he must send his brothers to act upon his dream to pluck out the tree. The fact that the brothers get rid of the tree pits the older generation that blocks libido against the younger generation, suggesting classic oedipal themes in the struggle between generations. In this case, however, the struggle, as I have suggested, seems to be between the primal mother and the phallic son.

Once the tree is plucked out, the libido it contains flows freely through the hole where it once stood and impregnates the man's wife. The husband now has mastery over this libido, for he blesses the tree "that had fallen through the earth for the sake of the new creation" and he blesses the new life, in the form of the young tree, that remained. He pushes his wife through the hole onto the newly created earth below where she propagates a new race of beings, called the earth-beings. His remaining behind suggests that he is the master of the events that follow. His position above is balanced by that of the mud-turtle below, which is the only creature powerful enough to bear the earth on its back and thereby to fulfill the "instructions given from above."

On earth, the wife gives birth to a daughter who had been conceived in the world above. When the girl is old enough, she desires to go to the water, the symbol of fecundity; however, the mother forbids her. Once again, the mother is the symbol of blocked libido. The daughter goes to the water against the wishes of the mother and conceives twins, one called good and the other called evil.

The motif of hostile twin brothers, Neumann says, belongs to the symbolism of the Great Mother. This motif appears when the male attains self-consciousness by dividing himself into two opposing elements, one positive and the other negative. This kind of struggle, Neumann suggests, marks the separation of the conscious ego from the unconscious. The separation of the male antagonist from the male-female uroboros, and the splitting of the Great Mother into a good mother and her destructive male consort, marks a differentiation of consciousness and a breaking down of the archetype – an important stage in the dissolution of the uroboros and consolidation of ego consciousness.[25]

The twins of the Iroquoian creation myth separate the forces of good and evil by their conflict in the womb. Although the twins are themselves separated by the death of their mother, they remain interdependent, just as the conscious ego and the unconscious are interdependent in the Iroquoian theory of dreams. The conflict between the twins kills the mother and thereby repeats the theme of the felling of the tree by the brothers in that this act releases libido. In breaking out of the mother's womb, the twins liberate her libido for the purposes of humans (as symbolized by the cornstalks that grow from her body, which are good for seed). At the same time, they become the masters of good and evil, symbolized by their subsequent creative acts. The Good Twin does the work of Eros in his acts of creation, whereas the Bad Twin does the work of the death instincts in undoing all that is done by the Good Twin.

The remainder of the myth is concerned with the creative and destructive acts of the twins, who are now distinguished as older and younger. The union of mother and son is again indicated in the stealing of the sun by the grandmother and the evil twin, who is designated as the younger brother. This theme is reminiscent of Neumann's observation regarding the splitting of the Great Mother into a good mother and her destructive male consort. In bringing the Sun back, the older twin masters the forces that seek uroboric union with the mother. The story ends with the struggle between the older, Good Twin, and his younger brother in a contest to decide who was the ultimate creator of the world. The final mastery by the older twin is achieved when the giant's nose is bashed against the side of the mountain. The older twin does not kill the younger, however. He asks the younger twin to "help the people and take them as his grandchildren"; these words suggest that the evil twin will play a role in the perpetuation of the generations. In return, the evil twin asks that his passions be nurtured so that he can give the people power against adversity. In this sense, he, too, achieves mastery. The mastery is reminiscent of the mastery of the unconscious achieved by acting out the wishes of the soul.

The focusing of desire in dreams and masked ceremonies

In dreams and masked ceremonies, the Iroquois externalized the unconscious and acted upon its demands. Human action and identity were thus ultimately derived from the consciousness of inner states. Subject–object relations were established by acting upon the desires of the soul. The objectively impure object that produced subject-consciousness in response to the dread of pollution, as described in Chapters 3 and 4, did not awaken the Iroquoian soul. Rather, it was the soul's awareness of inner demands and the dread of what would happen if these demands were unmet that produced subject-consciousness.

The dialectic of inner–outer is established by the objective action taken in response to the wishes expressed in the language of the dream. This dialectic is similar to Ricoeur's discussion of subject-object relations in the symbolism of sin. The terror that results in sin-consciousness, according to Ricoeur, is a transformation of the subjective dread of defilement into the fear of the wrath of God. This terror is not from the fear of pollution, as was the case in the symbol of defilement, but from the fear of annihilation due to the ruptured relationship with God. For the Iroquois, the subjective dread of defilement is transformed into fear of the wrathful power of frustrated desire. The Jesuits reported that the dream was the "God of the Hurons" and that the authors of dreams, the spirits, were "the real masters of the country."[26] The dream was "the most absolute master" for if a chief said one thing and the dream another, the dream was obeyed.[27]

In general, if dreams were not granted or symbolically satisfied, the soul became angry and might revolt against the body, causing illness or death.[28] Like the rite of purification, granting the wishes of the soul objectified subjective states while it subjectified the externality of consciousness experienced in defilement. Speaking in analytical language, the instinctual life, the id, was the god who was defrauded if the desire was not gratified.[29]

The dreams and wishes of the soul ranged from simple requests to give a feast or acquire a certain object to the acting out of sexual

136

desire, sometimes in sexual orgies. Nightmares of torture and personal loss were apparently quite common among warriors. A man
might dream that he had been taken and burned as a captive. The
response to such a dream might be to burn the dreamer in order
to avoid the ill fortune of such a dream. In one case, the dreamer,
after being burned, paraded through the cabins with a dog on his
shoulders, publicly offering it as a consecrated victim to the demon
of war, "begging him to accept this semblance instead of the reality
of his Dream." The dog was killed with a club, roasted in the
flames, and eaten at a public feast, "in the same manner as they
usually eat their captives."[30]

Dreams in which hostility was directed at members of other
nations would be acted out both in pantomime and in real life, but
bad dreams about members of the same community were acted
out only in some symbolic form, which had a prophylactic effect.[31]
The acting out of dreams as prophylaxes against the fate implicit
in the wish was based on the idea that a wish, although irrational
and destructive toward self or friends, was fateful, and that the
only way of forestalling the realization of an evil wish was to fulfill
it symbolically.[32] In addition, some dreams were supposed to reveal the wishes of the supernatural. Frustration of the wishes of
the supernatural was especially dangerous and could bring death
to the dreamer and disaster to the whole society, or could even
cause the end of the world. Thus dreams in which the Good Spirit
(a favorite dream-figure) appeared were matters of national moment. Chiefs met and discussed ways and means of satisfying the
demands of the dreamer, who represented supernatural wishes,
and of averting the predicted catastrophe. In his identification with
the gods, the dreamer in these cases assumed the role of prophet
and public advisor.[33]

Wallace notes that the manifest and latent content of Iroquoian
dreams reveals the strong active-passive dimension of Iroquoian
personality. The manifest content of dreams was mainly in the
active voice; the latent content, representative of the underlying
wish, was often passive or self-destructive. Dreams asked or demanded something of the community – that it rally around the
dreamer offering gifts or performing rituals. The dreamer might
be fed, danced over, rubbed with ashes, sung to, given valuable
presents, given an available female by the chief's council, or
burned, depending on the wishes of the dream.[34]

Membership in the Society of Faces provided another modality by which the Iroquois could express what they otherwise could not allow themselves to feel: "a longing to be passive, to beg, to be an irresponsible, demanding, rowdy infant, and to compete with the Creator himself; and to express it all in the name of the public good."[35] The "false faces" were masks donned in rituals held at certain times of the year to drive out witches and disease or to cure illness at any time. The Seneca referred to the False Face masks by the same word they used for the human face. These masks were hideous representations of oral aggression and rage. Painted black, red, or black and red, the masks put a face on desire. They had huge, staring eyes; long, protuberant, and frequently bent noses extended from brow to lips; and the mouths were open and dramatically distorted. The mouths had many forms: "There were wide mouths, upturned at the corners in a sardonic leer, sometimes with huge teeth showing; mouths rounded into a wide funnel for blowing ashes, sometimes with tongue sticking out; mouths puckered as if whistling, the lips everted into two flat, spoonlike disks; mouths with straight, swollen, shelflike lips; mouths twisted at one corner to accompany the bent nose, as if the face had been twisted by paralysis."[36]

According to the legend of the origin of the Society of Faces, the faces were first revealed to a lonely hunter in a dream. Whoever dreamed of a face instructing him to make a mask was obligated to do so. Once completed, the mask was "baptized" by being dunked in the councilhouse fire while the great False Face, of whom it was a living likeness and deputy, was supplicated by the burning of tobacco. Once baptized, the mask was alive and capable of doing almost limitless good or ill. The faces were nurtured and loved like children and most of them belonged to the members of the Society of Faces. Without the care of the society and the activities of the faces, a Seneca community would, in theory, have faced extinction.[37]

The adult who wore the mask impersonated the gods and exerted their power to cure disease, ward off deadly tornadoes, cast out malevolent witches, and bring order to the community. In this impersonation, the masked could vent attitudes and feelings otherwise not permitted. He might gurgle and coo like a baby, thump with sticks on walls and windows, bang open doors, throw fire and ashes around, throw people out of bed, smear them with human excrement, frighten the timid, and, in general, act out the forces of human chaos. The beings whom the masked represented were, according to Wallace, the prototype of the infant: "ambitious beyond their years, desirous of emulating their betters, mischievous and destructive, quickly enraged at neglect or frustration, careless of their parents' welfare, yet hopeful of forgiveness if their dreams of stolen glory were discovered. And at the same time the omnipotent infant was the omnipotent parent, able to cure disease, avert thunder, and scare away evil people."[38]

The manifest content of a torture ritual

The dialectic of active-passive, ego-id, and parent-child revealed in the analysis of the Iroquoian creation myth, dream theory, and masked ceremonies is also evident in a Jesuit account of the torture of an Iroquoian prisoner captured by the Huron. The Huron, who had captured eight Iroquois, brought seven of the prisoners back to Huronia, keeping only the head of the eighth. On the way back they held a council to decide which of the nations would receive the prisoners. When they arrived in Huronia, the old men, to whom the young men gave the prisoners to be distributed, held another council to determine which villages would be given the prisoners. It was customary to give a notable person who had lost one of his relatives in war an enemy captive "to dry his tears" and to assuage his grief.

One of the prisoners was given to a village in which the Jesuits resided. This prisoner was escorted into the village beautifully dressed in a beaver robe with wampum beads around his neck and draped around his head to form a crown. The captive was in very poor condition: "[O]ne of his hands was badly bruised by a stone, one finger had been violently wrenched away, the thumb and forefinger of his other hand had been nearly taken off by a hatchet blow, one arm joint had a deep cut, and both were badly burned."[39] As he came into the village, the captive, who was over fifty, was commanded to sing, and the chief addressed him, saying: "My nephew, you have good reason to sing, for no one is doing you any harm; behold yourself now among your kindred and friends."[40]

Several days later, after more feasting and traveling to another village, the chief addressed the captive:

My nephew, you must know that when I first received news that you were at my disposal, I was wonderfully pleased, fancying that he whom I lost in war had been, as it were, brought back to life, and was returning to his country. At the same time, I resolved to give you your life; I was already thinking of preparing you a place in my house, and thought that you would pass the rest of your days pleasantly with me. But now that I see you in this condition, your fingers gone and your hands half rotten, I change my mind. I am sure that you yourself would now regret to live longer. I shall do you a greater kindness to tell you that you must prepare to die. Is that not so? It is the Tohontaenrats who have treated you so ill, and who also cause your death. Come then, my nephew, be of good courage; prepare yourself for this evening, and do not allow yourself to be cast down through fear of the tortures.[41]

The captive asked how he would die and the chief said by fire. Meanwhile, the sister of the Huron replaced by the adoption of the captive brought food to the prisoner, treating him as if he were her own son. She was very sad and her eyes full of tears. The chief also showed solicitude for the captive, putting his own pipe into the prisoner's mouth, wiping the sweat from his face, and fanning him with a feather fan.[42]

About noon the captive made his farewell feast, which was similar to the feast given by any man before he thought he was to die. Before the feast began, the prisoner addressed the people who were there in crowds, saying: "My brothers, I am going to die; amuse yourself boldly around me; I fear neither tortures nor death." Then he and several of those present sang and danced. Food was given to those who had plates while the rest watched.[43]

The torture began that evening in the house of the war chief where all war councils were held. About eleven fires were lighted along the house and the people gathered. The old and young men were separated in a manner suggesting that the torture was the job of the young men alone. The old men took their places above on a sort of platform extending the entire length of the cabin on both sides. The young men were crowded below, seated by the fires so that there was hardly a passage along the fires where the victim was made to walk. The emotional tone and expectancy with which the torture began is vividly described by the Jesuits:

Cries of joy resounded on all sides; each provided himself, one with a firebrand, another with a piece of bark, to burn the victim. Before he was brought in, the Captain Aenons encouraged all to do their duty, representing to them the importance of this act, which was viewed, he said, by the Sun and by the God of war. He ordered that at first they should burn only his legs, so that he might hold out until daybreak; also for that night they were not to go and amuse themselves in the woods.[44]

Next the captive was brought in and sentenced by the war captain, who proclaimed who would take his robe, who would cut off his head, and who would receive his head, arm, and liver to make a feast. Then the spectators proceeded to burn him as he marched up and down the house making the whole cabin appear as if it were on fire. In response to the victim's shrieks, the whole crowd imitated his cries, "howling at the top of their voices, with firebrands in their hands, their eyes flashing with rage and fury." In addition to burning him, members of the crowd broke the bones in his body, pierced his ears with sticks, and bound his wrists with cords. When he fell on the embers of the fire, a hot brand was applied to his loins and others would have proceeded to stir up the fire to burn him had the captain not intervened ordering the torture to cease so that he would live until daylight.[45]

Most of the crowd then went away so that the captive might be revived with drinks of pure water. As he returned to his senses, he was commanded to sing. At first he sang in a broken, dying voice, and then in a voice so loud he could be heard outside the cabin. The youths reassembled and continued the torture. The Jesuits watching the scene were struck by the fact that, instead of anger and rage on the faces of the torturers, there seemed to be gentleness and humanity, their words "expressing only raillery or tokens of friendship and goodwill." While burning him cruelly on the legs and feet, they said: "Here, uncle, I must burn thee." Referring to him as a canoe, another torturer said, as he passed the brand along the captive's legs, "Let us caulk and pitch my canoe, it is a beautiful new canoe which I lately traded for; I must stop all the water holes well." Another one asked him, "Come, uncle, where do you prefer that I should burn you?" Others said: "Ah, it is not right that my uncle should be cold; I must warm thee"; "Now as my uncle has kindly deigned to come and live among the Hurons, I must make him a present, I must give him a hatchet." Another gives him a pair of stockings made from old rags and these were set on fire. When asked whether he had had enough, the captive replied, "Yes, nephew, it is enough, it is enough," to which the tormentors replied, "No, it is not enough," as they continued to burn him and demand if it was enough.[46]

This continued throughout the night with rests to revive and feed the captive. If he refused to eat, they said to him:

"Indeed, dost thou think thou art master here? . . . For my part, I believe thou wert the only Captain in thy country. But let us see, wert thou not very cruel to prisoners; now just tell us, didst thou not enjoy burning them? Thou didst not think thou wert to be treated in the same way, but perhaps thou didst think thou hadst killed all the Hurons?"[47]

The Jesuits remarked that during this ordeal the captive bore the pain with patience and that not one abusive or impatient word escaped his lips in the midst of the taunts and jeers. He spoke to the company on the state of affairs in his country and about the death of some Hurons who had been taken in war.

At daybreak fires were lighted outside the village to display the "excess of their cruelty to the sight of the Sun."[48] The captive was made to mount a scaffold six or seven feet high, where he was tied to a tree so that he was free to turn around. Three or four of the torturers mounted the scaffold for the last of the torture.

There they began to burn him more cruelly than ever, leaving no part of his body to which fire was not applied at intervals. When one of these butchers began to burn him and to crowd him closely, in trying to escape him, he fell into the hands of another who gave him no better reception. From time to time they were supplied with new brands, which they thrust, all aflame, down his throat, even forcing them into his fundament. They burned his eyes; they applied red-hot hatchets to his shoulders; they hung some around his neck, which they turned now upon his back, now upon his breast, according to the position he took in order to avoid the weight of this burden. If he attempted to sit or crouch down, someone thrust a brand from under the scaffolding which soon caused him to arise. . . . They so harassed him upon all sides that they finally put him out of breath; they poured water into his mouth to strengthen his heart, and the Captains called out to him that he should take a little breath. But he remained still, his mouth open, and almost motionless. Therefore, fearing that he would die otherwise than by the knife, one cut off a foot, another a hand, and almost at the same time a third severed the head from the shoulders, throwing it into the crowd, where someone caught it to carry it to the Captain Ondessone, for whom it had been reserved, in order to make a feast therewith. As for the trunk, it remained

at Arontaen, where a feast was made of it the same day. . . . On the way
(home) [the Jesuits said] we encountered a Savage who was carrying upon
a skewer one of his half-roasted hands.[49]

The focus of desire in torture rituals

The torture ritual just described condenses many of the themes
that have been mentioned so far and introduces others. Like the
Great Pandanus Rite, the torture by the Huron of their captive
constructed, broke down, and then introjected an ego ideal. Burning the victim defiles and breaks down the evil embodied in the
flesh; eating introjects the strength exhibited by the victim's stoic
endurance. Like the victim of the Bimin-Kuskusmin rite, the Huron torture victim, although brought from outside social boundaries, is identified with culturally valued models of personhood.
In the case of the Huron, the victim represents a loved and revered
compatriot. In the case of the Bimin-Kuskusmin, the male and
female victims represent a living model of the mythical, androgynous ancestors.

The behavior of the captive during the ritual – his patience, tol-
erance, courage, and passive acceptance of the torture – makes him
a model of and for the stoic endurance of great pain. In this behavior he reflects the power of the Evil Twin, who promised to give
people power, through the masks, to endure pain. Throughout the
torture, the captive endeavors to stand up to his captors, to be their
equal. The competition between the captor and their captive is
reminiscent of the competition between the Good and Evil Twins
for mastery.

More than personal pride may motivate the captive to accept his
role. Torture is witnessed by the Sun and the God of War, supernatural beings shared by all Iroquoian tribes. By playing his part
in the appropriate manner, by not dying before the morning of the
sacrificial offering (a feat that requires cooperation from the master
of the torture ritual), he becomes one with these supernatural
beings at the same time that he becomes one with the Huron nation. In the end, it seems that uroboric unity is reestablished.

To understand the immediate motivations of the torturers it is
necessary to digress somewhat and consider the Iroquoian response to death. The Iroquois and the Huron were deeply affected
by death. The following words, quoted from the Address of a

Seneca Condolence Council upon the death of a chief, depict the Iroquoian experience of grief in terms suggesting the clinical details of melancholia.

The organs within the breast and the flesh-body are disordered and violently wrenched without ceasing, and so also is the mind. . . . Verily, now, the life forces of the sufferer always become weakened thereby. . . . The disorder now among the organs within [the] breast is such that nothing can be clearly discerned . . . when a direful thing befalls a person, that person is invariably covered with darkness, that person becomes blinded with thick darkness itself. It is always so that the person knows not any more what the day light is like on earth, and his mind and life are weakened and depressed . . . the sky is lost to the senses of that person . . . such a person knows nothing about the movement of the sun [i.e., night and day and the passage of time are not noticed] . . . invariably the mind of that person is simply tossed and turned on the grave of him in whom he fondly trusted. . . . Verily, it is a direful thing for the mind of him who has suffered from a grievous calamity to become insane, [for] the powers causing insanity are immune from everything on this earth, and [insanity] has the power to end the days of man.[50]

Elaborate and lengthy burial rites helped the bereaved to sever their emotional and social ties with the deceased. A man who was approaching death made a feast to which he invited all of his friends and important people. After his death many feasts were held and gifts distributed among the relatives to dry their tears. Much time and effort were directed toward providing the dead with the proper clothing and the guests of the funeral with gifts and food. Gifts were given to console a person who did not consider himself comforted if given nothing but words. Intense mourning continued for ten days after the funeral and lesser mourning for a year thereafter. The soul did not immediately abandon the body after death. When the corpse, covered in a beaver robe, was taken to the grave, the soul walked in front and remained in the cemetery until the Feast of the Dead, which was held approximately every eight to twelve years. Until the dead were finally laid to rest in this feast, the soul might walk through the villages, take part in feasts, and eat what was left from the evening meal.[51]

The Feast of the Dead has been described as "the most brilliant and solemn of all observances among these savages."[52] At this time each family would exhume the remains of those relatives who had died since the last feast and cleanse the bones of flesh, dress them in new clothes, and adorn them with bead necklaces or with garlands. After a local ceremony everyone would then take the bones to a central meeting place, which might be quite distant. During the funeral procession, the dried bones – which were referred to as the souls – might give the bearers a "pain in the side for life" if they did not take the precaution of "imitating the cry of the souls."[53] The final rite was celebrated in the midst of an enormous crowd. In the name of the dead the chiefs distributed many presents, which went largely to strangers invited to the feast in order to admire the country's magnificence. Thus, the final ceremony had a pronounced collective character. Its purpose was "to reintegrate the dead into social communion."[54]

By means of the Feast of the Dead the Huron confirmed their friendships, saying that "as the bones of their deceased relatives and friends were united in one place, so they would live together in the same unity and harmony."[55] In this way the Huron reaffirmed the ties that united them. By establishing a society of the dead, they regularly recreated the society of the living. The final interment of the bones, one might add, also severed the living from the emotions they had invested in the dead.

A Huron who died a violent death did not receive the normal burial. If the body was brought back at all, his bones were not removed from the grave and reburied at the Feast of the Dead, as the people believed that those who died in war had no communication in the afterlife with other souls. Thus, a kinsman killed in war was lost in more ways than one. The normal procedure for handling grief was unavailable and the social being grafted upon the physical individual was permanently lost with no gifts to compensate the loss. The solution to this dilemma seems to have been to find someone who could fill the social and emotional gap, as well as the gap in the afterlife occasioned by the death of a warrior.

The socioemotional aspects of grief were worked out either by letting the victim live as a substitute for the dead warrior or by torturing and killing him. The torture ritual emulated the social processes of death and burial. The victim gave a farewell feast as was normal for a man about to die. The chief announced a burial feast to which all would be invited, including members of other villages. There is in all this a gruesome twist for it was the victim's body that provided the feast and the focus for expending the sadistic fury associated with melancholia.

Freud draws an analogy between the work performed in melancholia and in mourning. In the work of mourning, by declaring the object to be dead, the ego in time is impelled to give up the object. In melancholia the same work is accomplished through rage. By disparaging the object, by defiling, denigrating, and slaying it, the fixation of the libido is loosened. The final severance from the object comes as the fury spends itself.[56]

The uninhibited rage of melancholia that marks the torture of the victim is offset by the chief who ritually regulates the expression of this and other emotions. The chief directs the young men, the active agents in the torture, not to go and amuse themselves in the woods during the night and not to burn the victim to death too quickly. The social control of the unrestricted passion played out in the torture is also suggested in the projection of oedipal themes. The prisoner is burned in his "fundament," his fingers cut off, and, in the end, he is beheaded. The chief's position as ritual regulator of these actions suggests that he presides over his son's castration, symbolically deflected onto the body of the victim. But the victim may also represent the father who is executed by the young men in a classic acting out of the oedipal theme. By eating the victim, the chief as well as the youths incorporates desired masculine traits.

These images and actions are reminiscent of Freud's depiction of the primal oedipal struggle in *Totem and Taboo*.[57] Freud hypothesized that the solution to the primordial problem of evil lay in the killing and eating of the father by the sons of the primal horde, an event bringing guilt, remorse, instinctual renunciation, and the cultural superego into the world. Hatred and envy motivate the murder, which restores order and peace through the expiation of hatred and the renewal of love. Cannibalism combines a physical and spiritual identification with the victim. Forever lost, the victim is restored inside the ego, where the characteristics of the victim are assumed. The cultural superego – the source of restrictions and morality, the very foundation of the social order – is thus internalized in each individual in the most literal sense – by eating. A Freudian interpretation of Iroquoian cannibalism, thus, might see in the victim a surrogate for the original victim – the primal father.

Conclusion: The latent content of torture and cannibalism

George Devereux suggests that the primordial pull of intrafamilial bonding is at the basis of the incest taboo. In the incest taboo Devereux sees an attempt in part "to impede an excessive temporal prolongation of early intrafamilial affective bonding, as well as an extreme (and therefore desocializing) intensification of sexual bonding, which the permanent sexual receptiveness of the human female does render possible."[58]

The pull of intrafamilial affective bonding is the behavioral equivalent of what I have been calling the primordial pull of the maternal uroboros that collapses all opposites. This pull is evident in the Iroquoian torture rites and in the creation myth discussed in this chapter. Desocializing affective bonding between mother and son is described in the creation myth. It is the responsibility of the elder brothers of the myth to break this bond by plucking out the tree in the first part of the myth, killing the mother in the second part, and separating the grandmother and the younger grandson in the third part. Thus men seek to break the unity of opposites contained in the mythical female. Like the Gimi flute myth, the Iroquoian creation myth gives men the task of breaking up the paradise of the parthenogenetic woman. Having accomplished this task, the brothers of the Iroquoian myth then become locked in competition for mastery. The moral and power relationship between them is established when the older twin defeats the younger twin in the battle over who was to be the Creator. In return for his agreement to cooperate with creation and to harness his destructive powers for social purposes the Evil Twin is promised that his desires will be fed. Thus, order is instituted in exchange for allowing the animating power of chaos a place in human events.

Women do not play a passive role in the Iroquoian creation myth or in everyday life. They seek to reincorporate family members, just as Gimi women, in a different modality, seek to reincorporate their beloved family members. Iroquois women were entitled to publicly demand that a murdered kinsman or kinswoman be replaced by a captive. Male relatives were morally obligated to go out in a war party to secure captives for adoption or torture. Wallace notes that warriors and women played complementary roles in the revenge process, "each dependent on the other for validation and fulfillment of status."[59]

147

The rage of bereavement is given expression in the context of the torture. The torture itself can be understood as permitting the expression of intrafamilial psychic impulses through orgiastic rites culminating in the physical incorporation of a surrogate kinsperson. The torture indulges these impulses at the same time that it controls them, by restricting the actions of the torturers. The rite provides a model of unrestricted passion and a model for the regulation of such passion between close kin.

Unrestricted passion involves all family members, not just father and sons, in complex instinctual impulses including oedipal and counteroedipal desires as well as cannibalistic and countercannibalistic urges.[60] All surrogate members of the family romance played the role of victim in the torture ritual.[61] A Jesuit priest, captured by the Iroquois in 1653, describes the treatment of three women captives and their children:

They brought three women from the same nation, with their little children, and received them naked, with heavy blows of sticks; they cut off their fingers, and, after having roasted one of them over her entire body, they threw her, still alive, into a great fire, to make her die therein, – an act uncommon, even there. And, as often as they applied the fire to that unhappy one with torches and burning brands, an Old man cried in a loud voice: "Aireskoi, we sacrifice to thee this victim, that thou mayst satisfy thyself with her flesh, and give us victory over our enemies." The pieces of this corpse were sent to the other Villages, there to be eaten.[62]

The torture victim drawn from outside social boundaries becomes the surrogate target for the expression of impulses that might be directed within. In torture, violence is expressed; in cannibalism, violence is ritually devoured. The whole affair is the means by which maleficent violence is transformed into a beneficent substance, a source of peace, political strength, and fecundity. The monstrous acts perpetrated against the victim and his stoic endurance prove that humans are stronger than the forces of evil and that out of chaos it is possible to produce order. The sadistic burning of the Huronian victim physiologically transforms raw emotions. Individuals who are "cooked," Lévi-Strauss says, are those deeply involved in a physiological transformation from the natural to the cultural. Although Lévi-Strauss was not referring here to the symbolic meaning of the burning of torture his comments apply:

The putting onto the oven, like the roasting of women in childbirth or pubescent girls, may be a symbolic gesture intended to mediatize a person who, still unmarried, has remained imprisoned in nature and rawness. . . . The conjunction of a member of the social group with nature must be mediatized through the intervention of cooking fire, whose normal function is to mediatize the conjunction of the raw product and the human consumer, and whose operation thus has the effect of making sure that a natural creature is at one and the same time *cooked and socialized*.[63]

Seventeenth-century Iroquoian torture was both part of the need to socialize and regulate violence and an acting out of the dissymmetries of power among Europeans and the various Indian nations of this part of colonial North America. As observed in eighteenth-century European torture victims, Indian victims who did not bend under the torture gave proof of theirs and their nation's strength, which no power could succeed in bending. In these times, when death became a way of life and either lordship or bondage the options open to warriors, the torture complex channeled destructive energies needed for the development of warriors and taught men and women alike that even as victims they could dominate. Torture victims thus were essential for the individuation process. The enemy's body mediated the raw and the cooked of social relations and psychological development in a world torn by strife and competition. Where the enemy body was unavailable, a dog or a bear was substituted. When these animals were substituted, however, it was with the knowledge that the gods preferred human flesh. Torture and cannibalism were the means by which a nation facing bondage sought to dominate.

The ferocity of the torture rituals cannot be separated from the severity of conditions during the seventeenth century where death from hunger, disease, and warfare became a way of life. It was torture and warfare or give up altogether. In the end, the Huron did give up and fled. Two Huron "captains" came to the Jesuits and described their plight, saying, "Thou hast seen more than 10 thousand of us dead at thy feet; if thou wait a little longer, not one of us will be left to thee."[64] The utter despair of these men was evident in their resignation to death for themselves and their people. They said that whoever fled would only "find death, where they think to find life. . . . Hunger will attend them everywhere, and they will not be exempted from the scourge of war."[65] They saw themselves as "nothing but ghosts, and souls of the dead." They said of their land, "[It] is not solid; it will open very soon to swallow us, and to put us among the dead, among whom we therefore already reckon ourselves."[66] These are the words of a dismembered and incorporated nation.

7 · Raw women and cooked men: Fijian cannibalism in the nineteenth century

Cannibalism among this people is one of their institutions; it is interwoven in the elements of society; it forms one of their pursuits, and is regarded by the mass as a refinement.

Reverend Thomas Williams, missionary to Fiji from 1840 to 1853[1]

In nineteenth-century Fiji, cannibalism was a key symbol, the focal paradigmatic gesture upon which orderly social relations were mythically and ritually based.[2] The passions exhibited in cannibal custom – the rage, joy, fierce aggressiveness, and sexual excess – were deeply etched in the Fijian collective psyche and social foundation. In many respects, nineteenth-century Fijian culture can be characterized as "a pure culture of the death instinct," a phrase Freud used to describe the sadistic superego seen in melancholia.[3] Warfare was one of the bases of Fijian society. Periods of peace in epic tales receive special mention as interludes between the intertribal warfare. When a tribe settled for any length of time in one place without fighting, this fact was recorded as worthy of note. Flying over parts of Fijian territory, which is composed of numerous islands, one can see the surviving earthworks of scores of circular ditched or moated fortifications. The Fijian dictionary contains many obsolete terms referring to war and cannibalism, the names of war clubs, and numerous words pertaining to clubbing and spearing. Clunie relates that recent archaeological discoveries reveal that fortification and, therefore, warfare have been present in Fiji from at least A.D. 1200. The oldest reliable Fijian oral traditions, dating back several centuries, also emphasize the constant strife and intertribal warfare. About the Fijians, Captain James Cook wrote:

[T]hese [the men] of Feejee are formidable on account of the dexterity with which they use their bows and slings, but much more so on account

151

of the savage practice to which they are addicted. . . . of eating their enemies whom they kill in battle. We were surprised that this was not a mis-representation. For we met several Feejee people at Tongataboo, and, on inquiry of them, they did not deny the charge.[4]

Among the myriad gods in Fiji, the war gods were especially well known. These gods are variously described as "gigantic and cannibalistic," murderous and always "fresh from the slaughter," and vicious with an "over-riding passion for human brains."[5] Their lust for death was expressed by priests through whom the war gods spoke. In the middle of the nineteenth century, speaking through his priest, one war god said:

I am the god of war. I only am strong, and wise to fight. I can do as I please. War is that by which I amuse myself. I love it. I wish now to sport in war. War is the proper exercise of chiefs, it becomes them. There are two things worthy of gods and Chiefs – war and feasting. Go on. Build your walls, erect your fences. War is good: I will fight: my hand is strong, and long also; I can extend it to all lands; – to Somosomo, to Tonga, to Britain, to all lands. Well, prepare your fences. The people of Vungalei (a town near Viwa) are preparing theirs. All the towns are preparing for war; but none will prevail against Bau.[6]

The feasting referred to in this passage meant the feasting on cannibal victims.

For over two hundred years, Europeans best acquainted with Fijians speculated on why they ate one another. The most logical reason, at least in the minds of the Europeans, was a presumed shortage of other meat. Reasons given by the Fijians included revenge, a gourmet appreciation of human flesh, political ambition, masculine bravado, fear of the chief, or because it was the custom. All of these reasons were complementary to the cultural sense of cannibalism, yet, as Sahlins remarks: "[A]ll of them put together cannot logically motivate the meaningful content of a custom which, as constituted by relationships to other customs, is the condition of their own possibility as appropriate motives."[7]

Cannibalism and the origin of culture

In a discussion of myth and practice, Sahlins explicates the "cultural sense of cannibalism" in traditional Fiji. The cultural sense of cannibalism refers to its place in the total cultural scheme, its relationship to other categories or concepts. Thus, the meaning of the Fijian cannibal victim is found in an analysis of its relationships "to chiefs, gods, turtles, whale teeth, and women."[8] These relationships are paradigmatically expressed in a mythically based model of and for reality entitled "How the Fijians First Became Cannibals." This myth, which is ostensibly about the origin of cannibalism, is, as Sahlins notes, about the origin of culture. Its central problematic, the solution of which constitutes the social relationships of which cannibalism is a part, is the tension between senior and junior males in competition for the same women. Thus, I suggest, the myth also offers a paradigmatic solution for the problems of the psyche as well as for those of culture.

The "first man" lives alone with his aging wife and three daughters near Vatukarasa, on the western coast of Viti Levu. . . . The old man broods on killing his wife and replacing her with his daughters, there being no one else to marry them. But one day the daughters find a handsome young stranger washed up on the shore from the wreck of his canoe. They restore the half-drowned castaway and suggest he take them as wives. The stranger agrees and accordingly requests the daughters of their father, offering in return to plant the elder's food. Deeming the proposal impudent and the offer insufficient, however, the old man turns the youth out, saying he will have to do a work of mana to merit the daughters. The disconsolate hero, whose name [we now learn] is Tabua, "Whale Tooth," sleeps fitfully and next morning eats some Tahitian chestnuts and a snake he has managed to kill. Suddenly he remembers having seen a whale drift ashore the same time he did, and realizing the people here are still ignorant of whale teeth, he invents a disingenuous scheme to demonstrate his mana. In the difficult task of extracting the dead whale's teeth, however, he accidently knocks out four of his own front teeth. Still, he is able to fit the accident into his plan. He burns the whale carcass and returns after some days to the house of the "first man," whom he finds lecturing his daughters on the fickleness of youth, and proposing that his wife be strangled and they take her place. To the elder's chagrin, Tabua proceeds to tell a fabricated story about the whale teeth, a myth within the myth: that he had cleared some forest in the manner of a yam garden, and planted his own four

153

teeth, which in the course of eight days miraculously increased in number and size. The self-evident value of the whale teeth allows the ruse to succeed. Indeed, the evidence of Tabua's feat so delights the mother and daughters that they fall gleefully on the elder, in the course of which embrace his wife pulls out his beard. The old man reluctantly consents to his daughters' marriage, claiming in return the right to make certain laws: that hereafter whale teeth shall be called "tabua" after the hero's name; that such tabua *shall be used as payment for the woman in marriage; and that all further castaways who wash ashore be killed and eaten, lest they, like Tabua's teeth, should only increase in the land. Hence the title of this tale, "How the Fijians first became cannibals."*[9]

In his analysis of this myth, Sahlins demonstrates the cultural logic of Fijian cannibalism in the foundation of the Fijian social order. The myth begins with the relationships of nature, which are transformed into those of culture. Through trickery and agreement, antisocial and antagonistic elements are transformed into relationships of the social order. A foreign male, a castaway washed up on shore, is turned into a chief after demonstrating his reproductive powers in connection with growing whale teeth, which wins him wives in exchange for whale teeth. Whale teeth are Fiji's supreme riches, being considered "about the price of a human life."[10] The hero, who is named Whale Tooth, has magical qualities enabling him to save his own life by substituting whale teeth in place of himself. The old man's claim that in the future all strangers washed on shore will be killed and eaten adds cannibal victims to the equivalency established between whale teeth and chiefs.

In reality, whale teeth, chiefs, gods, and cannibal victims are equated. In his journal of 1840, the missionary-ethnographer John Hunt remarked about a particular king that he made a speech only when he distributed rebel corpses for his people's consumption or when whale teeth were divided. "These," Hunt said, "are their two great things."[11] The Great Thing was the title of the most powerful chief in western Fiji, which is the setting of the myth of Tabua.

Cannibal victims were generally acquired in battle outside the chiefdom. The ruling chief relied on his foreign sailors and turtle-fishers for the procurement of ritual victims needed for human sacrifice. The sacrificial victim was needed for the exchange of

154

mana between men and gods on such occasions as the construction of temples, chiefs' houses, and sacred canoes; ceremonial visits of allied chiefs; installation of chiefs, and first-fruit rites.[12] The phrase cooked men for raw women refers to the duty of the stranger-king to supply cannibal victims in exchange for the women originally ceded him by the indigenous people. The attribution of raw and cooked is actually made by the Fijians. One chief was quoted as having apologized for being unable to give the bodies of young men or else a woman "brought raw" to the master builder of his sacred canoe. This chief explained that Christianity "spoils our feasts."[13]

The developed Fijian chiefdom was organized around an exchange of raw women for cooked men between three general categories: foreign warriors, immigrant chiefs, and indigenous members of the land. The foreign warriors were needed to procure human sacrificial victims from beyond the land. Some of these warriors were "sea people" including turtle-fishers who were also referred to as "fishers of men." The several foreign allies, who might also include land allies, were originally attached to the chief and chiefdom by the gift of a royal daughter. The allies were thus wife-takers to the chiefly line, as the chiefs were wife-takers to the indigenous people. As the chief shared bodies with the people in return for women, so the foreign warriors brought bodies to the chief.[14] This flow of women against (cooked) men, Sahlins notes, is specifically a *founding transaction,* establishing the perpetual relationship between lines that is not necessarily continued as an empirical system of generalized exchange. The triadic structure of the Fijian chiefdom and the transformations between raw and cooked was "an organization of all of nature as well as all society, and of production as well as polity." Thus, from the myth of Tabua we see that cannibalism was a condition for the founding of Fijian society.[15]

The Fijian drama of creation and the symbolism of evil

Missing from the mythical events chartering Fijian cannibalism is the conceptualization or experience of evil as objective defilement or subjective sin. There seems to be no association of either good or evil with cannibalism. There is no suggestion that cannibalism was meant to physically introject the desired and destroy the un-

155

desired, nor did it bring to an end the torturous process of resolving unbearable grief and sadistic revenge. For the Fijians, cannibalism was largely an appetite that had to be fed and that was as natural and necessary as incest to the primal father of the Tabua myth.

The Tabua myth corresponds in structure to myths of primordial chaos discussed by Ricoeur, in which "chaos is anterior to order and the principle of evil is primordial, coextensive with the generation of the divine."[16] The events told in the Tabua myth regulate cannibalism and end incest. Tabua would have eaten the island's inhabitants or been eaten by them had he and the father, upon the urging of the daughters and mother, not arranged the exchange of wives for whale teeth. Tabua signifies his identity as a cannibal by his breakfast of snake and Tahitian chestnuts. The snake is the body of the autochthonous snake-god, the creator Degei. By slaying and consuming the snake, the hero is able to incarnate an indigenous divinity. By eating the Tahitian chestnut, he consumes the daughter of Degei, since ancient tales tell that the chestnut is the form assumed by Degei's female descendants. Furthermore, endocannibalism is symbolized by the hero's loss of his teeth, an affliction visited upon those who eat their own kinsmen.[17]

In the Tabua myth and in reality the stranger-hero represents the youthful, active, disorderly, magical, and creative violence of conquering princes. The divine, the natural, and the foreign are opposed to the human and the cultural. The hero comes as a terrible outside cannibal to a place where endocannibalism and incest reign. These are not associated with human fault, but with human desire. Redemption from the chaos represented by endocannibalism and incest is accomplished by the social contract with its substitutive satisfactions and its resolution of the power struggle between the native chief and the hero. This kind of scenario is evident in the investiture of Fijian kings.

The investiture of the Fijian king reproduces an original disorder in the establishment of order. Having committed monstrous acts against society, proving he is stronger than it, the stranger-hero is domesticated by the investiture ritual, which brings system out of chaos. One such ritual, described by Sahlins, consciously follows the legend of an original odyssey that brought the ancestral holder of the title into power. The chief makes his appearance from the sea, as a stranger to the land. Disembarking, he is escorted along a path of barkcloth recapitulating the correlated legendary passages of the men of his title from foreign to domestic, sea to land, and periphery to center. In general ritual usage, barkcloth serves as "the path of the god." Barkcloth is hung from the rafters at the sacred end of the ancient temple and is the avenue by which the god descends to enter the priest. Since the stranger-king is himself a triumphant warrior and cannibal, a god descended upon the land, the installation represents his descent as a god. During the ceremony the chief is escorted by elderly women between two rows of women who are seated alongside the barkcloth. Barkcloth is the preeminent feminine valuable in Fiji, the highest product of woman's labor, and the principal good of ceremonial exchange. Mediated by women and barkcloth, symbols of natural and social reproduction, the chief dies as a terrible cannibal to be reborn as a domestic god.[18]

The symbolism of death and rebirth is repeated in the kava ceremony. In this ceremony, the chief is symbolically killed by the indigenous people at the moment of his consecration when he is offered a deadly potion of kava that conveys the land to his authority. According to legend, the kava is grown from the leprous body of a sacrificed child of the native people. The kava the chief drinks poisons him. The kava is a sacred product of the people's agriculture. The installation kava is brought forth by a representative of the native owners who proceeds to separate the main root by the violent thrusts of a sharp implement. This kills the kava root (equated with the child of the land) whereupon it is passed to young warriors of royal descent who, under the direction of a priest of the land, prepare and serve the ruler's cup. Traditionally the warriors chewed the root in order to offer the cup: "The sacrificed child of the people," Sahlins says, "is cannibalized by the young chiefs." The water of the kava is referred to as sacred rain water from the heavens. When the ruler drinks the sacred offering, he is in the state of intoxication Fijians call "dead from kava"; to recover from this state is "to live." The cup of fresh water he is given revives him and he is brought again to life – in a transformed state.[19]

Thus, the sacrificed, cannibalized, child of the people gives birth to the chief. In consuming the cannibalized victim, however, the chief is himself sacrificed (by the poisonous contents of the kava he drinks). These symbolic acts of endocannibalism represent the chaos out of which a new order – that is, that of the new ruler – is formed.

Poisoned and reborn as a domestic god, the chief, instead of eating the people, must now send for real human victims from outside society and give feast to the people *"on bodies of his own kind."* The cannibal victims are like the chief himself – "terrible outside gods." Having consecrated the victims in raw form, the chief distributes a certain portion of the cooked bodies to the native owners whose power he has usurped – the priests and other chieftains of indigenous lineages.[20] The cooked bodies represent in another modality the chief whose investiture has cooked (i.e., socialized) him for a different fate, at least for the time being. The analogy between the cooked body of the newly installed chief and those of the cannibal victims is evident in the final rites of the installation, when the ruler is once more escorted along a path of barkcloth. This time the path is lined with warriors whose victory song as the chief passes between their lines is the same as the one they chant over the body of a cannibal victim.[21]

In time the chief himself will be killed for, as Hocart says, quoting a Fijian: "[F]ew high chiefs were not killed."[22] The king ushered to the throne in the ritual described above was the successor of parricides. According to legend his title originated in bloody exploits of the slaughter of a younger brother by the son of the elder, followed by the son of the murdered man taking revenge on both the murderer and his father.[23]

Indo-European legends of divine kings display a structure that is similar to the Fijian philosophy of polity. The king is an outsider, an immigrant warrior prince whose father is a god or a king of his native land. Exiled, perhaps because of his love of power or banished for a murder, the hero is unable to succeed in his own land and takes power elsewhere. Through a woman – a princess of the native people whom he gains by a miraculous exploit involving feats of strength, ruse, rape, or murder – the heroic son-in-law from a foreign land demonstrates his divine gifts, wins the daughter, and inherits half or more of the kingdom. "Before it was a fairy tale," Sahlins says, "it was the theory of society."[24]

Fijian cannibalism

Chaos, order and the Fijian oedipal drama

The generative core of Fijian cannibalism includes two central features: (1) the generation of the social order from chaos; and (2) the resolution of oedipal tensions in the succession of generations. The play of unrestricted passion between all family members is evident in the Tabua myth and in cannibal practice. The desire borne by these wishes represents the chaos that the Fijian system of order indulges by bringing "foreigners" from other shores.

The Tabua myth opens with a compelling version of the primal horde archetype. The father has blocked his daughters' sexual energy by reserving it for himself. The stranger-hero appears from outside society and is used by the daughters in the ruse to free their sexual energy from the father's possessive hold. These events recall the central problematic of the Iroquoian creation myth created by the blockage of libido. Who will control the succession of generations is at issue. The struggle for control is between the primal father, on the one hand, and the alliance formed between the stranger, the daughters, and the wife, on the other. Thus, this myth presents women acting to break the uroboric hold of a male, contrary to the Iroquoian myth, in which men alone play this role.

The absence of sons in the Fijian primal horde prompts us to ask whether the stranger washed up on shore is a banished son returning to kill the father and claim the libido of his mother and sisters, in the manner of Freud's primal horde. Luc de Heusch's analysis of royal incest among several peoples of East Africa and Rank's analysis of Indo-European hero myths prompt this suggestion. Addressing the question of the source of the East African kings' charismatic appeal, de Heusch notes the frequency with which these kings ritually marry their real or symbolic mothers. Such a marriage grants power, just as the barbaric outsider from the sea has power on Fijian shores. By being removed from normal rules of kinship, descent, and marriage, the East African king is sacralized and superhuman. His incestuous marriage also serves to reunify the royal lineage, which in the struggle for sucession is torn by fratricide. The royal installation and marriage with the Queen Mother are further interpreted by de Heusch as a playing out of the oedipal drama. Adding to de Heusch's remarks, Paul notes further that the political and sacred authority of divine kings is always accompanied by oedipal symbolism. This symbolism, in Paul's opinion, is not just a template for a psychological drama of individual proportions but constitutes a template for human social organization in general and the succession of generations in particular.[25]

The interpretation of the Tabua myth in terms of oedipal themes is further suggested by Rank's analysis of myths of hero births in which he shows that hero status is granted to the banished son who returns and claims hegemony over the father. Referring to but one among many of the themes in these myths, Rank suggests that the hero who kills the father who refuses to give his daughter to any of her suitors kills "the man who is trying to rob him of the love of his mother; namely the father."[26]

The relations of Freud's primal horde pit father against son. The killing of the father by the sons results in the institutionalization of the moral and the social orders because the sons, overcome by guilt, renounce their desire for incest and introject the ego ideal represented by the father's restrictions (see discussion in Chapter 6). The primal horde represented in the Tabua myth also pits father against son, but here the social order is not based on instinctual renunciation as Freud suggested was true in the origin of culture, but on the renunciation of one basic instinct (incest) and the regulation of another (cannibalism). The transformations and exchange effected in the Tabua myth constitute culture by introducing the foreigner who, because he is an outsider, is more powerful than the indigenous people. He is, however, a symbol of disorder by virtue of his killing of the father. In showing he is more powerful than the father, the stranger forces the father to renounce his daughters. By giving up incest, the father gains whale teeth, the Fijian equivalent of human flesh. However, the stranger is not exempt from renunciation for he must renounce endocannibalism (symbolized in the eating of the snake). By giving up endocannibalism the stranger gains wives. Thus, renunciation, substitution, and exchange lead the Fijian social order from the undifferentiated level of the primal horde to a developed chiefdom, as Sahlins says, "organized by an elaborate cycle of exchange of raw women for cooked men between a basic trio of social cum cosmic categories: foreign warriors, immigrant chiefs, and indigenous members of the land."[27]

Fijian cannibalism

Channeling basic instincts in cannibal practice

In *The Future of an Illusion* Freud argues that culture began with the prohibition of ancient desires – incest, cannibalism, and the lust for killing.[28] In Fiji, however, as already mentioned, cannibalism and lust for killing motivate basic cultural themes and establish basic cultural categories. For example, gods demand cannibal victims, chiefs send armies to war, and young men seek the title of manslayer, which gives a man his identity.

Training for violence began at birth. The umbilical cord of a baby boy was loaded into a musket "and shot away that he might kill in a war."[29] Girl babies might be killed by their mothers or a hired woman because they were not of direct service in war. Pieces of human flesh were rubbed over the lips of little children and infants and a portion put into the mouth so that they might be "nourished by its juice and trained in the practice of cannibalism." Mothers taught their young to hate tribal enemies by kicking and trampling the dead enemy bodies brought in for sacrifice and eating. Children orphaned by war or murder were disparagingly known as "the children of the dead" until they grew up and avenged their parents' deaths. In games one child would take the role of the enemy body while the others would drag him about singing the cannibal song.[30]

As they grew older, boys were tossed the less desirable cuts from cannibal feasts. They learned the martial arts in mock battles fought with clubs and scaled-down spears and bows and arrows. They also learned to become skilled with the various Fijian weapons from more formal training by their fathers. When a large number of enemy children were captured, they were sometimes brought home alive to give boys practice, shooting them, spearing them, or clubbing them to death. Boys might also gain experience in killing by practicing on adult prisoners who would be tied or held down while the boys beat them to death with their toy clubs. Training also occurred on the battlefield. Boys who accompanied the army to carry extra weapons were encouraged to help by killing the helpless wounded and by mutilating the dead.[31]

A boy became a man only when he had killed an enemy with a war club, as distinct from all other weapons excepting the musket in later years. The war club was the mark of the phallus and the

manslayer its living embodiment. A man whose club was still unstained with blood at death was doomed to pound human excrement with his dishonored weapon in the afterworld. Special rev-
erence was attached to the war club of the manslayer and there
were ceremonies to title the warrior and his club after he had killed
an enemy regardless of his victim's age or sex. Killers were honored by giving them new titles and commemorative names. If a
chief or notorious warrior was the victim, the slayer received the
special honor of being allowed to take his victim's name. Such a
killer also received a title commemorating and representing his act.
Thus, a man might take his name from the chaos and slaughter he
caused or his name might commemorate the stench arising from
the rotting bodies caught in the mangrove roots after he had engineered a memorable slaughter.[32]

Warriors who had slain ten people received an honorary title and
a special decoration, a black and white cone shell to wear on each
arm. Those who had killed twenty and thirty received distinct
titles and were presented with a second and third decoration.
When warriors to be titled returned with their victims, they were
met before the temple of the war god by the chiefs, priests, old
men, and the general populace. Here the battle reports and offering
of the captured bodies to the gods were conducted. Reed tokens
were taken from the killers by the priests as symbols of their loyalty and service to their gods and chiefs. Each killer was called out
in turn by name. The presiding chief or priest exhorted each man
to throw away his old name "like a circumcised foreskin, and to
take a new one to commemorate his new killer status."[33]

Castration and phallic themes are reflected in the treatment
given to the victims' bodies and in the licentious dancing and sexuality associated with the cooking of the victims' bodies. The sexual organs of both male and female victims were cut from the
bodies and hung up on display in the sacred trees growing near the
temple, and left there to rot. The head and penis of an enemy chief
or leading warrior might be tied to a pole or sent back to his home
town as an ultimate insult, reminding all that the victory was as
much sexual as it was political.[34]

The castration of the victims had a fertility aspect. The sexual
organs were referred to as fruit and hung in sacred trees. As the
flesh cooked, the warriors and women danced the lewd death
dance. As the women danced naked, they compared their genitals

with those of the stripped carcasses of the enemy warriors, prais-
ing the sexual prowess of the killers, and sexually insulting the
naked enemy bodies.[35] Feeling mounted during the cooking and
feasting until the tension was broken in a frenzied sexual orgy.
Normal social restrictions were abandoned for the night (the first
night of the warriors' return) and women copulated indiscriminately with the warriors. The next morning, one observer noted,
the women were unable to move.[36] Thus, unrestricted sexuality is
temporarily expressed along with the destructive aggression channeled through the acts of cannibalism, castration, and murder.

Women add to the phallic, castrative themes at the naming ceremony by singing erotic songs as they present the warriors to be
titled with bowls of red paint (the color of war paint) with which
to anoint their bodies. The warriors are then stripped naked by a
senior man and they stand naked astride the corpses, plastered
with red paint, holding their clubs over their heads before all the
people. In some places the women were charged with stripping
and painting the warrior. The chief or priest then swathed the warrior in folds of barkcloth.[37]

The phallic masculinity of warfare, an inverted fertility cult of
death, is also indicated in the sacred status given to newly returned
killers. The warriors fasted during the day and were allowed to eat
only at night when they were fed with a fork by attendant boys.
They spent the first night and much of the following morning in
dancing the death dance while a party of women danced the lewd
death dance in return.[38]

Activity during the four days after the warriors' return alter-
nated between unrestricted sexuality and aggression, and forced
observation of rigid rules of behavior. During this time they were
treated as short-term chiefs and were given special privileges.
They were allowed to club other men's pigs and were openly lusted
after by women. On the other hand, they had to observe special
restrictions such as not being allowed to enter any building other
than a special hut erected for their use and the temple of the war
god. They kept their clubs on their shoulders for the duration of
the four days, even sleeping sitting up with them held in position.
On the final evening they went through a bathing and cleansing
ritual. Other ceremonies on the fourth day were held while the
rest of the population was subjected to strict silence. Canoes were
sent to fetch water from a certain stream; the water was taken to

the temple where the killers assembled to drink it. While this was going on everyone else retreated to their houses and all noise, even the crying of infants, was prohibited.[39]

The swathing of the newly returned killers in barkcloth and the fresh water they drink at the end of the four days of ceremonies is reminiscent of the barkcloth path that conducts the king from the sea at the beginning of his investiture, and the fresh water he drinks at the end of his investiture. The cup of fresh water drunk by the chief revived him, transformed his death as a terrible outside god to his life as an indigenous, domesticated chief and god. Similarly, the killer is transformed from a state of terrible outsidedness and unrestricted passion to a titled and controlled manslayer of renown.

The relationship between senior and junior men and between chiefs and their allies is clarified in the context of warfare. This relationship places junior men in the active, aggressive role vis-à-vis senior men, who hold the passive but powerful role of the paternal lawgiver and enforcer. These roles are rehearsed in pre-battle ceremonies. The allies assemble before the chief, who gives a string of whales' teeth and a bundle of spears to the allied chiefs. The military reviews and property presentations held at the gathering of the forces for war were exciting, dramatic spectacles. As each tribe of allies arrived to reinforce an army they were given a chance to prove their loyalty to the fighting chief. He, in turn, displayed his power by expounding on his policy and rewarding the allied troops with handsome preliminary gifts of food and property. In response, the allied groups each demonstrated their aggressive commitment to the host chiefs, their leaders.[40]

Such ceremonies unified an army made up of diverse and often antagonistic groups of allies. It was not unknown for a group of enemy warriors to infiltrate such a scene and, disguised by their war paint, to crash their clubs down on the heads of the fighting chief and his staff instead of beating the ground in symbolic loyalty. Such an act would be followed by a general slaughter of the assembled troops.[41] Thus, the inherent antagonism felt between senior and junior generations or between chiefs and their allies might achieve direct expression.

The chief, as the incarnation of the war gods, desired human

flesh. The religious aspect of cannibalism was based in the appetites of these gods. The bodies brought back from war were offered to them. The priests played a prominent part in the dissection
of the bodies and the cooking of the meat in the pit-ovens, which
were either close to the temple or within the temple compound.
The cannibal feast nearly always took place in the temple of the
god on whose behalf the flesh was being eaten.[42]

The gods, who spoke through the priests, displayed the raw
passions at work in the Fijian psyche. When possessed, a priest is
described as being gripped by severe convulsions, speaking in an
unnatural voice, and talking in a hysterical, incoherent fashion.
When the god speaks through him,

the priest's eyes stand out and roll as in a frenzy; his voice is unnatural,
his face pale, his lips livid, his breathing depressed, and his entire appearance like that of a furious madman. The sweat runs from every pore,
and tears start from his strained eyes; after which the symptoms gradually
disappear. The priest looks round with a vacant stare, and, as the god
says, "I depart," announces his actual departure by violently flinging himself down on the mat, or by suddenly striking the ground with a club,
when those at a distance are informed by blasts on the conch, or the firing
of a musket, that the deity has returned into the world of the spirits.[43]

In the distribution of the victims, the chiefs and priests received
the large choice shares of meat. On taking a particularly notorious
enemy, a chief might decide to keep him all for himself in supreme
sacrifice to the war god. If there was enough meat, the warriors all
got cuts according to their social standing. The choicest pieces,
such as the hearts, thighs, and upper arms, went to the chiefs and
priests, while the less desirable cuts such as the hands, head, and
feet went to the lowliest warriors, with boys getting the scraps.
Generally women were not permitted to eat human flesh, but
women of rank were reputed to eat it surreptitiously, and if the
supply was large, common women also consumed human flesh.[44]

Just as important as the erotic nature of the cannibal feasts was
revenge. Notorious enemies, unfortunate enough to be taken
alive, were subjected to far more than the standard abuses and were
cruelly tortured to death before being cooked and eaten. As in
Iroquoian torture, fire played a key role. In one form of torture
the victim was set on fire and turned loose to run free among the

165

spectators, whose exultation mounted as the agony of the sufferer became more intense. In another form of torture the parts of the body of an especially hated captive – such as the ears, nose, fingers, toes, or limbs – were cut off, cooked, and eaten before his eyes with the captors gloating over its flavor and inviting him to partake of his own flesh.[45]

The extent of cannibalism is suggested by Sahlins's review of the nineteenth-century reports. Cannibalism was frequent in the wars waged in the earlier nineteenth century. One source estimated that during a five-year period in the 1840s, no fewer than 500 people had been eaten within fifteen miles of his residence. Massacres of more than 300 people were known to follow the sacking of large towns. On such occasions, more cannibal victims were available than could be consumed. One notorious chief made an alignment of 872 stones, one for each victim.[46] European trade and the beginnings of colonial settlement in the early nineteenth century "fueled the ovens of cannibalism in Fiji to the point of incandescence."[47] Muskets acquired in trade enabled tribes to enter warfare that might otherwise have made peace with their enemy. The Fijian reaction to European trade, Sahlins says, "was distinctively an intensification of transactions in whale teeth and cannibalism."[48] The Fijians "literally assimilated" the competitive ideals of capitalism "as a consuming passion."[49]

Conclusion: Regulating desire in myth and cannibal practice

Following Sahlins's analysis of Fijian cannibalism, I have tried to show how the practice of cannibalism can alternately serve "as the concrete referent of a mythical theory or its behavioral metaphor."[50] But behind myth and practice lurks desire, and I have also tried to say something about the nature of the psychic energy that fueled the nineteenth-century Fijian cannibal complex. Although I do not wish to claim that this energy caused the complex, I suggest that this energy was an integral part of it and must therefore be included in any attempt to unlock the mystery of Fijian cannibalism.

Some say that Fijian cannibalism began out of respect for the gods – of wanting to present the most costly offering that could be made. Since all presentations of food were eaten, the human sacrifice was treated in the same way. The gods told the people to go to war and bring back cannibal victims; thus divine guidance ensured that destructive aggression was satisfied outside social boundaries. Just as whale teeth satisfied material desires and substituted for cannibal victims, cannibal victims taken in war satisfied projected desire and indulged basic instincts.

The Tabua myth is a paradigm for grounding culture in the resolution of problems posed by incest, endocannibalism, and (by implication) lust for killing. These desires, which Freud identifies as the most ancient human desires, are resolved by means of substitution and regulation. Guilt and renunciation did not help the Fijian individual obtain mastery over the death instinct, as Freud suggested; rather, the death instinct was encouraged from birth and channeled by gods who demand cannibal victims, by chiefs who send armies to war, and by priests who title the Manslayer. The death instinct was regulated, not sublimated.

The Tabua myth is reminiscent of the Iroquoian mythical version of uroboric unity. The two myths are structurally similar in that both begin with a kind of paradisal state in which libido is blocked. Both relate events in which this libido is freed. The difference lies in the role played by male and female figures in the symbolic representation of the unity and its symbolic liberation. The Iroquoian myth clothes uroboric unity in maternal symbolism and the Fijian myth in paternal symbolism. It seems reasonable to suggest that where the female body is the predicator of primordial human identity, uroboric unity will be presented in the form of maternal symbols. On the other hand, where conflict between males is the predicator of identity, one might expect that the primal horde led by the father will constitute the unitary symbol of primordial human life.

As the symbol of the unity of opposites, the mediator of raw and cooked, order and disorder, the Fijian chief is structurally analogous to the Hua female body, the Bimin-Kuskusmin androgynous ancestor, and the mother of the Iroquoian creation myth. Like these figures, he attracts qualities of the numinous and his symbolic domain is reconstructed and fragmented in ritual. Unlike these figures, the chief is culturally rather than primordially constructed. His being is not predicated by natural substances or by a primordial splitting of good and evil. His being is due to an alliance with the primal women of the Tabua myth and a primordial contract with the primal father; his perpetuation also depends on the actions of women. It is the job of women to constellate the chief by symbolically transforming him from raw to cooked, and the job of men to usurp his power, kill, and eat him.

Another important difference between the Tabua myth and the primordial characters described in previous chapters concerns the construction of gender. There is no hint of a monistic origin of the sexes in the Tabua story – the sexes come ready made, their roles in the primal drama precast. There is no struggle to physically separate from a uroboric female; the struggle is to release the hold of the primal father. The primal father, however, repeats uroboric symbolism in his desire to contain the women of the primal horde. Unlike the uroboric mother, he does not contain the opposite sex in his physical being; he contains his female counterparts by sexual union and his male counterparts by eating them. Such differences are explainable in terms of the physiological differences between the sexes. The physicality of the uroboric male can only be phrased in terms of killing, eating, and sexuality. The uroboric female, on the other hand, displays these modes as well as the natural processes associated with pregnancy and birth. Birth from the uroboric male can only be culturally produced.

Finally, like the Iroquoian creation myth, the mythical paradigm of Fijian cannibalism illustrates Ricoeur's point that the expression of the experience of evil can be embodied in myths about the beginning and end of the social order as well as in the primary symbols of evil. Ricoeur's myth of primordial chaos corresponds with the structure of the Tabua myth. Here, the problem of chaos is not a problem of human actions or motivations, but a fact of the nature of existence. Redemption from chaos is accomplished by the creation of order, a deed performed continually by the gods and by humans in their ritual activities. In this view, violence and the struggle for power are part of the scheme of things. Evil is overcome by reenacting the original chaos and its solution. In the Fijian case, reenactment is seen in the continual exchange of cannibal victims, an act that regenerates and reproduces basic sociological and cosmological categories.

8 · Precious eagle-cactus fruit: Aztec human sacrifice

And things being so, they [the captives] were made to arrive at the top [of the pyramid], before [the sanctuary of] Uitzilopochtli. Thereupon one at a time they stretched them out on the sacrificial stone. Then they delivered them into the hands of six offering priests; they stretched them out upon their backs; they cut open their breasts with a wide-bladed flint knife. And they named the hearts of the captives "precious eagle-cactus fruit." They raised them in dedication to the sun, Xippilli, Quauhtleuanitl. They offered it to him; they nourished him. And when [the heart] had become an offering . . . these captives who had died they called eagle men. Afterwards they rolled them over; they bounced them down. They came breaking to pieces; they came head over heels; they each came headfirst, they came turning over and over. Thus they reached the terrace at the base of the pyramid. . . . They took them there to their *calpulco*, where the taker of the captive had made his undertaking, had said his say, had made his vow. From there they removed him in order to take him to the house of [the captor], in order to eat him.

From Sahagún's description of the second month's rites.[1]

On April 21, 1519, Hernando Cortés anchored off the coast of Vera Cruz in the Gulf of Mexico. Later, he marched with 300 Spaniards and thousands of Indian warriors hostile to the Aztec into the realm of Moctezuma II, the Aztec ruler of Mexico City. Founded in 1369, Mexico City (Tenochtitlan) was one of the Three-City League that had united the forces of three Aztec kingdoms in subjugating almost the entire Mesoamerican world.[2] Upon meeting Cortés, Moctezuma II referred to himself and the others who inhabited the land of Anahuac (the realm of the Aztec) as strangers, people who were not native to the land but who had come from "far outer parts." The rightful heirs to the land were the Toltec, deposed centuries before by the Chichimec ancestors of the Aztec. Moctezuma II believed Cortés was the Toltec god Quetzalcoatl returning to claim his patrimony.[3]

According to legend, before the Chichimec invaded Tula, the center of the Toltec empire, a prince named Topiltzin represented and was heir to Quetzalcoatl's divinity on earth. This prince was noted for his prohibition of human sacrifice. The gods envied his righteousness and tempted him to sin. His fall from grace brought about his expulsion from the city. He immolated himself by fire and his heart rose upward and became the morning star. Before dying he prophesied that he would return on the anniversary of his birth date, Ce Acatl ("one-Reed"), to reclaim the empire of Tula as his, ruling as Quetzalcoatl's anointed one. This took place near the end of the Toltec empire and prior to the ascension of Aztec rule.[4]

During the centuries thereafter, the Aztecs supposed that Quetzalcoatl brooded in a faraway land patiently waiting to reclaim his imperial rights. New rulers were adjured to look forward to this divine return. When the Spaniards who preceded Cortés were first sighted off the coast of Vera Cruz, the Mexicans rushed to the coast to gather information. This group of Spaniards did not stay, however. They left a present of beads and announced that they would return in a year. That year was one-Reed, the year of the prophecy. After viewing the beads and hearing the newcomers described, the rulers of the Aztec League convened for the purpose of determining the identity of the visitors who had come by sea from the direction of the morning star. They decided that Topiltzin Quetzalcoatl had shown himself and that the time had come to offer him the kingdom he had returned to claim. An embassy of five ranking magnates was enjoined to seek out the newcomers, who by then had departed, for the purpose of discovering their intention toward Moctezuma II – whether they wished him to die or to live out his life under them as their *calpixqui* (local officials who collected tribute for the Aztec king).[5]

In the year Ce Acatl, the year of the prophecy, the gods returned. Moctezuma's envoy carried the full regalia of the god Quetzalcoatl to offer to the strangers who had come in his name. When several months later Cortés entered Mexico City, Moctezuma II placed around his neck a necklace from which hung the distinctive wind jewel of Quetzalcoatl and addressed him saying:[6]

O our Lord, thou hast suffered fatigue, thou hast endured weariness. Thou hast come to arrive on earth. Thou hast come to govern thy city of Mexico; thou hast come to descend upon thy mat, upon thy seat, which for a moment I have watched for thee, which I have guarded for thee. For thy governors are departed – the rulers Itzcoatl, Moctezuma the Elder, Axayacatl, Tizoc, Auitzotl, who yet a very short time ago had come to stand guard for thee, who had come to govern the city of Mexico. . . . O that one of them might witness, might marvel at what to me now has befallen. . . . I do not merely dream that I see thee, that I look into thy face. . . . The rulers departed maintaining that thou wouldst come to visit thy city, that thou wouldst come to descend upon thy mat, upon thy seat. And now it hath been fulfilled; visit thy palace.[7]

Moctezuma II abdicated his leadership to the Spaniards and was murdered not long after. He had not convinced any significant portion of the Aztec nobility that the Spaniards were the sons and ambassadors of Quetzalcoatl. Indeed, their behavior led everyone to the opinion that Mexico had been invaded by enemy gods. On his march toward Mexico, Cortés was lured to Cholula, the center of the Ce Acatl Quetzalcoatl cult, to test his power and divinity. There he gave the nobility good reason to suspect his connection with Quetzalcoatl when he destroyed the divine house and, upon hearing about a plot against him, massacred vast numbers in the city.[8] Wherever he went, Cortés made a speech saying that his lord and king had sent him to give warning to the people and command them not to worship idols, nor sacrifice human beings, nor eat their flesh.[9] He ordered a stop to human sacrifice and cleansed the blood from all shrines. While his order could be interpreted as a reinstatement of Topiltzin's charge against human sacrifice, his cleansing of the shrines was undoubtedly understood as a destruction of the gods and thus the life and soul of the Aztec people.

The shrines that Cortés cleansed were devoted to the worship of gods who lived on the transfigured energy of human hearts torn from the living body in solemn sacrifice. The outstanding feature of these sacrifices, which occurred as a regular feature of the divine calendar, was the enormous outpouring of symbolic, social, and physical energy fused into one wholesale gushing of blood bringing gods and humans into symbolic and physical communion. The

Aztec, not only in human sacrifice but generally, cast their most comprehensive ideas of the way things are and the way humans should therefore act, into physical symbols and acts focused on the body. The fusion, and thereby the regeneration, of the individual, social, and divine was more than a matter of mere belief. What occurred in the mind at the level of belief was concretely enacted in the sacrifice of the hearts of humans. The gods ate offered hearts and drank human blood. Humans ate parts of the offered victims (the rest being reserved for Moctezuma) and donned their skins in order to become the god represented by the victim, for in these sacrifices only gods could be offered to gods. Thus, the divine was brought to earth and the human raised to the divine in bloody and fetid (for after a while the skins smelled) transubstantiation.

Detailed knowledge of Aztec sacrifice and cannibalism comes from several sources, among which the most well-known is the work of Father Bernardino de Sahagún. Upon reaching Mexico in 1529, only a few years after the Aztec kings were hanged by Cortés, Sahagún learned the Aztec language (Nahuatl) and under the dictation of Indian nobles and with the help of Indian scribes proceeded to record the monthly rites and much else in a work entitled *General History of the Things of New Spain*. Sahagún specifically refers to cannibalism in the context of sacrificial rites that took place during the ceremonial feasts of the second, thirteenth, and sixteenth months of the eighteen month solar year. It is likely that human flesh was included in the feasts following the human sacrifices of other months as well. The most detailed information on the practice of cannibalism is found in Sahagún's description of the second month's rites.[10]

On the first day of the second month, the Aztec celebrated a feast in honor of the god called Totec or Xipe at which time they slew and flayed many slaves and captives. On this feast day all who had been taken captive died – men, women, and children. After the hearts, the "precious eagle-cactus fruit," were sacrificed to the sun god – to "nourish" him – each body was rolled down the side of the pyramid and taken to the house of the captor to be eaten. At the house of the captor they portioned the body out:

they cut him to pieces; they distributed him. First of all, they made an offering of one of his thighs to Moctezuma. They set forth to take it to him.

And as for the captor, they there applied the down of birds to his head and gave him gifts. And he gathered together his blood relatives; the captor assembled them in order to go to eat at his home.

There they made each one an offering of a bowl of stew of dried maize, called *tlacatlaolli*. They gave it to each one. On each went a piece of the flesh of the captive.[11]

The cannibalism on the ground was paralleled by the hunger of the gods for the blood and hearts of the newly sacrificed. The climax of the gladiatorial sacrifice of the second month came when the priest "gashed [the captive's] breast, seized his heart, raised it in dedication to the sun," and then gave the blood "standing in the captive's breast [cavity]" to the sun to "drink." The captor took the blood of his captive "in a green bowl with a feathered rim . . . to nourish the demons," meaning the gods. The captor "went everywhere; . . . nowhere did he forget in the *calmecacs,* in the *calpulcos.* On the lips of the stone images, on each one, he placed the blood of his captive. He made them taste it with the hollow cane."[12]

The meaning of precious eagle-cactus fruit

In the dominant symbol of the second month's rites – precious eagle-cactus fruit, the name given to the consecrated hearts offered to the sun – there is a powerful condensation of meaning. Seen from without, these rites point toward a public dramatization of divine and human tyranny. The social inequality produced by the obsession with war, which made nobles out of commoners who had managed to capture sacrificial victims, was a device to provide nourishment for the gods. Warriors were honored on the ground while the hearts of their victims, the precious eagle-cactus fruit, were dedicated to the sun at the top of the temple and the blood splashed all around to nourish the idols. To this spectacle, which included flaying and donning the skins of the captives as well as feasting, dancing, and sexual orgies, Moctezuma invited guests from enemy cities as well as the leaders of the Three-City League. The whole affair was at once a microcosm of the supernatural order and the material embodiment of political order. In all of this the precious eagle-cactus fruit served as a dominant symbol drawing the cosmological, the sociological, and the biological together into one bloody reenactment of the founding of the Aztec universe.

The Aztec sacrificial complex was part of a cosmo-magical-biological schema for social, physical, and sacred being. Aztec ontology merged the physiological, the cosmological, and the divine. Metaphors for sacred and physical being were based on the body and projected onto the screen of cosmology. The psycho-biological nature of the person was formed from cosmological projections, clothed in divine form just as the state and the collective psyche were formed by the divine demands of cosmic beings. The sacrificial complex is explicable only in terms of this basic schema, as Sahlins suggests (see Chapter 1). The decisive quality of the Aztec sacrificial complex lay in the way the Aztec developed an ancient Mesoamerican ontological schema in reaction to the material–historical constraints and opportunities they experienced in the course of their history. The scale of Aztec sacrifice – a scale that exceeded anything known in the Mesoamerican world – is understandable as a predictable response in terms of this schema to political and ecological exigencies threatening the stability of the Aztec system of authority.

Carrasco characterizes Aztec worldview as illustrating cosmo-magical thinking – a mode of thinking that projects models for being onto the cosmos and derives from these models guidelines for ritual action and daily living. The perception of the divine programs human behavior because only the sacred is real; the purely secular is trivial. Cosmo-magical thinking dramatizes the cosmogony by constructing on earth a reduced version of the cosmos, usually in the form of a state capital. As Wheatley describes it, "reality [is] achieved through the imitation of a celestial archetype, by giving material expression to that parallellism between macrocosm and microcosm without which there could be no prosperity in the world of men."[13] The parallellism is between the "regular and mathematically expressible regimes of the heavens and the biologically determined rhythms of life on earth as manifested in the succession of the seasons, the annual cycles of plant regeneration and, within the compass of an individual life, birth, growth, and procreation and death."[14]

Cosmo-magical thinking is evident in the structure of the Aztec city and in the Aztec theory of the body, both of which give material expression to a celestial theory. López Austin demonstrates the isomorphism in Aztec conceptions of the body and in their political, religious, and mythical orders. The body contains three

174

major life centers, or forces: the heart, the top of the head, and the liver. The heart is the center most frequently referred to in the Aztec sources and consists of the following attributes: vitality, knowledge, affection, memory, habit, inclination, will, and direction of action and emotion. The top of the head, or the brain, was associated with conscience, reason, and analytical and logical thought. The liver's attributes were mainly vitality and affection, the forces making an individual brave, vigorous, and strong.[15]

These body parts constitute life centers, that is, areas where the life forces that generated the basic regulatory impulses conferring life and psychic functioning on the organism were concentrated. The life forces corresponding to each of the three body parts are *tonalli* (head), *teyolia* (heart), and *ihiyotl* (liver). *Tonalli,* the best-known force or substance, is defined in terms of irradiation, solar heat, astrological destiny, soul, and spirit. It established a link between man and the divine will, since it was infused into the fetus by the creation gods and was maintained there during life by exposure to the sun, a principal god. The principal location of *tonalli* was the head and the forelock; thus, in capturing a prisoner the Aztec would grasp his forelock to capture his life force. The antiquity of the *tonalli* concept is suggested by the fact that it appears as a ubiquitous iconographic symbol of pre-Columbian Mesoamerica.[16]

Teyolia, defined as the giver of life to people, is an inseparable force essential to life. It is also identified as the entity that "goes beyond," to the world after death. The heart could be made divine by receiving divine fire – an infusion experienced by rulers and those who excelled in the fields of divination, art, and the imagination. The heart could be damaged by immoral conduct, ailments due to other sources, and by sorcerers. The third force, *ihiyotl* (breath), is identified as "night air." Sinners emitted harmful *ihiyotl* inadvertently; certain sorcerers emitted it voluntarily. All three of these forces had to function harmoniously because a disturbance in one could affect the other two.[17]

Health was maintained by keeping the three forces in balance. Imbalances could be due to nature, as in the birth of twins, or to environmental factors. Work, long hikes, and tiredness altered the heat distribution within the body by making *tonalli* hotter, the stomach and the feet colder. The supernatural was also implicated in the theory of disease because the human body was intimately associated with the spirit world. The head was associated with heaven, the sun influenced the heart, and the liver was related to earth. Thus diseases could be viewed as forms of aggression by supernatural forces.[18]

López Austin argues that the ideology of the body was used as an instrument of social control by the Aztec ruling class. Attendance at the temple-schools was compulsory, a stipulation supported by law and the belief that failure to attend might result in punishment by supernaturally inspired disease or death. Another mode of control lay in the belief that nobles were biologically superior to commoners owing to their stronger *tonalli* and *teyolia*. In their investiture ceremonies, nobles underwent symbolic death and rebirth, which included the infusion of divine *tonalli*. Slaves, on the other hand, were conceived as having lost a vital physical attribute that had to be symbolically returned if they were set free by a baptismal ceremony.[19]

The idea that the divine force is more intense in some individuals explains the divine–human status granted to sacred specialists who exercised considerable political control by communicating the wishes of the gods vis-à-vis the frequency and scale of human sacrifice. Such individuals corresponded to an ancient leadership paradigm, which López Austin calls *hombre-dios,* or man-god. As defined by Carrasco, "the *hombre* had the capacity to be possessed, to have inside his body the *dios,* temporarily becoming a divine man." The human figure Topiltzin Quetzalcoatl provided an exemplary model of the *hombre-dios* which was imitated by Aztec priests.[20]

The priests communicated the wishes of the gods to the people and offered life force to the gods in the form of precious eagle-cactus fruit or in the form of drowned, burned or beheaded victims. The second month's rites (described at the beginning of this chapter) emphasized the heart and the top of the head, the two major life centers. The victims were brought to the sacrificial stone "by the hair of the tops of their heads" where their hearts were torn out to "nourish" the sun. This act kept the sun on its daily course, increased the stature of the captor, and conferred godhood on the captive, assuring him a place in the house of the sun and the joy of accompanying the morning sun on the first part of its daily journey for a period of four years. There was no feeling of hate or cruelty in sacrificial slaughter and the victim willingly accepted death on the sacrificial stone.[21]

Body symbolism, then, was part of an elaborate schema uniting the divine and the human. The divine and human were also united in the symbolism of the city, which embodied the divine in spatial terms and dramatized the cosmogony. In addition to feeding the gods vital life forces, the sacrificial ritual repeated the legendary image and charge upon which the city of Mexico was founded.

The Aztecs entered the Valley of Mexico as tribes of hunters, gatherers, and horticulturalists known as the Chichimecas. Long before they entered the valley, warring city-states consisting of small capital cities surrounded by dependent villages and towns flourished there. The most prestigious settlements were founded on the Toltec paradigm of urban center and authority. When a new wave of Chichimec tribes entered the region in the thirteenth century, they encountered a long-standing Lake Culture dominated by the Toltec paradigm. This was the paradigm upon which the Aztec grafted their sacred traditions in founding their universe.[22]

According to their sacred history, the Aztecs emerged from a place called the Seven Caves, which was on an island surrounded by a lagoon. Their patron deity, Huitzilopochtli, commanded their shaman priest to lead the people south to a place where the god would appear in the form of a great eagle devouring its prey on a cactus-tree. After his death Huitzilopochtli, once a human leader of the Aztec, became a god in the form of a mummy inside a bundle, from which he directed his people in their migration southward.[23] He told his people:

Verily I shall lead you where you must go. I shall appear in the shape of a white eagle, and wherever you go you shall go singing. You shall go only where you see me, and when you come to a place where it shall seem to me good that you stay, there I shall alight (come down) and you shall see me there. Therefore in that place you shall build my temple, my house. . . . Your first task shall be to beautify the quality of the eagle.[24]

When they came upon the sacred tableau of the prophecy on the shores of the present site of Mexico City, the eagle, gripping a snake in its beak, was perched on a cactus-tree that stood in a boggy pool of white water – the color of sacrifice.[25] Here the Aztecs built the first shrine to their patron, Huitzilopochtli and

founded the city of Tenochtitlan, which according to divine promise would become "the queen and lady of all the others of the
earth," where they would receive kings and lords who would
"come as to one supreme among all the others."[26] The tableau of
eagle-snake-cactus became the emblem of the city and later the
national emblem of the Republic of Mexico.

In one depiction of the legendary scene, the eagle is shown gripping a scroll-like sign in the shape of a serpent, the Aztec hiero-
glyph meaning war. According to Brundage, this sign stood for
the command of the Mexican god (as symbolized by the eagle) to
his people that he be served with blood and hearts gained in
battle.[27] Among the eagle's multiple associations, the most important were those of sun and war, both of which were represented
by Huitzilopochtli. In his solar manifestation this god was an eagle
because both the sun and eagles "fly high" in the sky. Hunt says
that since eagles are birds of prey = carnivores = killers, eagles
represented warriors. As the divine war leader of the Aztec, Huitzilopochtli was the warrior par excellence. The highest military
order of the Aztec was known as the Eagle Knights, "warriors of
the sun," "probably in memory of this mythical transmutation."[28]
Thus, Tenochtitlan was founded on the principle of warfare.

Tenochtitlan's status was that of *axis mundi* of the empire. During the two hundred years of its existence, an elaborate ceremonial
center, the Templo Mayor, was constructed around the original
shrine. The Aztec divided their city into four quarters for the four
directions of the winds. Their perception of the universe as a four-
cornered world surrounding the center influenced the spatial structure of the city, at the center of which was the Templo Mayor.[29]

The Templo Mayor contained twin temples to Huitzilopochtli
and to Tlaloc, the rain god and synthesis of all sacred manifestations of fertility. Most of the sacred rituals associated with the
eighteen-month calendar were conducted in these temples and
centered on human sacrifice. Cannibalism was the festive after-
math of these more sacred events. Each month was dedicated to
certain gods whose sacred role was in some manner related to the
functioning of the solar system. In most cases of human sacrifice
these gods were impersonated by human victims and the sacrifice
was a self-sacrifice to regenerate or vanquish celestial manifestations of the gods. For example, as has been noted, the precious

eagle-cactus fruit was torn from the body of gods to revitalize the dying sun.

The paradigm for human sacrifice is associated not just with the foundation of the Aztec universe, but with the origin of life itself. This was an ancient paradigm in prehispanic Mexico, the Aztec version of this paradigm being one of many local sociohistoric variations. The ubiquity of primordial chaos and division from a uroboric entity is a striking characteristic of the central Mexican cosmogony.

The Aztec version of primordial chaos

The central Mexian cosmogony, according to Nicholson, begins with two great creative deities described by Hunt as a dual deity, half male and half female.[30] These deities exist in the thirteenth heaven and are self-created, eternal, immutable, the source of all life. They engendered four varicolored sons, "quadrupartite manifestations of the omnipotent Tezcatlipoca: (1) Red Tezcatlipoca (Mixcoatl-Camaxtli or Xipe), (2) Black Tezcatlipoca, (3) Quetzalcoatl (white?), and (4) Huitzilopochtli (blue)." To Quetzalcoatl and Huitzilopochtli fell the job of creation. They produced fire and a half-sun followed by the first man and woman. After that the calendar was fixed, the lords of the underworld were created, and the heavens and the waters were established. After the creation of the rain god Tlaloc, and his spouse, the water goddess, Chalchiuhtlicue, the earth was formed from a great crocodilian monster who had been created in the waters.[31]

Historical time is accounted for in terms of a sequence of suns or world ages, each possessing a distinctive set of characteristics and each terminated by a different kind of cataclysmic destruction. Various accounts of these eras have been preserved. In the summary given by Nicholson, which is based on the "apparent canonical version of Tenochtitlan," the first sun, 4 Ocelotl, was "assigned to the Earth, with Tezcatlipoca presiding." This age was terminated by a swarm of devouring jaguars. The next sun, 4 Ehecatl, "assigned to the Air or Wind, Quetzalcoatl presiding, was destroyed by great hurricanes." The next sun, 4 Quiahuitl, "assigned to the element Fire, Tlaloc presiding, was destroyed by a great fiery rain." The fourth sun, 4 Atl, "assigned to Water, presided over by Chalchiuhtlicue, was terminated in a great deluge."[32]

Tezcatlipoca and Quetzalcoatl were responsible for reviving the shattered universe and initiating the fifth, present sun. The waters, which still covered the earth, had to be dispersed and the earth restored. According to one of several accounts, this was accomplished by the two gods transforming themselves into great serpents in order to battle a horrendous earth monster swimming in the primeval waters. They split the earth monster in half, forming the earth with the upper half and carrying away the other half to the heavens. This angered the other gods who decreed that from her would issue all the necessary fruits to sustain the life of man. From her hair they created trees, flowers, and herbs; from her skin, grass and tiny flowers; from her eyes, wells, springs, and small caverns; from her mouth, rivers and large caves; from her nose, mountain valleys; and from her shoulders, mountains. Thus, the physical characteristics of the earth and its surface are created from and, hence, participate in a generalized cosmic force. This creature cried out in the night, however, and refused to bring forth fruit if not soaked with blood and fed with human hearts. Thus, despite her sacred nature, she depends on humans for sustenance.[33]

The interdependence of human and divine, death and life is evident in subsequent events told in connection with the creation of the fifth sun. Humans were restored to earth before the creation of a new sun. The fundamentals of the various accounts show Quetzalcoatl descending into the underworld to obtain from its ruler the bones and ashes of the previous generation of humanity from which to recreate man. He delivered the bones to the gods. Cihuacoatl-Quilaztli ground the bone fragments into a mass, which was placed in a precious vessel. The gods then performed autosacrifice, permitting their blood to drip thickly on the mass. After four days a male child emerged and, after four more days, a female infant. From these two all mankind was descended.[34]

The daily journey of the sun was conceived in similar terms. The sun rose in the morning, traveled the sky, and at night descended to the underworld where he died, swallowed by the earth monster. In the underworld the sun became the Night Sun, moving like a blind monster through the galleries under the earth shedding a gloomy light for the dead. The rising sun at dawn is thought of as the reincarnation of the dead sun in the person of his son and successor. Each day's sun was believed to be connected by descent with the previous one.[35] The rejuvenation of the sun was accomplished in the monthly rites by the offering of blood and precious eagle-cactus fruit. Here, the rejuvenation was not based on the daily cycle, but on the annual cycle of the seasons. The second month's rites, specifically dedicated to the sun, occurred in the springtime when the sun was renewed in order to provide the strength needed for newly planted crops to grow. In myth and reality blood carried the vital force that conferred divine life.

The events described so far in connection with the creation of the fifth sun transpired in darkness for the new sun had not yet been created. According to one version, the sun was created from the suicide by fire of two gods, Nanahuatl and Tecciztecatl, who were transformed into the sun and moon. In another version, it is the sons of Quetzalcoatl and Tlaloc who become the sun and moon after being hurled into a great fire by their fathers.[36]

After the immolation, the gods waited for the sun to rise. They looked in all directions not knowing which direction would produce the sun. Only Quetzalcoatl knows that the new age will dawn in the east. When the sun appears it is described as "swaying from side to side," as Carrasco says, "an unstable, threatening cosmic orb born out of the self-sacrifice of the gods."[37] Because the sun and moon were unable to move, the gods then decided to sacrifice themselves to ensure the motion of the sun. They say, "Let this be, that through us the sun may be revived. Let all of us die."[38] In one account, Xolotl, the monster god who is a manifestation of Nanahuatl, executes the other gods. In another, it is Quetzalcoatl who executes the gods when Xolotl fails in the task. In performing this self-immolation, the gods set an example followed by man in their human sacrifices. Because gods must die in behalf of cosmic motion, the human victims are first made into gods, a destiny that many warriors felt was their just reward for living. The primary purpose of warfare was to acquire victims whose sacrifice invigorated the cosmos by nourishing the insatiable craving of the sun and the earth for blood and hearts.[39]

Cosmic anxiety and political instability

Hence the fabric of Aztec life was woven from chaos, destruction, and conflict. The myths describing the creation of order convey a message of instability, uncertainty, and paranoia. For the Aztec, the cosmos "is not so much a ballet of great rhythms in which order is accomplished against the forces of chaos, but a revolutionary pattern of ferocious attack by one part of the cosmos against another."[40] In myth the battle was waged between members of the cosmic family while on the ground the battle was waged between the center of the Aztec state and surrounding city-states.

Carrasco points out that the control exercised by the Aztec warriors and priestly nobility of the internal organization of conquered city-states was uncertain. While expanding its territory and tribute controls, the Aztec capital was faced with numerous rebellions demanding complex and organized military and economic reprisals. The antagonism between the core area of Tenochtitlan and the surrounding city-states created immense stresses that were resolved by the human sacrifices carried out at the Templo Mayor. "In this situation," Carrasco says, "the ritual strategy of feeding the gods became the major religio-political instrument for subduing the enemy, controlling the periphery, and rejuvenating cosmic energy."[41] The precious eagle-cactus fruit strengthened the political as well as the cosmic heart of the Aztec universe.

The paranoia of the sacrificial complex was part of the Aztecs' perception of their historical experience. When they were led by their god to the shores of their city, what they saw was later described in gargantuan terms:

This clump of reeds and cane secreted in a great lake of glaucous water, a dreaded lake where seethes fresh water against salt, a place of fish and of birds flying, the place where the great serpent fearfully writhes and hisses and where the majestic eagle dines, Mexico Tenochtitlan, founded by Aztecs and Chichimecs.[42]

The lake surely must have caused bafflement with its combination of fresh and salt water and its underground springs, which formed, in one place, a dangerous whirlpool that sucked canoes down into its dark "abyss." During times of severe drought, the fall in the lake's level exposed this abyss as a deep hole in the mud. Such an underground, and seemingly unnatural source of energy, could have only enhanced the Aztec notion of the dreadful duality of their divine. From the beginning this natural wonder was the

scene of cults connected with Tlaloc, one of the divine manifestations of fertility.

In 1454 a terrible drought and famine was experienced in the
Valley of Mexico. Merchants came from other areas and bought
children from their parents for a few handfuls of dried maize.
These children were bought for sacrifice and probably cannibalism
in other areas. At least 50 percent of the population in the valley
was lost through emigration and starvation. About the emigration
Brundage says:

Older people were sold, and long files of them with wooded yoke collars
at their necks moved daily out toward the mountains beyond which lay
death. In a desperate and no doubt fruitless effort to control this loss of
population, Mexico set a bottom price on its people who wished to sell
themselves into slavery to foreigners: four hundred ears of maize for a
Mexican woman, five hundred for a man. This way it was hoped that
some food might be kept in the city to feed the dying inhabitants. Of
those who left the cities voluntarily, unnumbered thousands left their
meager bones on the trailsides with their tumplines still clamped around
their skulls.[43]

The nobles were probably relatively unaffected but, no doubt,
could feel their society crumbling away. It was decided "that the
gods were raging in their anger at the nations of Anahuac and that
before all reliefs [*sic*] must come acts of placation."[44] This meant
sacrifice and sumptuous performances of key festivals. Among the
numerous shrines built for Tlaloc, Moctezuma I (king at the time)
presented the divine sump hole in the lake with a great carved
stone on which children were sacrificed to please the offended god
of water and to plead for the return of the life-giving rain.[45]

So serious was the famine that the Aztec rulers came together to
discuss the charge made by the priests that the disaster had befallen
their world because the gods were angered at the niggardliness of
human sacrifice. The priests demanded that the sacrificial cult be
expanded to pacify the gods and to prevent a recurrence of their
wrath. In the discussion an agreement was reached on ways to
provide more sacrificial victims during times of drought or other
natural calamities.[46]

The Aztec response to famine will, no doubt, be taken by some
as good evidence for the materialist hypothesis (see Chapter 1). I

suggest, however, that the sacrificial code was expanded, not created, in response to famine and drought. When famine, drought, or political unrest threatened to tear the social fabric apart, this code provided the major cultural support in the struggle against anomie and social dissolution. The idea of sacrifice, of physical communion with the animating forces of the universe, was there from the beginning, available not only to the people who became the Aztec but also to many of the peoples of the Americas. Sacrifice was particularly exemplary for the Aztec, who made it part of their understanding of the origins of their universe and of their city. The sacrificial complex created bonds that cut across kinship ties and thus enabled the Aztec to change from a social structure based primarily on kinship ties to a hierarchically organized urbanized society. Temple offerings provided a center around which a small, insecure, but proud, kinship-based society forged and maintained an empire. Like usurpation by the stranger-hero discussed in Chapter 7, the sacrificial code constituted a theory of society and provided a template for behavior.

The primal mother and the phallic son: Archetypes of uroboric existence

The collective psyche of the Aztec, which emphasized war to appease hungry gods, was based on a theory of birth, death, and reproduction conforming in general outline to Neumann's definition of uroboric existence. Neumann defines uroboric existence as the domination of the ego and group consciousness by the symbol of the "circular snake, standing for total nondifferentiation, everything issuing from everything and again entering into everything, depending on everything, and connecting with everything."[47] The circular snake symbolizes the exteriorization of the ego and its embeddedness in a circular psychological process in which its end is its beginning; its death is its rebirth. The circular structure of the Aztec ego is seen in the symbol of the daily journey of the sun, which rises in the morning from the bosom of the Earth Mother, travels through the sky, and descends to the underworld at night, swallowed by the earth monster.

The merging of maternal, paternal, phallic, procreative, and divine imagery in the second month's rites exemplifies the Aztec version of uroboric existence. The merging took place symbolically on the sacrificial stone and actually in the flaying and donning of skins. For example, during the gladiatorial sacrifice the warrior-victims were tied around the waist with an umbilical–like cord called the "sustenance rope" to the center of the sacrificial stone. Tied in this fashion, the victim was given weapons with which to defend himself against his captor. If he was particularly brave he then fought the "ocelot and eagle warriors," high–status names given to captors and to newly delivered mothers. Upon being sufficiently weakened, the victim was grabbed, thrown down, "stretched out on the edge of the ground stone of gladiatorial sacrifice," and slaughtered by the presiding priest.[48] The bodies of the victims were then flayed and taken to the captor's home, where they were cut up for eating. The identity of captor and captive was merged as the captor did not eat the flesh of his captive, saying, "Shall I perchance eat my very self?" This identity was based on the father–son relationship. When the captive was taken, the captor would say, "He is as my beloved son." And the captive would respond, "He is my beloved father."[49]

The relationship between the captor and captive also paralleled that of mother and child. When a woman had given birth she was said to have "become as an eagle warrior . . . an ocelot warrior" and to have "returned exhausted from battle." Labor was likened to taking up "the shield, the small shield" in order to give off, to cast out, "her heaviness, her pain." The moment of birth was referred to as the "moment of death."[50] When the baby was born, the midwife gave "war cries, which meant that the little woman had fought a good battle, had become a brave warrior, had taken a captive, had captured a baby."[51] The newborn was called "precious necklace," or "precious feather." The creator of the newborn, called "our lord," was said "to hath *inclined his heart*" (emphasis mine). "In his absence," the text continues, "the maiden hath cast forth the baby, our child."[52] Thus, death by sacrifice (inclining his heart) is birth, and birth through woman is death. One is born into this life not to live and prosper but to die on the sacrificial stone and be united with the gods. Sacrifice reconstitutes the original primordial unity.[53]

Neumann interprets the sacrifices of the second month as an exteriorization of the fight of the ego to disassociate from uroboric existence. The reproductive imagery surrounding the sacrificial victim recreates uroboric unity. This unity is fragmented when the victim is killed and the heart is torn from the body, a symbolic disassociation of the ego from its uroboric union with the mother. Tearing the heart from the victim, according to Neumann, also implies castration, mutilation, and sacrifice of the essential male part at the same time it is birth and a life-giving deed for the benefit of giving strength to the nascent ego (symbolized by the early morning sun). Within this context, Neumann explains that the merging of father and son is the symbol of the emancipation of the individual from the domination of the Great Mother. The voyage that the slain victim takes with the sun signifies the development toward the relative independence of an ego endowed with such attributes as free will. However, the ego's emancipation is only temporary, for although the heart sacrifice invigorates the morning sun, enabling it to rise to its zenith, the coming of the evening depletes the sun's vigor and causes it to fall back into the darkness of uroboric unity with the Earth Mother.[54]

The emancipation of the ego from uroboric existence is epitomized by the myth of Quetzalcoatl's return. The relevance of this myth for the final breakdown of the Aztec structure of authority and the abandonment of the sacrificial complex was described in the first part of this chapter. The myths involving Quetzalcoatl – his birth, departure, and return – as well as Moctezuma's peculiar relationship to the mythologem of Quetzalcoatl's return, suggest a series of transformations whereby the experience of fault and ego development is internalized rather that projected onto cosmic entities. Along with the emancipation of the ego from bodily metaphors, we can see in these archetypal events a sequence that spans Ricoeur's symbols of evil: defilement, sin, and guilt.

Quetzalcoatl: From chaos to guilt

For more than a thousand years, from Teotihuacan's empire (A.D. 250) to the end of the Aztec empire (A.D. 1521), the symbols of Tollan and Quetzalcoatl contributed to the organization of political authority in the major capitals of central Mesoamerica by symbolizing sacred space and authority in a trembling world.[55] The Aztec sought legitimacy in their new world by grafting their sacred traditions onto the Quetzalcoatl-Tollan paradigm. They built their city according to the Tollan model of the four corners with the sacred center. There is a reference in one version of the foun-

dation of Tenochtitlan to an association of Quetzalcoatl with Huitzilopochtli at the site where the shrine to Huitzilopochtli was first
built. In another text, Aztec citizens are called "the noble sons,
precious green stones, descendents of Topiltzin Quetzalcoatl."[56]

The most outstanding example of Quetzalcoatl's influence in
Aztec institutions was in the priesthood. Quetzalcoatl was the archetype for the highest Aztec priestly orders. The authority of the
high priests was equal to that of Moctezuma. Moctezuma considered himself to be of the same lineage as Quetzalcoatl, in whose
name he exercised authority. The throne of Tezcoco, one of the
Three-City League, was said to be created by Quetzalcoatl, in
whose name all kings, including Huitzilopochtli, ruled. When one
of these kings was crowned, he was told that the throne did not
belong to him but to the ancestors to whom it would eventually
return.[57]

The symbols of Tollan and Quetzalcoatl had a double-edged
influence on the Aztecs for they contained not only the principle
of order and stability, but also the promise of disjunction, collapse,
and abdication of order and authority. The mythical figure of
Quetzalcoatl represents a transition from chaos to order, and from
the objective to the subjective experience of evil. According to
most accounts of Quetzalcoatl's beginnings, he is born into a
world of ferocious warfare in which it is his job to bring order. He
is described as the lawgiver who was imitated by the priests. It was
by his life "that the laws were ordained and applied, the rituals
practiced, and the customs established in Mexico."[58]

Quetzalcoatl is presented as a two-sided figure: He stands for
order and yet is also known to participate in the fundamental chaos
from which the cosmos is born. In one source Quetzalcoatl
avenges his father's murder at the hands of his paternal uncles by
torturing and killing them and cutting open their breasts. As a
result of this victory, it seems, his reputation was established and
he became king.[59] Accounts such as this and others noting Quetzalcoatl's role in establishing the fifth sun by sacrificing his son suggest that chaos and order are synthesized in Quetzalcoatl's being.

Such versions of the drama of creation are analogous to the
myth of primordial chaos discussed by Ricoeur. To repeat, these
myths illustrate the idea that "chaos is anterior to order and the
principle of evil is primordial, coextensive with the generation of
the divine."[60] Evil is external to humans and is not related to any

human deeds or human fault. Redemption from evil is not a "history of salvation distinct from the drama of creation."[61] Salvation comes with the creation of order out of an ever-threatening chaos, a deed performed continually both by virtue of divine and ritual activity.

The creation of order out of chaos presents one side of Quetzalcoatl that was emulated by the Aztec in their monthly sacrifices. Another side recognized the subjectivity of fault. Quetzalcoatl was famous for his penances, bloodletting rituals, and offerings of snakes, birds, and butterflies instead of humans. Carrasco describes a ritual episode, called a religious breakthrough into the world of the gods, which highlights this side of Quetzalcoatl.[62]

After Quetzalcoatl was installed as king in Tollan, he built a special temple in conformity with the cardinal directions and began intense ritual activity to make himself the human link to the Creative Pair. Quetzalcoatl sought union not through the bodies of others, but through his own subjective and physical self. At the temple, he "worshiped, did his penance and also fasted." He "set thorns into his flesh," and

sent up his prayers, his supplications, into the heart of the sky and he called out to Skirt-of-Stars, Light-of-Day, Lady-of-Sustenance, Wrapped-in-Coal, Wrapped-in-Black, She who endows the earth with solidity, He who covers the earth with cotton. And they knew that he was crying out to the place of Duality which lies above the ninefold heavens. And thus they knew, they who dwell there, that he called upon them and petitioned them most humbly and contritely.[63]

By his penances, Quetzalcoatl became united with the great divinities of the Toltec heaven, which he visits in an ecstatic experience. In ecstatic experience Quetzalcoatl turns on himself some of the sadism of human sacrifice.

The Quetzalcoatl who builds the temple and establishes a model for worship is closely associated with the divine Quetzalcoatl of Tollan who admonishes the people saying: "There is only one god; [he is] named Quetzalcoatl. He requireth nothing; you shall offer him, you shall sacrifice before him only serpents, only butterflies."[64] The god who "requireth nothing" is predicated by subjective rather than objective metaphors for being. Internalization rather than projection represents the process for reaching the divine. The god who "requireth nothing" is one who does not feed on others and does not need others to constitute his being. He embodies the principle of the autonomous ego.

Quetzalcoatl's primordial connection with the original chaos shows that he symbolizes defilement; his awareness of the importance of the relationship of humans to the gods and his call for penance and expiatory sacrifice illustrates his understanding of sin; and his willingness to accept full responsibility for his own sin, which leads to his self-banishment from his capital, shows that he has internalized both the experience of evil and redemption from evil.

The story of Quetzalcoatl's fall, which leads to his self-banishment and the promise of his return, describes the alternation and conflict between two mythic and ritual paradigms for the religiopolitical structuring of the Aztec state. As told in one of the earliest and most reliable primary sources, the political setting of these events involved a religious controversy concerning the appropriate victims for sacrifice. Quetzalcoatl had designated quail, butterflies, snakes, and large grasshoppers for sacrifice but the gods Huitzilopochtli and Tezcatlipoca demanded human victims and forced Quetzalcoatl to leave Tollan with a number of his followers.

The sacrificial paradigm established political boundaries by designating certain areas as sources for sacrificial victims, whereas offering butterflies broadened boundaries and integrated groups. Although Quetzalcoatl was frequently tempted into sacrificing humans, it is said "he would not consent. He would not comply, because he greatly loved his subjects who were Toltecs. The offerings he made were always snakes, birds, and butterflies."[65] Quetzalcoatl sought to break down social boundaries by prohibiting sacrifice and substituting self-sacrifice. One of the sacred cities associated with Quetzalcoatl, Tollan Cholollan, was called a pilgrim's paradise, a place where warring heads of states could meet and worship together. Cholollan was a truce city to which all the "governors and kings of New Spain" came "to do obedience to the idol of Quetzalcoatl." Following a war there was a massive ritual pilgrimage to the city to initiate a period of peace. The pilgrims visited "the house of the oracle of Quetzalcoatl, offering *quail, serpents, deer, and rabbits*"[66] (emphasis mine). Although at the time of Cortés, human sacrifices in great numbers were offered in

Cholollan shrines, earlier the benign, integrating principle of Quetzalcoatl's message may have reigned.

The story of the confrontation between the two paradigms is as follows:

And it is told and related that many times during the life of Quetzalcoatl certain sorcerers attempted to shame him into making human offerings, into sacrificing humans. But he would not consent. He would not comply, because he greatly loved his subjects who were Toltecs. The offerings he made were always snakes, birds, and butterflies. And it is related, they say, that he thereby angered the sorcerers, so that they took to mocking and taunting him. And the sorcerers asserted and willed that Quetzalcoatl be vexed and put to flight.

Then they tell how Quetzalcoatl departed: it was when he refused the sorcerers' decree that he make human offerings, that he sacrifice humans. Thereupon the sorcerers deliberated among themselves, they whose names were Tezcatlipoca, Ihuitmecatl, and Toltecatl. "He must leave his city, for we shall live here," they said. And they said, "Let us make pulque. We will have him drink it, to corrupt him, so that he will no longer perform his sacraments."

And then Tezcatlipoca said, "I, I say we must give him his body to see!" . . . Tezcatlipoca went first, carrying a two-sided mirror the size of an outstretched hand, concealed in wrapping.[67]

In Tezcatlipoca's mirror Quetzalcoatl sees his own evil: "[T]he eyelids were greatly swollen, the eye sockets deeply sunk, the face much distended all over and bilious." Shocked at his image, Quetzalcoatl goes into refuge and has a mask made to cover his face. Looking again in the mirror, he is pleased with his new image and comes out of refuge. The sorcerers then got Quetzalcoatl drunk with pulque and in this state he has a sexual encounter with his sister, a high priestess. When he wakes from this, he is heartbroken and realizing that his authority has been betrayed, he leaves Tollan, with the result that the city falls.[68] When he left Tollan, he promised to return and reestablish his kingdom. The rulers of Tenochtitlan were aware of this prophecy and awaited his return to claim the kingship.[69]

The confrontation between Tezcatlipoca and Quetzalcoatl in this scenario illustrates the Aztec belief that the cosmos was not perfectly balanced between elements representing chaos and those representing peace and order. In this scenario, Brundage suggests, the Aztec thinker was expressing his belief that the "inexplicability of God exceeded his resources of justice." The figure of Tezcatlipoca represents passion and untrammeled will, which were, in the Aztec view, just as necessary for living as was Quetzalcoatl the priest, with his penances and his wisdom.[70] In other words, there is a time when the ambivalent nature of the human spirit emphasizes the dark as opposed to the light, the objective experience of evil as opposed to the subjective knowledge of it. As Carrasco says about the Aztec cosmic order, "[it] was marked by combats, sacrifice, and rebellion, as well as by harmony, cooperation, and stability. But the former actions always seemed to overcome the latter."[71]

In tempting and being tempted, both Tezcatlipoca and Quetzalcoatl show an awareness of the human participation in the cosmic dimensions of chaos. The mirror and the drunkenness indicate the knowledge that evil is internal as well as external and part of human interaction. The story of Quetzalcoatl's fall, like the Adamic myth, portrays evil as residing within the actions of humans and as distinct from good. In the Adamic myth, Ricoeur sees the ambiguity of human nature as destined for the good but inclined toward evil.[72] The serpent, like the pulque with which Tezcatlipoca tempts Quetzalcoatl, represents "that aspect of evil that could not be absorbed into the responsible freedom of man."[73] Thus, even in the subjective experience of fault an objective element is retained.

Neumann interprets Quetzalcoatl's fall as a symbol of a return to uroboric existence through uroboric incest, which he defines as the ego's tendency to dissolve back into unconsciousness.[74] Quetzalcoatl's sister is a symbol of the Great Mother. By being seduced, Quetzalcoatl regresses to son-lover and loses his position as autonomous ego. After the deed, Quetzalcoatl laments his fall:

> Our mother
> The goddess with the mantle of snakes,
> Is taking me with her
> As her child.
> I weep.

"Even Quetzalcoatl," Neumann says, "could not withstand the power of the Terrible Mother. . . . the Feminine proved stronger than the Masculine."[75]

Quetzalcoatl's fall is due to the trickery of Tezcatlipoca in a religious and political struggle for authority. Thus his fall must be understood in terms of political usurpation as well as in moral terms. The Aztec linked their priestly tradition to the Quetzalcoatl line, but they completely discarded his anti-sacrificial policy. The Mexica version of the Quetzalcoatl tale admits the truth of Mexica intrusion and usurpation. The enduring tie the Aztec felt to Quetzalcoatl is demonstrated in an Aztec lament mourning his departure and crying out for his return.

> The turquoise house, the serpent house, you built
> them here in Tollan where you came to rule.
> Nacxitl Topiltzin! Never can your name be lost, for your
> people will be weeping.[76]

According to Paul's generative paradigm for the succession of kingly generations, accepting the usurper's role meant that eventually the Mexica would themselves face defeat (see Chapter 7, note 25).

As the holder of Quetzalcoatl's status and believer in the prophecy of his return, Moctezuma had no other choice but to abdicate to Cortés. Moctezuma was particularly vulnerable because in response to a devastating famine, he had elevated himself from the position of temporary successor to Quetzalcoatl to a king-god in his own right.[77] Moctezuma's knowledge of his usurpation and illegitimacy is suggested by his response to the news that Cortés, whom he assumed was the returning Quetzalcoatl, was coming: "[H]e was . . . terror struck . . . he was filled with great dread, swooning. His soul was sickened, his heart was anguished."[78] In abdicating to Cortés, Moctezuma capitulated his status as both king and god in an act that differentiates king, god, and man. According to Cortés, upon admitting that he claimed to be a god, Moctezuma "raised his clothes and showed me his body, saying, as he grasped his arms and trunk with his hands, 'See that I am of flesh and blood like you and all other men, and I am mortal and substantial.'"[79]

And thus another king gave way in the progress of generations.

Conclusion

Sacrifice is an idea that animated many peoples in their obsession to build a society or to hold one together. About the sacrifices of early Christianity, Feeley-Harnik notes that Jesus "sacrificed to confound what Jews traditionally sacrificed to keep from being confounded." The Jews sacrificed to build a tightly knit social unit; Jesus sacrificed himself to "make one new creation in which there were no divisions" between Jew and Gentile.[80]

The early fathers emulated Jesus' sacrifice as they struggled to build the institutional church. They conceived of martyrdom as "a sacrifice for God while there is an altar at hand."[81] It is significant that an eyewitness to the martyrdom of Saint Polycarp in one of the oldest accounts of the martyrdom of a Christian outside the pages of the New Testament stresses that it was "a martyrdom conformable to the gospel." This means that Polycarp "waited to be betrayed, just as the Lord did, to the end that we also might be imitators of him, 'not looking only to that which concerns ourselves, but also to that which concerns our neighbors.'"[82] After an auspicious death, Polycarp was "crowned with the wreath of immortality" and the faithful attempted to seize his corpse in order "to have fellowship with his holy flesh."[83]

Like the Aztec sacrificial victims, the martyrs died in order to be reborn in the company of the divine. But they also desired to make a public statement with their death. Ignatius, another early martyr, wrote to the faithful: "Grant me no more than to be a sacrifice for God while there is an altar at hand. Then you can form yourselves into a choir and sing praises to the Father in Jesus Christ that God gave the bishop of Syria [i.e., Ignatius] the privilege of reaching the sun's setting when he summoned him from its rising."[84] Thus, the martyrs were after more than communion and transcendence. They were obsessed with building a church. Just as the sacrifice of the Aztec victim clearly marked the lines of social status and recruited people into those statuses, the death of the early martyrs forced people to declare by their acts where they stood vis-à-vis the religious statuses of the times. They either "formed into a choir" to sing praises to the God for whom the martyrs died, or joined forces with those seeking new martyrs to feed the appetites of those who came to feast on the spectacle of the arena.

Sacrifice formed the basis of the Aztec state and empire. Had the Aztec adopted the antisacrificial policy of Quetzalcoatl, it is doubtful that they would have succeeded in building an empire, for this empire depended on the hearts and blood of their neigh-

193

bors. When the Aztec entered central Mexico, their social order differed from the social order of the surrounding city-states. Theirs was a simpler system, based primarily on kinship ties, which contrasted with the highly complex, hierarchical, social order of their neighbors. In order to reign supreme, the Aztec adapted to city life and expanded the sacrificial complex according to a hierarchical view of the cosmos.

Gods, humans, and animals were ordered according to a chain of being in which each segment participated in a common essence and depended on other segments to survive. The first four ages were conceived as being populated by lesser orders of beings. In each age the prehuman version of mankind had been transformed into fishes, monkeys, dogs, butterflies, and turkeys. The present version of mankind was considered a better creation of the gods and placed below the gods and above all other animals in the ladder of power, merit, and perfection. This ladder was revealed in the eating order. Lower orders of animals ate one another and plants, humans ate all of them, and the gods ate humans to subsist. According to Hunt, "[t]his basic idea of an arrangement of the living orders of the universe as a phagohierarchy was the theological justification for human sacrifice."[85]

The spectacle of an eagle gripping a snake conveyed more than a charge to the Aztec people to feed the gods on human hearts. The divine scene bespeaks the majesty of a people whose destiny was constructed on empowering a ferocious universe capable of destroying all life on earth. In this dominant symbol, this "eternal object," emblem of the Aztec nation, ritual and social norms are infused with emotional and physiological stimuli, locking principles of the social with those of the purely sensory in unbreakable interconnection.[86] The eagle's animating power appealed to the senses; its social power lay in the endless round of ritual slaughter that moved a nation; its psychological power lay in merging the physical and the divine.

Sifting through the layers of meaning interwoven in the letting of blood on the Aztec sacrificial stone and in the subsequent cannibal meal, one can identify virtually any of the moods and motivations associated with cannibalism anywhere in the world ranging from the sensory to the sublime: revenge, a gourmet appreciation of human flesh, political ambition, masculine bravado, and the desire to communicate with and feed the gods. As was true of Fijian cannibalism, however, Aztec cannibalism is comprehensible only by considering its place in a larger cultural system. The Aztec placed unregulated cannibalism in the world of darkness, death, and destruction, as happens during the eclipse of the sun when the gods come down and eat men.[87] But it is from this very world, according to the Aztec origin story of the primal sun, that the present world was formed.[88] To maintain their sanity, to convince themselves that the universe will not return to its original state of chaos, and to build and maintain an empire, the Aztec fit sacrifice and cannibalism into an overarching logic of death and reproduction in which humans regulate and dominate controlling forces. The cosmo-magical thinking of the sacrificial complex was expanded by an inward-turning political system that sought ascendancy by waging a cosmic battle against environmental and political enemies.

9 · The transformation and end of cannibal practice

They came back, they returned and settled near Tewara. They turned into stones; they stand in the sea. One of them cast her eyes on Dobu, this is Murumweyri'a; she eats men, and the Dobuans are cannibals. The other one, Kayguremwo, does not eat men, and her face is turned towards Boyowa. The people of Boyowa do not eat man.

Myth of the Flying Canoe of Kudayuri, Trobriands[1]

He promoted a Modawa festival to attract the people out of the bush and back into the village, and when it was concluded after a year he distributed food and pigs among the whole of Nibita. He told the people that fighting and cannibalism must finish; that henceforth they must fight only with food.

From a condensation of Kalanuna, Goodenough Islands, folk-history[2]

Is [there not] a possible religion of life, a religion of love? . . . In the famous myth of the primal murder, Freud encounters an episode that remains unexplained, although it is ultimately the pivot of the drama: this episode is the forming of the covenant among the brothers whereby they agreed not to repeat among themselves the murder of the father. This covenant is highly significant, for it puts an end to a repetition of the act of parricide; by prohibiting fratricide, the covenant engenders a history. But Freud is much more preoccupied with the symbolic repetition of the murder in the totem meal than with the conciliation among the brothers, which makes possible the reconciliation with the father image henceforward engraved in the hearts of men. Why not link the destiny of faith with this conciliation, rather than with the perpetual repetition of the parricide?

From Ricoeur's critique of Freud[3]

In myth or in reality the practice of cannibalism may be transformed in the interest of the social order. The Iroquoian story of the origin of the confederacy and the Fijian myth of the origin of culture are examples of transformation by means of displacement and projection. The culture hero of the Iroquoian story, Deganawidah, who sets out to bring peace to the nation, differentiates righteousness, health, and power from "such evils [as cannibalism]." In this act, Deganawidah introduces an "ethical sense," which makes the law a bond among individuals and among the nations of the confederacy. The bond between an individual and the wishes of the soul, which I have called the dialectic of id and ego, was retained but subjected to social control within the confederacy. Outside the confederacy, the demands of the id were given free rein in the aggression directed against members of other nations. The cannibalistic urges projected onto the Iroquoian god, Aireskoi, also expressed inner wishes.

A similar process of control, displacement, and projection is seen in the Fijian story of the origin of culture. In this story, endocannibalistic urges and incestuous desires are tempered by providing substitutive satisfaction through exocannibalism introduced by the contract between the stranger and the primal father. The contract constitutes a new system of social relationships by differentiating new social categories. Again, the dialectic of subject and object (in this case chaos and order) is transferred from relationships predicating intrasocietal relationships to intersocietal relationships.

Substitution is another mechanism discernible in the transformation of cannibal practice. In equating pig with human flesh, the Melpa substitute the former for the latter in mortuary ceremonies. As I suggested in Chapter 2, cannibalism may have been a variant of an ancient highlands ritual model that channeled vital essence from the dead to the living and the ancestral repository of life force.[4] If groups were primarily inward turning and did not rely on an extensive network of exchange links, mortuary cannibalism is one model for the exchange of substance in regenerating the sources of social reproduction. If, on the other hand, groups were linked to exchange partners in other groups and depended on these links for their ritual and economic status, then cannibalism can be considered a model that negates exchange. I suggest that these models presented alternative exchange paradigms to highlanders

197

just as the two political models symbolized in the figure of Quetz-alcoatl presented alternative political paradigms to the Aztec.

When they entered the Valley of Mexico, the Aztec had a choice between two paradigms for structuring their relationship with the all-important gods. Quetzalcoatl embodied in his dualistic nature both the creative power of chaos in his sacrifice of human victims and the epitome of the loving god in his substitution of butterflies on the sacrificial altar. The first sacrificial paradigm enabled the Aztec to build a state based on the principle of cosmic dominance of the human world. The second paradigm, however, remained a model for an accommodating and integrating social network guided by the moral imperatives of the Quetzalcoatl penitential religion.

Alternative ritual paradigms are also evident in the islands of the Massim, Papua New Guinea, as the myths cited in the Preface and at the beginning of this chapter demonstrate. An examination of the cultural context of these myths indicates that the characteriza-tion of cannibalism as evil does not always imply projection, dis-placement, or substitution, as has been described in previous chap-ters. Another process, evident in the Quetzalcoatl religion of integration, is similar to what Ricoeur calls the "religion of life," or the "religion of love," in his criticism of Freud noted at the opening of this chapter. The "religion of life" that seeks concilia-tion rather than domination is analogous to Freud's Eros: "the in-stinct to preserve living substance and to join it into ever larger units."[5] As the death instinct patterns ritual activity in some in-stances, as shown in the discussion of Fijian cannibalism, the fol-lowing examination of the Trobriand islanders and their neighbors in the Massim demonstrates the influence of Eros.

In his survey of the Massim at the beginning of the twentieth century, Seligman said that "no well-marked groups which can be called tribes" were present. He identified two geographical group-ings under the heading of the northern Massim (the Trobriands, the Marshall Bennetts, Woodlark Island, and the Laughlans); and the southern Massim, of which the D'Entrecasteaux Islands make up the largest portion, with the Island of Dobu at its center. Com-menting on one of the most obvious differences distinguishing the two areas, Seligman said that "the northern portion is character-ized by the absence of cannibalism, which until put down by the

Government, existed throughout the remaining portion of the district."[6]

More recently, several authors have noted the differences between the two areas, particularly between the Trobrianders and the Dobuans, represented by disjunctive orientations manifested not just in the presence or absence of cannibalism, but also displayed in mythical references to cannibalism. An analysis of these myths illustrates Ricoeur's point that myths offer models *of* and solutions *for* existential conflicts.

Several Trobriand myths end with a disjunction between cannibalism and abstention from cannibalism. The first myth, quoted in the Preface, concerns three people, two brothers and a sister, who are migrating for unknown reasons to the Trobriand district. When the two brothers alight on an island in their travels, the brother who looks toward the jungle is a cannibal and the one who stays on the beach and looks toward the sea is not. Malinowski points out that the noncannibal brother is said to be "good" because the story is told by Trobrianders who, unlike the Dobuans, for example, are not cannibals.[7] Indeed, according to Malinowski, in normal times the Trobrianders regard cannibalism "with scorn and moral disapproval."[8] This disapproval, I suggest below, discloses the possibility of cannibalism, a possibility that the myth presents in terms of a moral choice.

The second myth (The Myth of the Flying Canoe) is very long and ends with the disjunction between cannibalism and abstention from cannibalism (see the selection quoted at beginning of this chapter). Malinowski refers to this myth as "perhaps the most telling of all myths from this part of the world" and considers it truly a charter.[9] He calls the myth a "good example" of the proposition "that the identical conditions, sociological and cultural, which obtain at the present time, are also reflected in mythical narratives."[10]

Tambiah's interpretation of this myth touches on themes raised in the preceding chapters. He suggests that the opposition of cannibalism and noncannibalism with which the myth ends – in which one sister casts her eyes on Dobu, where the people are cannibals and she eats men, while the other sister "does not eat men, and her face is turned towards Boyowa" (i.e., the Trobriand Islands) – indicates that "the Dobuans and Boyowans separated by

the divide of cannibalism are nevertheless in a reciprocal relationship (as represented by Kula exchange), an idea nicely represented
by two sisters sharing ties of kinship but standing back-to-back
facing opposite directions and representing disjunctive orientations."[11]

The disjunctive orientations include more than just the presence
or absence of cannibalism, however. Correlative types of behaviors, reminiscent of themes raised in previous chapters, are associated with these orientations. First, it should be noted that the
events told in this myth do not occur in the Trobriands but on the
island of Kitava, directly to the east of the Trobriands; Malinowski
says that the people of this island differ "only very little" from the
Trobrianders.[12] The location of the events on the island of Kitava,
I suggest, is a projection by the Trobrianders of excesses they fear
in themselves.

The Kudayuri Myth of the Flying Canoe begins with the exploits of an older and younger brother who live with their sisters.
The family is a prototypical family, anchored in the area as original
inhabitants who had emerged from underground as the first pos-
sessors of adze and creeper canoe magic. Excess and domination
characterize the activities of the brothers for they build their canoes
not on the beach, as do the other inhabitants of the island, but on
the hill in the middle of the village where it is impossible to launch
the canoes without extraordinary magic. This magic enables the
older brother to fly his canoe from island to island and to arrive
before his kula rivals and thereby monopolize kula exchange activities. Later in the tale there is a drought in Kitava, and the older
brother uses his magic to provide a rainfall that fertilizes his garden
exclusively. The younger brother, thinking he has learned his older
brother's magic, kills him with the help of his subclan brothers
and maternal nephews. However, the following year, when he tries
to build a canoe in the middle of the village, he discovers that he
has not acquired his brother's magic for the canoe will not fly.
Because they are angry with their brother for having killed the
elder brother and having failed to learn his magic, the sisters fly
away. They cut through rocks and follow flight paths analogous
to that of the magical canoe and similar to the path that would be
taken today by kula fleets starting from Kitava. One of them lands
where she turns into a rock and stands in the sea. The other two
travel further south toward Dobu and then return to the location

where they turn into stones. The one who looks toward Dobu is cannibal and the other who looks toward the Trobriands is not.[13]

Tambiah compares and contrasts the events of this myth "with the *social norms* of everyday life incumbent on present-day Trobrianders."[14] He suggests that the myth explores the implications of violence and excess. First, the brothers are coresident with their sisters, in violation of Trobriand residence norms, which send sisters to live with their husbands. The coresidence of the brothers and sisters, he says, "carries connotations of violating the norm of brother–sister social distance; indeed it smacks of an 'involuted' incestuous relation between brothers and sisters."[15] This involution is reinforced by the practice of building the canoe in the center of the village on clan land, rather than taking the canoe to be completed on the beach in a public ceremony. The isolation of the family is marked by their refraining from the obligatory ceremonial proceedings on completion of the canoe, proceedings that "emphasize exchange and reciprocity between villages (or settlements/canoes building and owning groups)."[16] According to Tambiah,

The myth conveys a strong impression that the "involuted" non-exchange relations of the Kudayuri group are the basis for its strong ("excessive") magical powers, and that the proper state of affairs is the *dispersion* and *differentiation* of this group (the separation of brothers and sisters), with the converse implication of its becoming open to relations with the outside world. This outcome necessarily also results in a *weakening* (a partial inheritance) of the original magic in its supra-normal potent form.[17]

About the fratricide, Tambiah suggests that were it not for the fratricide, men would know how to build flying canoes and there would be no flying witches "to haunt and ravage the real crews of ordinary real canoes."[18] Thus fratricide reduces men's magical powers and enhances the natural, malevolent magic of women, represented by the image of flying witches.

In his second reading, Tambiah suggests that the older brother violates the social norms of gardening by practicing magic that brings rain to his garden alone. In contrast to the competitive activity of the kula, gardening should be "informed by communal and cooperative norms."[19] Garden magic should be practiced on behalf of the community of gardeners, not for the individual garden owner. In particular, the chief and his garden magician must practice garden magic for the benefit of the whole district. Thus, Tambiah points out, there is good reason for killing the older brother, who is the headman and who violates communal norms by practicing evil rain magic.[20]

Tambiah concludes that the myth leaves Trobrianders with "the permanent loss of flying canoe magic, but the existence of flying witches as an experiential reality."[21] Trobrianders associate flying witches with evil and with cannibalistic excess. During a storm at sea the full force of the elements may be released in "the cannibalistic attack of flying witches from 'above' and of creatures from 'below' the sea."[22] On land witches may kill and eat their unfortunate victims. In summarizing Malinowski's description of flying witches Spiro notes,

Pouncing on them [their victims] from some hidden – usually high – place, the invisible witch removes their insides, together with their eyes and tongue, before eating them (SLS:45). Possessed of "ghoulish instincts," witches not only eat their living victims, but also devour entire corpses, thereby becoming "more than ever dangerous to the living" (Malinowski 1955:153). This is why, following a death, Trobrianders refuse to walk around the village or to enter the surrounding cultivated land. Although they are especially dangerous at that time, witches are "objects of real terror" at all times (ibid.).[23]

The Kudayuri myth, I suggest, reminds Trobrianders of the dangers of cannibalistic excess at the same time it conveys that there is a choice in this matter, because, as will be remembered, the witch who looks toward the Trobriands is not a cannibal, whereas the witch who looks toward Dobu is. In this connection it is interesting to note Fortune's comment that "Dobuan men are quite certain that the women of the Trobriands do not practice witchcraft spells, as they are equally certain that their own women do so practice."[24] This fact suggests that the disjunctive orientations involve more than cannibalism. The Kudayuri myth pits competition against cooperation, the destructive consequences of the selfish use of magic against its benign social uses, the neglect of an older brother to teach canoe magic to his younger brother against the expectation that this magic is transmitted from brother to brother, and incest against exogamy. This myth acts as a reminder of the two paradigms for living and what can be expected from each.

In the two myths cited so far there is a distinction between land and beach/sea as well as between cannibalism and noncannibalism. The associations contained in these myths suggest that an orientation to the land implies cannibalism and an inward-turning antisocial quality of social life, whereas an orientation to the beach/sea implies the absence of cannibalism and an outward-turning emphasis on sharing and cooperation. Such disjunctive orientations are reminiscent of the Hua and Bimin-Kuskusmin maternal symbolism described in previous chapters, which was compared with the Melpa symbolism predicating peaceful exchange relations.

In Trobriand thought, land has female connotations whereas the sea has male. The depths of the land, Tambiah says, are the habitation place of the lineage spirits, reborn through women. Land implies "anchoring" and constitutes the "belly" for life and growth. Yams, like people, are anchored in the land. Like the *baloma* essence from which people are born, yams emerge from below onto the land surface to manifest themselves.[25] The sea is associated with the oversea voyages of men in search of kula valuables and specialized goods not locally available. In the Kudayuri myth, the shore is the locus of communal canoe building and kula ceremonies. Standing on the shore thus symbolizes communal cooperation and turning outwardly to other groups in kula exchange. Turning toward the land, on the other hand, suggests an endogamous monopolization of economic and sexual power. The myth of the emigrating brothers (quoted in the Preface) echoes these themes. The brother who looks toward the jungle "eats men" while the brother who stands on the beach and looks toward the sea is "good."

Uberoi suggests that the disjunctive orientation outlined in the two myths discussed above differentiate Trobriand from Dobuan culture as politically separate entities engaged in mutual exchange. He says, for example, that "the particular difference of custom between the two tribes, in respect of cannibalism, is primarily a symbol of their fundamental political separateness. . . . A tribe without government has no figurehead to express its unity in inter-tribal political relations; some striking custom therefore receives significance as a symbol of its separate identity and political autonomy."[26] I suggest, referring to the discussion of dialectical opposition in the construction of self and society mentioned in

Chapter 2, that these two groups of people define themselves in dialectical opposition to one another. This opposition should not be interpreted in terms of isolated traits, however, but as internally consistent paradigms for living.

These paradigms embody complexes of traits I have associated with the presence and absence of cannibalism in previous chapters. For example, the Trobrianders exhibit cooperation, the Dobuans delight in competition and suspicion. Dobuan women are feared as witches, Trobriand women are not.[27] Dobuan men "feel safer in the Trobriands among a strange people of a strange speech than they do in their own homes – in direct and striking contrast to their greater fear in the Amphletts and in parts of Fergusson Island than in their own homes, and in contrast also to their greater fear in other Dobuan districts than in their own home districts."[28] Trobriand garden magic is to be used for the benefit of the community, whereas Dobuan garden magic is employed for the benefit of the individual. Trobrianders can walk about alone in their environment without fear but the Dobuans cannot.

Fortune relates two tales from the Dobuan perspective that highlight the differences between the two societies. First, there is a historical event, "vividly remembered by eyewitnesses," that illustrates the destructive aggression that rules Dobuan life, even life within the family. As told to Fortune, a man who commits adultery with his sister's son's wife is killed by the sister's son. The killer's mother sends her village brothers to kill her son in order to avenge her brother's death. Months later, when the true brothers of the slain son come into the area, they kill his slayer, roast the corpse, and eat it.[29] This tale of adultery, vengeance, counter-vengeance, and cannibalism contrasts markedly with the Kudayuri myth in which fratricide is punished not by an outbreak of vengeance and countervengeance but by events that end with a disjunction between a cannibalistic and noncannibalistic sister. The Dobuan tale, on the other hand, ends with cannibalism – no moral choice distinguishing acceptable from unacceptable solutions to incest and murder is offered.

The second tale is a myth suggesting that the Dobuans are aware of the differences separating them from the Trobrianders. In this story, "women who are evil in appearance" are asked to stand on the side of a tree that points them toward the Trobriands while women "who are handsome" are supposed to stand on the side that points them toward Dobu. However, as the tree crashes to the ground after being cut, it picks up the evil-looking women and flings them inland while the handsome women are flung "seawards and into the Trobriands."[30]

The case of the Trobriand Islanders is intriguing because, despite the evidence of periodic drought and famine in an area where cannibalism was culturally elaborated, there seems little evidence that cannibalism was practiced, at least in recent times, by the Trobrianders themselves. Malinowski's informants told him stories, which they had been told by their grandfathers, of people being killed and eaten in times of drought and famine. Malinowski suggests there might be some elements of truth to such stories and believes that some sort of endocannibalism was probably practiced in times of real famine. He notes that although the Trobrianders live "on the outskirts of cannibalism" and in normal times "regard it with scorn and moral disapproval, in times of hunger they might be tempted (as some people in post–War Europe were tempted) to help themselves to an easily available meal."[31] Malinowski was not able to confirm the stories of famine cannibalism, however. He mentions that a cave full of bones supposedly from such a cannibalistic feast "were certainly not relics of such endo-cannibalistic feasts; neither could they have dated from a few generations back, since most of them were covered with soil and some of them were even overgrown with stalagmites."[32]

Even if we agree that famine cannibalism was periodically practiced, there is no evidence that cannibalism played a key role in Trobriand ritual, as we know it once did in Dobu. Fortune reports that, in addition to practicing vengeance endocannibalism, Dobuan men went on raids of neighboring islands to obtain victims for cannibal feasts, and the affinal relatives of the members of the village of the dead gave "a freshly-killed man . . . to the village of the dead," as part of a mortuary rite.[33]

As a symbolic system, however, cannibalism plays an important role in Trobriand consciousness. Strathern presents evidence that kula valuables may have substituted for human victims. A Trobriand "epic poem" that he cites tells the story of a chief who is killed by his enemies, burned "like a pig over a fire," and treated like "a rare *mwali* shell."[34] Strathern remarks that "the symbolic equivalence between a human victim and an item of wealth is here made explicit."[35] Additionally, the poem twice refers to paying ransom for a chief captured in war by means of the valuables exchanged in the kula ring. Strathern suggests that in terms of its own symbolism, "the kula appears indeed to replace warfare with exchange, hostility with friendship, antagonism between males with a model of reciprocal benefit."[36]

Attributes of a "cannibalistic consciousness" can also be noted in the Trobriand beliefs in cannibalistic witches. Like the Melpa, the Trobrianders associate cannibalism with the internal biological functioning of female witches. The feminine quality of Trobriand witchcraft stems from the fact that witchcraft is a substance that is an inherited, as opposed to an acquired ability, such as sorcery. According to Tambiah, the biological nature of witchcraft is a projection of the procreative powers of women and the Trobriand notion that lineage identity is physically transmitted by women through pregnancy and birth.[37] The most feared of witches, the flying witches, he says, "carry their powers inside the 'belly,' which is the seat of emotions and understanding, the storehouse of magic and the seat of memory."[38] Trobriand sorcerers, on the other hand, are usually male and never eat their victim's flesh. Male sorcery is learned, not physically transmitted, as is true of witchcraft.

This comparison of the Dobuans and the Trobrianders in the light of Strathern's discussion of the Melpa raises the question of whether the same environmental factors associated with cannibalism in the highlands of Papua New Guinea might not also characterize the distribution of cannibalism in the Massim. It will be remembered that Strathern associated the absence of cannibalism with agricultural intensification in the highlands and its presence with the sparsely populated fringe regions where there are no large herds of domestic pigs. The little evidence that exists suggests only that the Trobriand Islands are agriculturally richer than Dobu. "The Trobriand Archipelago," Malinowski says, is

a group of flat coral islands, surrounding a wide lagoon. The plains of the land are covered with fertile soil and the lagoon teems with fish, while both afford easy means of inter-communication to the inhabitants. Accordingly, the islands support a dense population mainly engaged in agriculture and fishing, but expert also in various arts and crafts and keen on trade and exchange.[39]

Malinowski notes that the magical thieving of crops characteristic of Dobu and absent in the Trobriands "is no doubt connected with the fact that the Trobrianders are much richer in food."[40]

Fortune refers to Dobu Island as "an infertile volcanic cone for the greater part of its area," "where population presses heavily on very poor and scanty land" and "each year the saving of enough seed for the next year is accomplished against the pressure of hunger."[41] According to Fortune, "[t]he natives go through an annual season of privation when the yam supply is running low, when they live mainly on roots and wild leaves of certain trees with small remnants of yams or early yams taken from the new gardens before they are grown – and with the usual rare pigs taken hunting or small fish that are caught with much trouble and scant reward in the poorly stocked seas."[42] To this picture of want must be added Fortune's observation that, according to the local missionaries, "bumper native crops, such as are not known now, used to be harvested in the earlier days of the Mission in good seasons." It is also relevant that the Dobuans produced a surplus of sago, which they made particularly for export to the Trobriands and the Amphletts, who had none.[43]

Although the Trobrianders also face annual periods of hunger, Malinowski does not describe Trobriand agricultural potential as poor or scanty. However, years of drought-induced hunger (*molu*) were certainly known. Up to 1918, Malinowski says, no cases of *molu* had been recorded for some twenty-five years. The incidents of cannibalism that Malinowski's informants reported to him occurred before this time and during a period of "really bad *molu*."[44] The difference between the two groups, then, is not that both did not know drought-induced famine or that the Dobuans did not experience a surplus, but that the Dobuans cultivated infertile land. Thus, the source of life, the "belly of the earth," was less generous to the Dobuans than it was to the Trobrianders. However, both societies were sufficiently wealthy to play the leading roles in kula exchange. On the basis of environmental circumstances alone one cannot build a case for the dialectical opposition between the two groups.

The same dialectical opposition can be observed in the disjunction between the ethos of Dobuan community life and the ethos of Dobuan kula trade relations. The kula is phrased in terms of Eros, both in Dobu and in the Trobriands. Success in the kula is based on a man's physical attractiveness, and the relationship between partners is phrased in terms of marriage. "In native thought," Fortune says, "courtship of women and courtship of a *kula* partner are closely bound together."[45] In the Trobriands, Weiner reports, the gifts given to initiate a kula relationship between two men are described as gifts of love and likened to "two friends meeting, but they are not yet sleeping together."[46]

In the Dobuan tale of the origin of the kula, the contrast between the emotions that bind kula partners and the rivalry among kinsmen illustrates the opposition of Eros and destructive aggression. The hero of the legendary founding of the kula is described as "a man of diseased skin covered with sores – inside his skin a handsome man."[47] Upon arriving on the shore during an expedition, he secretly performs magic that causes his diseased skin to fall away and the handsome man to emerge. His magic also charms his kula gifts, making them "grow and ripen." When he goes to the house of his kula partner, the daughter of the house trembles before the handsome stranger. Similarly, when he goes to the house of the partner of his crosscousin, "his beauty, the charmed potency of his gifts, his beauty move them. Their hearts tremble with desire for him."[48] Each time he returns to his Dobuan canoe he resumes his diseased skin and hides the valuables he has been given "on his head beneath an ulcer."[49] When he reveals his valuables to his grandson, his son and other kula companions become angry and leave him marooned on a sandbank. He eventually returns to his village and turns the villagers into birds. Another version states that he becomes an evil spirit. Today the hero of the tale lives as a supernatural being "of the greatest importance in the Dobuan *kula* ritual. . . . His legend is not only not secret, but the Dobuans consider it as their most important legend and tell it *ad nauseam* with unfailing verve and grand gesticulation."[50]

This tale dramatically opposes the libidinal ties binding kula partners and the rivalrous feelings separating Dobuan kinsmen. The same rivalry is evident in the Myth of the Flying Canoe; however, as noted earlier, the mythical solution to the conflict disperses rather than perpetuates the magic that causes the conflict. The positive emotional value attached to the kula is also expressed in the Trobriand attitude toward the kula valuables. These objects constituted a physical symbol of good. Malinowski says the objects were treated as "supremely good in themselves, and not as convertible wealth, or as potential ornaments, or even as instruments of power. To possess *vaygu'a* is exhilarating, comforting, soothing in itself. They will look at *vaygu'a* and handle it for hours; even a touch of it imparts under circumstances its virtue."[51] In other contexts kula valuables put before snakes or crabs, which were believed to be evil spirits, were meant to exercise a direct action on their minds to turn them to benevolent action and, as the Trobrianders say, "to make their minds good."[52] I agree with Malinowski's conclusion that the kula is "connected with fundamental layers of human nature."[53] The kula demonstrates the social channeling of a generic human potentiality for benevolence that can be contrasted, as I have done in this and previous chapters, with the social channeling of the death instinct.[54]

The social channeling of the death instinct and its transformation with the coming of the Europeans is evident in Young's description of the end of cannibalism on Goodenough Island. Goodenough Island is the westernmost of the D'Entrecasteaux Islands in the southern Massim. These islands, although first sighted in 1782, were not explored until 1874.[55] Dobu is sometimes referred to as the heart of the D'Entrecasteaux, whereas Goodenough Island is more peripheral. In the twentieth century Goodenough Island has had four serious droughts resulting in "crop failures and human privation of famine proportions."[56] In addition, according to Young, "innumerable local droughts have been recorded and scarcely a year seems to pass without some part of the island suffering food shortages."[57] Goodenough has been relatively isolated and has not participated in the kula ring because, as Jenness and Ballantyne observed during fieldwork conducted in 1911–12, "the land is not remarkably fertile like the Trobriands, and so does not invite the same amount of trade and settlement."[58]

Jenness and Ballantyne report several instances of cannibalism. During the great famine of 1900,

so terrible was the distress at this time that children were exchanged for food with Belebele and Kwaiaudili, where they were killed and eaten. Friends even exchanged children with one another, and in at least one instance a father murdered his own child, and all his relatives joined in the feast. It was dangerous for a child to leave his parent's side for a single moment lest he should be carried off to swell the cannibal pots.[59]

The famine cannibalism of children can be distinguished from the raiding for cannibal victims by canoe war parties. Jenness and Ballantyne report that the Dobuans were the dominant power and regularly sent raiding parties to Goodenough Island in search of cannibal victims.[60] The Goodenough Islanders also fought against the Dobuans and against other neighboring groups. The motives for these fights and the cannibal feast was revenge. Prisoners suffered torture, dismemberment, and disembowelment. Informants described the fate of one victim who, upon being burned alive, began "to count aloud all the enemies he had slain." The importance of revenge was noted in the treatment of the body:

As a rule the body was cut into segments and laid upon a mat; nothing, not even a drop of blood, was allowed to escape, lest the victors should be cheated of part of their revenge. Each family received a portion, which it cooked like ordinary meat, and every one down to the smallest child shared in the feast. Where only one prisoner had been taken, his head and hands were given to the wife or nearest kinsman of the man for whom the prisoner was the atonement.[61]

According to the folk history and myths of one of the Goodenough villages, cannibalism ended when the mission and the government came. The tale that tells the story of the end of cannibalism indicates that excessive competition and jealousy between leaders is responsible for famine, cannibalism, and near social extinction. For example, about one leader the tale relates:

Everyone was afraid of him because he was very strong and knew how to kill by sorcery. Tomonauyama [another leader] was jealous and resentful of Malaveyoyo's authority and tried unsuccessfully to spear him. Malaveyoyo was about to retaliate when Tomonauyama challenged him: "Wait! If I finish all my taro, yams and bananas first then you can kill me."

This challenge refers to the practice of hoarding food by self-denial. As the story continues, the two men attempt to spoil each other's food and use their magic to make the other hungry. The whole island then suffers famine

and the people began killing each other for food. Malaveyoyo himself led raiding expeditions to Eweli and overcoming his follower's disgust, taught them to eat their captives raw. Soon only Malaveyoyo and Tomonauyama . . . remained in Nibita village; everyone else had fled to the bush in vain search for food. There they exchanged their children to eat.

Later in the story Tomonauyama is left with only one huge yam, because he has traded all of his food. This yam is stolen by one of his kinsmen while he is asleep. Upon waking and finding the yam gone, Tomonauyama weeps and flees the village leaving Malaveyoyo supreme. The latter kills Tomonauyama and eats him with his brothers. He buries the bones with hunger-suppression magic and with rites to end the famine in order to attract the people out of the bush.

He told the people that fighting and cannibalism must finish; that henceforth they must fight only with food. But Tomonauyama's sister wanted revenge. She cooked pots of food with shell valuables hidden inside and took them to a Kwaiaudili village. After eating her food and finding the valuables, the Kwaiaudili men asked her what she wanted. She told them. They set up an ambush and invited Malaveyoyo and his kinsmen to come for pigs. They came and only Malaveyoyo's son escaped alive. Before being speared to death Malaveyoyo doctored his own body with sorcery, and the whole village, save one girl, died from eating his poisoned flesh. Soon after this event, the Mission and the Government came to Goodenough. Men still sometimes want to "chase away" the food with their sorcery, but Christianity is "changing their minds." Men still sometimes want to fight with spears, too, but the Government stops them so now they fight with food instead.[62]

Today the Goodenough Islanders actually fight with food in competitive food exchanges called *abutu*. The purpose of *abutu* is to outgive one's opponent, whereas in the story the competition between the protagonists is to outdeprive one another. This mythical inversion, Young suggests, is a

statement of how *not* to conduct *abutu*. . . . instead of obeying the code of rules which ensure that *abutu* is a controlled, integrative surrogate for fighting, the rivals in the mythical contest used destructive magic indiscriminately with a disintegrative effect more calamitous than their fighting could ever have been; while as to their conduct, Tomonauyama was too generous and too careless to win the contest, and Malaveyoyo too ruthless and vindictive to escape ultimate retribution.

Thus, the tale provides a model of and for behavior in terms of how not to behave. It also demonstrates, Young says, "the absolute dependence of community and culture upon food resources" and Islander response to famine:

211

Famine means not only individual suffering but the attrition of kinship values and ultimately the total negation of social life. This is expressed by the abandonment of the village for the bush, the fragmentation of kin groups, the eating of uncooked human flesh, the theft by Tomonauyama's brothers of his last yam, and that terrible symbol of cultural suicide, the eating of children.[63]

Conclusion

The Goodenough Islander cycle of revenge and counterrevenge can be likened to the Dobuan response to incest in the tale cited in this chapter and contrasted with the response to drought-induced famine and fratricide in the Myth of the Flying Canoe. Although the selfish activity of the older brother of the Trobriand tale is punished by rivalrous fratricide, the latter act does not result in the perpetual repetition of such acts; rather, a new order based on the dispersion of female magic and the watering down of male magic emerges. The dispersion of female magic also implies the dispersion of the sisters from the residence of their brothers, where they are living contrary to Trobriand residence norms. These opposing solutions to conflict cannot be traced simply to environmental circumstances. Although the Trobrianders experienced famine and Malinowski describes hunger-suppression magic and rituals similar to those described for the Goodenough Islanders, the social paradigms formulating and channeling social energy in the two groups differ. One paradigm expresses competitive aggression in channeling social relations and the other is founded on the dispersion of power and emotional ties in building cooperative relationships among social groups. Dobuan and Goodenough Islander reliance on competitive aggression that may lead to murderous vengeance is an expression of the death instinct – or, rather, of its social usefulness. The Trobriand dispersion of power seen, for example, in the interlinking economic ties between lineages through the generations (as described by Weiner and noted in Chapter 1) is a social expression of Eros. When Eros formulates social ties, the solution to social conflict, as evidenced in the Myth of the Flying Canoe, is accommodation and integration. When destructive aggression channels social energy, the solution to social conflict, as evidenced in Dobuan myth and ritual, is submission, death, and, sometimes, physical incorporation by the other. As

212

the paradigm of the hero–stranger–usurper discussed in Chapter 7 represents a theory of society, these two modes for channeling social energy express qualitatively different models for moral style and social mood.

The social form of the kula is unique among the institutions discussed so far. Unlike pig flesh that substitutes for human flesh in Melpa mortuary rites; unlike the Fijian, Aztec, and Iroquoian victim who is the recipient of displaced aggression; unlike *abutu* that provides "a controlled, integrative surrogate for fighting," kula magic and kula objects transform, rather than derive from, destructive emotions. The kula magic of the Dobuan hero has the power to transform his diseased skin and make him into a "handsome man" who charms his kula partners. Trobriand kula valuables are described as "supremely good in themselves" and as having the power to turn the minds of evil spirits to benevolent action – "to make their minds good." Indeed, according to Strathern, when seen in terms of its own symbolism, "the kula appears . . . to replace warfare with exchange, hostility with friendship, antagonism between males with a model of reciprocal benefit." All of this suggests that the expression of Eros in the kula ethos is paradigm forming rather than deriving from an existing paradigm, in other words, that the "religion of life" mentioned by Ricoeur in his critique of Freud is as primordial as the religion of death. Indeed, the religion of life and the religion of death are inextricably linked by the dialectic of negation, because by affirming one the other is negated.

10 · Conclusion: Other symbols and ritual modalities

Man is to be defined neither by his innate capacities alone, as the Enlightenment sought to do, nor by his actual behaviors alone, as much of contemporary social science seeks to do, but rather by the link between them, by the way in which the first is transformed into the second, his generic potentialities focused into his specific performances.[1]

Cannibalism is a complex human image with many meanings. As a practice it may simply be a response to famine or enter into the transformation and social formulation of psychic energy. In many cases, ritual cannibalism physically enacts a cultural theory (of order and chaos, good and evil, death and reproduction) that enables humans to regulate desire, to build and maintain a social order. As a symbol of chaos, cannibalism is equated with all that must be dominated, controlled, or repressed in the establishment of the social order. Evil is projected onto enemies, animals, the cosmos, or harbored as a basic human instinct. In ritual cannibalism, the victim becomes the symbol of evil – the living metaphor for chaos, which must be dominated in the interest of social well-being.

As a life-giving symbol or a symbol of order, ritual cannibalism physically regenerates social categories by transmitting vital essence between the dead and the living or between the human and the divine. Society is reproduced in the social power that these rites confer and in the reaffirmation of the social hierarchy. For example, Bimin-Kuskusmin and Hua acts of mortuary cannibalism reproduce social personhood in the recycling of vital essence from the newly dead to the living. The fertility of the Bimin-Kuskusmin plant and human world depends on the ritually constituted flow of this energy from an enemy victim to participants in the Great Pandanus Rite. As the gods are fed vitalizing energy,

214

men are recruited into the Aztec nobility; the power of a Fijian chief is affirmed by the number of cannibal victims he supplies; and Iroquoian warriors earn a place in the social hierarchy through their bravado. Even the cannibal monsters of the Kwakiutl or of northern North America are involved in the regeneration of the social order because their appearance provides the occasion to re-iterate distinctions between acceptable and unacceptable behavior.

On another level, I have suggested that ritual cannibalism is part of a system of key symbols and oppositions that channel energy from the realm of the diffuse, inchoate, and unconscious in sub-jective awareness to the realm of the intersubjective and social. Inchoate psychic energy is transformed by projecting inner feel-ings onto outer persons, where the feelings can be clarified and given social form. The transmission of energy is itself culturally constructed. In the first cases considered, energy is transmitted directly through the vital essence believed to adhere in human flesh or body parts (see the discussion of the Hua, Bimin-Kuskusmin, and – for the projection to the plane of the divine of this mode of transmitting energy – the Aztec). In the next group of cases, en-ergy is transmitted to humans from their animal counterparts or from the other-than-human masters of the animals. Finally, in the last cases, energy is transmitted through the expression of rage, grief, or desire for cannibal victims in the acts of phallic sadism characteristic of Iroquoian torture rites and Fijian warfare. In all of these cases, the physical transmission of energy through culturally constituted channels is equated with individual and social well-being. The case of the Trobriands provided a contrast with those that use the body as a physical channel for social force and intro-duced Eros as a model for social bonding in opposition to the forces of chaos.

There are other modalities for predicating social and individual self-identity in the transformation of inchoate psychic energy ob-servable cross-culturally. One obvious example of a physical mo-dality that does not include cannibalism is seen in Michelle Rosal-do's description of Ilongot headhunting. Two additional examples, the Mbuti and the Navajo, illustrate modalities that are not cen-tered on bodily parts or biological functioning. Although the mo-dalities differ in these cases, the existential problems are similar.

Michelle Rosaldo's description of Ilongot headhunting demon-strates how the intense feelings of Ilongot males are resolved through severing a head and throwing it on the ground. The Ilongot associate severing a head with social and individual well-being. Rosaldo claims that the well-being and vitality gained in severing a head can only be explained by examining

Ilongot understandings of the interlinked facts of health and emotional well-being, of social processes like envy and emulation, and of the sorts of attitudes they associate with productive success. Because, for Ilongots, most effort is born of envy, beheading provides a sort of model of the process by which human energy is created, organized, and renewed. Killing, conceived in "angry hearts" that are "distressed" by grief or "weighted down" by envy, is an acting out of processes by which anxieties are "cast" aside and troubled "breaths" are "lightened"; it creates the fame and confidence which makes the killer's "life" or "name" a thing that radiates and travels widely – a model of the "opening out" and "lengthening" in terms of which Ilongots describe both health and joy. And finally, in converting "angry" and potentially disruptive thoughts into a source of personal satisfaction, killing also "angers" fellows – and so provides for a situation in which the "energy" born of "anger" can be perpetually reproduced.[2]

Rosaldo suggests also that the powers communicated by taking heads come not from victims but from Ilongot senior men "who would see 'concentrated' their waning reproductive force and so transmit it, through cooperative violent deeds, to sons."[3]

Rosaldo's description provides an excellent ethnographic example of the transformation of intense, inchoate ("cloudy" and "distracted") psychic energy by means of ritual killing. Severing a head and throwing it to the ground alleviate the "angry heart" that is "weighted down" by grief or envy and release positive psychic energy that is interpreted as bringing vitality to the community and well-being to the individual. By his act the headhunter demonstrates to the community that he is an autonomous, reproductive male who has the courage to release and transform energy born of anger or grief to work for the social good.

Ilongot emotions can be compared with the Iroquoian experience of grief described in the address of a Seneca Condolence Council upon the death of a chief (see Chapter 6): "The organs within the breast and the flesh-body are disordered and violently wrenched . . . and so also is the mind." The disorder is "such that nothing can be clearly discerned . . . when a direful thing befalls a person, that person is invariably covered with darkness, that per-

216

son becomes blinded with thick darkness itself." The grief-stricken may become "insane, [for] the powers causing insanity are immune from everything on this earth, and [insanity] has the power to end the days of man."[4] In order to prevent the consequences of extreme grief, such as that experienced when a chief died, a Condolence Council was held to cleanse the mourners of their despair.[5] War-caused bereavement, however, was treated as a "state of unavenged insult and shame." Until the bereaved had evened the score with retaliatory killings and tortures, "it was as if the blood of the murdered one had not been wiped away and his corpse not covered."[6]

The examples of Iroquois and Ilongot emotions projects an image of the anxious male whose creatural viability depends on a kinesthetic transformation of inchoate psychic energy achieved through the projection of inner states onto outer persons. Lopping off a head lightens an inner load, torturing a victim clarifies inner feelings and passes on inner pain. The victim's body provides the ground for acting out inner feelings, which releases the energy of inchoate emotions. The transformed energy strengthens and ripens a man, making him attractive and reproductive. The same kinesthetic transformation of energy is projected by the heart torn from the sacrificial victim to invigorate the Aztec universe, or by the Fijian manslayer whose body is painted all over in a blood red and whose war club receives a title. Similarly, the Bimin-Kuskusmin Great Pandanus Rite transmits certain psychological states through the meticulous social carving and eating of the victim's body.

Turning to the Mbuti of the Ituri Forest in the Northeast Congo, we can see the same mechanisms at work channeled through a different array of symbols. The Ituri Forest is the mirror through which the Pygmies see themselves. The reciprocal flow of life-giving energy (channeled through sound and formulated in song) between the people and the forest is the means by which inchoate, anxious psychic energy is transformed and formulated into the symbols of intersubjective reality.

The Mbuti believe that each individual has a personal force that derives from a larger source that is embodied by the forest. All moving, living things are animated by a life force that has the connotations of air and wind. Breathing is a manifestation of this force, and a gale of wind is interpreted as the breath of the forest

217

or of the disembodied spirits who are independent manifestations of the forest. The body is believed to be inhabited by this force (*pepo*) and any abuse or mutilation of the body is thought to drive away *pepo* and cause death.[7] Thus, as Turnbull says, "physical violence as a means for settling a dispute is abhorred as a sacrilege."[8]

The Mbuti are completely dependent on the forest environment, which provides them with abundance and thus permits each band to be independent.[9] The certainty of economic sufficiency and the general lack of crisis in their lives, Turnbull says, "lead the Mbuti to the conviction that the forest, regarded as the source of *pepo* and of their whole existence is benevolent, and that the natural course of life is good."[10] The forest is conceptualized as a source of physical and emotional nurturance. Physical merging with the forest is seen in the use of vine and wooden charms to convey the strength of the forest to the child, an act that is said to be "pleasing to the forest."[11]

The anthropomorphization of the forest is evident in the belief that the forest talks, that it can be awakened by sound, and that it shows its displeasure through bringing death and hunting failure. The forest tells people how they must act, it is the source of major moral imperatives. The forest's expectations regarding proper behavior make it the mouthpiece for the Mbuti ethos.

Song is the major means for communicating with the forest. Song attracts the attention of the forest and "pleases it." In song the Mbuti express their concerns and their joys, ask for help and give thanks. The fact that songs must be sung in groups illustrates the Mbuti concern for cooperative activity. Parts of songs are sung by different social categories of people – males, females, youths, hunters, or elders.[12] All songs share the same power of sound. "The sound 'awakens' the forest . . . and the nature of the song indicates the particular area of interest of the Mbuti at that moment, thus attracting the forest's attention to the immediate needs of its children."[13] The control of sound through song is considered the "strongest" and most powerful use of the life force that emanates from the forest.[14] Thus, song becomes the means by which the Mbuti harness the innate as conceptualized by them, in the interest of the social order.[15]

In times of chaos, when hunting fails or after certain deaths, the Mbuti believe the forest is disturbed and that they must reinstitute order by rejoicing the forest. At these times men take out the *molimo* trumpets that are represented as animals and make noises (in imitation of the elephant and leopard) to scare women and children and keep them in their huts.[16] Played in the forest by men alone during the night, the trumpets emit an eerie sound that models the element of chaos. The communication between the song of the trumpet played in the forest with the song of men sitting around the camp fire engages men in a dialogue with life, death, and the forest. The ceremony creates and resolves an opposition between male and female, chaos and order, forest and camp.

The opposition of chaos and order at this time separates the disorderly power of youths from the vulnerability of women and children. Shut up in huts away from the youths and mature men, women and children are not privy to the transformation and ordering of masculine reproductive energy. As with Ilongot headhunting, the lessons learned when the *molimo* trumpets are played in the forest at night involve younger men and calmer older men. However, unlike Ilongot socialization and social ordering, which does not involve women in any significant ceremony of transformation, the Mbuti *molimo* ceremony includes acts that not only transform the reproductive energy of women, but also involve women in the tempering of masculine energy.[17]

Changing Woman: The symbol of progressive synthesis

The Mbuti dialectic of forest and camp demonstrates accommodation and integration in the face of divisive forces. Domination, mastery, and control are antithetical to the Mbuti worldview. The Navajo worldview demonstrates a similar attitude of accommodation and integration, which is closely associated with the Navajo intellectual style that responds to diversity by seeking creative synthesis. The image of synthesis is represented by the major Navajo deity, Changing Woman, who is the product of the marriage of darkness and dawn, static and active, male and female. Changing Woman illustrates the predicating role of metaphysical modalities in Navajo ontology for she is animated by a small White Wind in her right ear and a small Dark Wind in her left ear, placed there by her parents.[18]

Responding to Turner's suggestion that the body is universally the basis for concepts of being, Lamphere suggests that the Navajo derive their model for being not from bodily experiences, but

219

from their model of the natural-supernatural world. The Navajo do not project bodily processes onto the cosmos; rather, they project cosmic processes onto the body.[19] Navajo orientation to reality focuses primarily on nonphysical symbols. Air, knowledge, thought, and speech are the power source of all creation, transformation, and regeneration.

Navajo cosmogony begins with matter existing in a neutral, unformed, and unordered condition, which had to be transformed into an ordered and formed condition by thought and speech. The inchoate subject is without thought and speech and is unguided by the knowledge borne by air. It is said that before the Holy People made this world, "they went around like sheep. Like sheep they did not talk. Their eyes governed their actions. . . . There was no language, so they merely looked at one another."[20] Thus, the inchoate human is one who has not synthesized knowledge, thought, and speech in his or her being.

Air is the vitalizing life force. Air is the only substance in the Navajo world that has the inherent capacity to move and to bear knowledge; it is the ultimate source of all knowledge and animation. The body has no inherent capacity for thought, speech, or movement, but acquires these capacities from air. A baby who never receives an "in-standing wind soul" has no life. In addition to being the only source of human life and animation, air is the source of plant and animal life. Without air, all animate objects stop growing or moving. Even the source of the apparent capacity of water to move is found in air. The Navajo agree that food is also an energy source, but they point out that there would be no food without air, and that air allows the plants and animals that provide food for humans to live and to grow.[21] Air possesses knowledge. Wind is the supreme mentor or informer, continually imparting information to the various beings that will guide their actions. The Navajo say that "the wind soul is the means 'by which [we have] life, movement, speech, dream, and thought.'"[22]

The goodness or badness of a person is attributed to the nature of his wind-soul. Like the inner forms of natural phenomena, these wind-souls exist independently of the body they occupy. They are dispatched into the body at birth and become its source of life. At death they leave the body and return to report on the life of the person controlled by the soul.[23]

When the fetus acquires human form, it receives a "small wind" that is different from the in-standing wind-soul acquired at birth. The small wind causes the fetus to move and this movement gives evidence to the mother that the small wind has taken its place inside the growing fetus. The small wind controls the digestive system of the body and its growth and maturation. The in-standing wind controls thoughts and movements as well as the capacity to think "far ahead" and to speak a language. The latter capacities distinguish humans from other animals who have only calls and cries.[24]

Because it is the source of all life and motion, air is the source of well-being called *hozho*. *Hozho* is the Navajo image of wholeness; it is not primordial, as *hozho* only came into existence with the creation of this world, the fifth world of the Navajo mythos. *Hozho* is most often translated as "beauty"; Wyman translates *hozho* as everything that the Navajo thinks of as being good as opposed to evil, favorable to humans as opposed to unfavorable. According to Wyman, it expresses "such concepts as beauty, perfection, harmony, goodness, normality, success, well-being, blessedness, order, and ideal." Reichard defines the term as "perfection so far as it is obtainable by man." She believes that it represents the end toward which humans, supernaturals, time and motion, institutions, and behavior strive. Kluckhohn comments that *hozho* "is probably the central idea in Navajo religious thinking."[25]

The opposite of *hozho* is *hochxo,* which Witherspoon glosses as "the ugly, unhappy, and disharmonious environment." Evil is not considered to be part of the natural cycle of the universe, but comes about only as a result of evil intentions and evil deeds.[26] Air can have an evil aspect that enters the person during breathing and through bodily orifices or it can influence thought through the ear. This evil aspect of air includes winds that have departed from the bodies of individuals who died before reaching old age. Other winds may be controlled by witchcraft to exert harmful effects. Particular winds associated with hostile deities can bring the powers of these deities to harm the individual.[27]

Good comes into the world when evil yields to the controlling power of ritual. Evil comes into the world when what can be controlled goes out of control and becomes disordered.[28] Today, the desirable condition of *hozho* is disturbed by the improper or inadvertent contact with things defined as dangerous or by the witchcraft of others. More than sixty curing rites are designed to purify the patient made ill by contact with dangerous things or to neutralize or reverse the effects of witchcraft.[29]

Healing does not entail the ritual manipulation of natural substances but the ritual restoration of the individual to a proper and harmonious state of relatedness to the universe. The preponderant aim of Navajo religion is to create, preserve, and restore harmony "between man and all elements of the universe, among which man and all social groups are important units."[30] This means that the rites restore one's relationship not only to the sacred but also to society.

This world, the fifth world of the Navajo cosmogony, was thought into existence by the Holy People, who represent the Navajo conceptualization of the spirit world. The Navajo do not propitiate the Holy People by means of blood sacrifice. About the psychology of offerings to the Navajo gods, Matthews wrote in 1897:

The sacrifices of the Navahoes are innocent and bloodless. Their kindly gods are easily propitiated. Like their worshippers, they are all fond of tobacco, and they prize a few feathers and beads. Even the chief war god demands no smoking hearts or blood of captives; a little painted cigarette is all he asks in return for his favors.[31]

The physical act of expiation and restoration of relatedness is accomplished in song, prayer, and making corn cakes (in some cases) and by positioning the individual in an elaborate and harmonious sandpainting that physically and spatially reintegrates the individual in the universe. These sandpaintings visually reflect the dynamic symmetry of the Navajo worldview. It is a symmetry that characterizes the relationship between the sexes as well as the flow and flux found in nature and in the proportions of the human body and the growing plant. In this symmetry the Navajo seek order and peace and love. They liken themselves to the beauty of nature from which they take their model for living. They say:

> We Navajos
> are always learning,
> it is our way,
> it is our eternal transformation
> like a seed.
> We are seeds,
> and we plant ourselves.[32]

Conclusion: Other symbols and ritual modalities

Because there is a primordial clarity about gender in Navajo origin mythology, there is no need to separate male from female in ritual or to emphasize splitting things apart. Diversity does not need to be created because it "is inherent in the primordial condition of things."[33] Creative synthesis and reaching for unity is the means by which diversity is overcome. Diversity and synthesis are represented in the Navajo story of origins in terms of the union of male and female beings. Evil is introduced when these beings separate and live separately; harmony is restored when male and female reunite.

Changing Woman, the creator of this, the fifth, world of Navajo cosmogony, incarnates the Navajo image of well-being. She is considered to be "the Supreme Mother of the Navajos . . . the most benevolent of all the Holy People."[34] She is the child of two beings, one identified with thought and the other identified with speech.[35] As their child, Changing Woman represents the creative synthesis of the two processes believed to have brought the present world into existence. In addition to being considered the mother of the earth surface beings, Changing Woman is also the source and sustenance of all life on earth's surface.[36]

Changing Woman unites in her being the oppositions of Navajo ontology. She represents fertility, health, and good. Through identification with her a person gains her extraordinary powers. She is considered the "mother" of the Navajo who brings the individual good and no harm.[37] According to Lincoln, Changing Woman was born to become the mother of the hero twins who are charged with ridding the world of the monsters.[38] The birth of these twins is also a union of opposites, this time in the body of Changing Woman. The union is between elements of the cosmos: According to one tale, the twins are born from their mother's union with the sun and then the moon. Another tale relates that the twins are born from the joining of two opposing elements, both necessary for life: "the celestial, fiery sun and the terrestrial, moist water."[39] Thus, Changing Woman is the physical manifestation of accommodation and synthesis. Contrary to the Aztec tales of cosmological conflict or the Iroquoian tale of the Good and Evil Twins, the twins born to Changing Woman are not in conflict. Their job is to conquer evil.

In Navajo ritual, Changing Woman is associated with the Blessingway cycle of rites in which she symbolizes safety, propriety,

223

fertility, and proper behavior vis-à-vis the cosmos. The twins are associated with the Enemyway ceremonial cycle in which they are represented as fighting and conquering evil. This mythical family, as Lincoln says about Changing Woman, represents "the triumph of cosmos over chaos, humanity over monsters."[40]

The Navajo myth of emergence, culminating in Changing Woman and the twins, conforms to a dialectic of mediation rather than contradiction and negation (see Chapter 2 for a definition of these terms). The splitting of good and evil, male and female, subjective and objective, in-group and out-group was accomplished prior to the establishment of the worldview characteristic of this, the fifth, Navajo world. The emphasis in this world is on synthesis rather than splitting, relatedness rather than separation, harmony rather than control. The fundamental pattern of the Navajo worldview, as Mills and Witherspoon stress, is one of progressive synthesis. Oppositions of the past are synthesized and become the polar term in oppositions of the future. As Mills says,

The fundamental pattern of the Navaho world view is dialectical: thesis, antithesis, synthesis. . . . For the Navaho . . . raising life to the highest degree of power and control, is the consummation of the Navaho way. The synthetic symbols, however powerful, are far from static. The harmony that earth people attain is not a resolution of conflict but a transformation of unbearable tensions into bearable and constructive ones.[41]

This pattern of relatedness and harmony is associated with the Navajo use of life, symbolized in the mother–child bond, as a template for behavior. The mother–child bond is the most powerful, intense, and enduring of social bonds. Because it provides the ideal pattern or code for all social interaction, maternal nurture (a derivative of Eros) is extremely important as a model of and for behavior. A physical referent, however, does not formulate consciousness of this bond. Witherspoon emphasizes that Navajo relations of kinship are symbolized in and defined "by actions and not substances."

It is the *act* of giving birth and the *act* of sharing sustenance that establish and express bonds of kinship. Although Navajos believe or will acknowledge that through sexual intercourse and birth some kind of common substance is shared, their culture attaches no meaning in terms of affective solidarity to this alleged common substance. Navajos never mention common substance in discussing, discovering, or invoking kinship ties and norms. Kinship is discussed in terms of the *acts* of giving life and sharing sustenance.[42]

The constellating power of Eros is underscored by the fact that even affinal relationships are subsumed under the rubric of kinship. Affinal terms are rarely used in address because affines usually use kin terms and think of themselves as kinsmen.

To conclude, Navajo ontology differs from what has been described in previous chapters in three respects. First, the primary symbols predicating self-consciousness are not focused on physiological processes of birth or digestion. Second, the primordial images of myth and ritual do not denote attack or conquest (negation), but accommodation and union (synthesis). Third, the cosmic order is marked by the ascendency of the forces of light over the forces of evil.

These distinctions, as in the cases of the Aztec and the Fijians, are best seen in a comparison of the Navajo myth of emergence with the myths of primordial chaos. The Navajo emergence myth illustrates a conflict between good and evil in which the forces of harmony win at the expense of the forces of disharmony. Whereas the Aztec believe that the motion of the world is based on the desire of the sun for human bodies, the Navajo believe that the dead persons fed to the sun produce the terrible mother of the monsters called "Snapping (Biting) Vagina" who must be killed along with her children by the Hero Twins, the sons of Changing Woman.[43]

The Navajo retain the idea of cannibalistic monsters in the fantasy that there are humans who, in the guise of wolves, may prey on other humans. Luckert suggests that the Navajo "human wolf" is comparable to the Northwest Coast Man Eater and that both are part of the ancient Athapaskan hunter tradition shared by these groups.[44] The Navajo attitude toward these monsters is certainly similar to the Kwakiutl attitude toward the Man Eater: These monsters symbolize evil that must be destroyed. However, unlike the Kwakiutl Man Eater who appears in pageants, the Navajo human wolf is a creature of Navajo fears and fantasies.

Like the serpent of the Adamic myth, the Navajo human wolf shows that ancient symbols are retained in the contemporary conceptualization of the innate. The serpent and the Navajo human wolf represent the aspect of evil that cannot be absorbed in the contemporary Navajo understanding of human freedom and human fault. The human wolf is a vestige of a prior merging of good and evil when animals and humans participated in the same general essence in the Navajo hunter past and the actions of humans could not be separated from those of animals. This was a time in the Navajo mythological stages when good and evil were neither distinct nor under the control of humans. As the Navajo mythos moves from one world to the next, good and evil are progressively placed under the control of humans.[45] The transformation may be connected with the Navajo adoption of agriculture and sheep herding in the Southwest. Despite the attempt to conquer evil, the human wolf phenomenon demonstrates that evil remains a part of human relationships. The difference between the Navajo and the Aztec or Fijian relationship to evil is that by founding their social order on harmony, peace, and love, the Navajo relegate disharmony, strife, and hatred to the realm of human feelings and actions that must be conquered, not expressed, in rites of reconciliation.

Two patterns of social bonding

Two patterns of social bonding are evident in many of the contrasts of this book: the Melpa versus the Hua, Gimi, and Bimin-Kuskusmin; the Dobuans versus the Trobrianders; and the Aztec versus Quetzalcoatl. The integrative mechanism of one pattern is found in acts of ritual killing; the integrative mechanism of the other is seen in exchange relations or in rituals of accommodation and integration. The difference between the Navajo and the Aztec styles of adapting to their new circumstances provides another example of the contrast. Both of these peoples were nomadic hunters who wandered into their homeland and who possessed an ethos and worldview that was at once markedly similar and dissimilar. Their origin myths conceptualize a progression of five worlds, each giving birth to the next. Whereas each Aztec world is initiated by death and cosmic conflict, each Navajo world is initiated by a movement "upward" from one world to the next. Whereas the contrary elements in the Aztec mythos are always in conflict, the Navajo solution to conflict merges oppositions. In their new land, the Aztec chose competitive emulation of their neighbors; as they adopted new ways, they became fiercely committed to giving these ways the stamp of Aztec imperialism. The Navajo moved into an area where synthesis had been developed as a cultural style; as they accommodated the symbols and rituals of their neighbors in their nomadic movements, they accommodated rather than conquered massive numbers of Pueblo refugees.[46]

The styles represented by the Aztec and the Navajo supply equally plausible models for channeling psychic and social energy and equally workable adaptations to ecological and political adversity. One style expresses cannibalism and the other does not. I suggest that these differences are best explicated by ontological rather than ecological considerations, although ecological considerations (as suggested in several cases) may intensify rituals for the regeneration of ontological and social categories.

One might well ask how people in societies for which there is no evidence of cannibalism respond to famine. Are the mechanisms for regenerating ontological categories strengthened or replaced by a focus on appetites and the body? The evidence suggests that although rituals may be curtailed or even eliminated, identification with the key symbols predicating being is strengthened, not produced, during such times.

One of the most compelling examples of a response to famine – one that does not include any evidence of cannibalism or attempts to master and dominate – is Turnbull's description of the Ik. The Ik's acceptance of and accommodation to their life of deprivation can be seen in the absence of physical violence or any concerted attempt to survive. Birth and death are the main events that draw their attention and energy. Sociality means nothing; all that counts is the few years in which the individual survives. There is no altruism and no bonding. Neither is there any attempt to master and control death by using death. The only object that holds the Ik's attention as a people and gives them a sense of shared identity is their sacred mountain, which they believe bore them and to which they will return at death. It is to this mountain that the lonely and starving turn their gaze as they sit silently in the village "sitting place." "A group of men," Turnbull says, "might sit for a day without saying a word while looking intently at Morungole" (the sacred mountain).[47] Their powerful respect for the mountain is also manifest in the accepted prohibition against hunting there. Even the young seemed to Turnbull respectful of the mountain. "The sentiment evoked by the mountain," he suggests, "was certainly as ideologically coercive as the physical environment was structurally coercive."[48]

Although the physical environment may determine the lack of altruism and sociality among the Ik, the sentiment evoked by the mountain formulates self-consciousness and a sense of common identity. The Ik's response to famine can be contrasted with the Huron perception of their near social extinction when their "famished teeth ceased to discern the nature of that they ate" and they saw themselves as "nothing but ghosts and souls of the dead," whose land, they said, "will open very soon to swallow us, and to put us among the dead."[49] The image of a land that swallows its people is a projection of the dialectic of lordship and bondage. At the same time, the mountain that accepts the dead and gives birth to the living is a projection of a dialectic of accommodation.

Another description of response to famine comes from Firth's observations in Tikopia during a period of famine in 1952. Firth notes that although the major effects of the famine were curtailment and limitation of most activity, organized dancing and public meetings were stimulated by the crisis. Dancing provided a distraction and was said to make the land "good." The public meetings provided a forum for leaders to discuss their concern with the maintenance of the social order and to control the action of thieves.[50] In his conclusions regarding the social effects of the famine, Firth says,

As a community they did not lose their identity and dissolve into a set of fiercely competing individuals struggling for food. . . . they made many organizational but few structural adaptations. But they did not act as an undifferentiated group. There was great variation in their ability to meet their difficulties, and their corporate survival owed much to the sense of responsibility of some of their leaders. . . . In the sphere of convention, they retained their manners; throughout the famine they followed out in practice their code of etiquette. Their morality suffered more. Their morality of action as regards theft was in many respects deplorable, a widespread breach of the rule. But the moral ideals themselves survived, given lip service to by all, though pursued in practice by only a few. . . . the retention of the moral ideal [allowed for] a more rapid return than otherwise to a state of comparative honesty when sanctions of force were introduced. . . . This moral continuity was very important for the survival of Tikopia social life in its systematic form.[51]

Thus, Firth demonstrates that the Tikopians retained the basic moral guidelines for social behavior, even though these guidelines were frequently ignored during a time of severe stress.

I suggest that during the formulation of a people's relationship to the world and to other beings ontological considerations take precedence over the utilitarian concerns given priority in the materialist point of view (see Chapter 1) and that these considerations frame a people's response to stress. This is not to say that the environment plays a passive role; indeed, it plays a most active role. As people learn a language by communicating with one another, they also learn an ecological language by communicating with their environment. An ecological language is a communicative form, acted in ritual, whereby culture and environment are synthesized and mutually enveloped. This process of communication is the ground for what is thought and symbolized. Such a communication is seen in its starkest form in the above description of the Ik's lonely dialogue with the mountain that bore them and the mountain that will claim them at death.

With regard to the effect of the forest environment on Mbuti culture, Turnbull says that the dependence of the Mbuti on the forest is a determinant of their value system. The character of the forest provides the symbols for both the projection of inner energy and its transformation into articulate form. Sound envelops the transformation process, and song is the form by which the Mbuti reflect back what they hear and feel in the forest, which is described as "nearly always full of sound."[52] Sound is intimately related to wind, which carries sound and blows through the trees of the forest, making it a living thing. "If the forest stops 'talking,'" Turnbull says, "then it is a sign that something is very wrong and alerts the Mbuti to imminent danger."[53]

The ecological language of the Mbuti is ongoing and intimately related to daily sociality. The sentiment evoked by the forest cannot be separated from the manner in which the forest structures daily life. In times of deprivation, however, the Mbuti believe that if they behave in certain ways they have the power to evoke well-being once again through communicating with the forest. In the process, potentially opposed and divisive forces – such as male and female, camp and forest – are separated and reconciled. Such rituals of reconciliation project not only problematic states but the Mbuti's perception of the causes of these states. The manner by which they incorporate their environment in rituals of reconciliation tells us how the Mbuti perceive themselves to be affected by their environment.

Turning briefly again to the Ilongot, I am intrigued by M. Rosaldo's comment "that the bright red flowers of the fire tree in bloom are said to taunt the novice with the knowledge that he has not killed." [54] The image of bright red flowers of the fire tree in bloom is striking for its intensity and the analogous intensity felt by the young man who severs a head to cast off an anger that oppresses his saddened heart. One can suggest that emotions are cast in immediately available metaphors or that emotions are culturally constituted by what is seen and heard in conjunction with what is felt.

It is hard to imagine a young man of the Ik severing a head. Not only is the Ik environment devoid of images of such passionate psychic intensity, but absolutely nothing social would accrue to the individual who performed such an act. There are no problematic states that can be resolved or transformations that can be effected by the Ik who severs a human head. The same can be said for the Mbuti male who performed such an act. Additionally, in the Mbuti case the concentration of intense psychic energy in a single act is antithetical to the flow of psychic energy characteristic of the Mbuti communication with their forest. Indeed, such an act would insert a shrill break in the nurturant communication between forest and camp.

To conclude, I suggest that as a people pass on a language from one generation to the next that predicates communication among humans, they also pass on a communicative form that frames and structures their relationship to nature, life, and death. Understanding the grammar and meaning of this language is the key to comprehending cannibalism. An analytic framework that concentrates on the cultural logic of life, death, and reproduction in particular circumstances is necessary in order to break through the facts of cannibalism and open up "the empire of meaning."

In this book I have attempted to illuminate a powerful human image by seeking cultural meaning in ethnographic particulars and by seeking explanation in the theoretical programs of such diverse thinkers as Ricoeur, Freud, and Jung. The analytic framework I have developed is not meant to integrate or resolve the disagreements among these men; rather, this framework applies particular ideas and concepts to the task of "breaking the charm of facts" in order to comprehend the generically human problems resolved by the phenomena of cannibalism. Interwoven with the analytic endeavor and the related task of opening up meaning has been the application of a sustained reflection on the webs of significance formulating a people's relationship to the world, to other beings, and to being itself.

Notes

Preface

1 Malinowski (1922:331).

Chapter 1. Cannibalism cross-culturally

1 Brown and Tuzin (1983:2–3).
2 Geertz (1973:52).
3 Murdock and White (1969). See also Sanday (1981, Appendix A).
4 Tuzin (1983:63).
5 Ibid., p. 70.
6 Sahlins (1983:89).
7 Williams (1930:171–2).
8 Lindenbaum (1979:21, 24).
9 McIlwraith (1948:2:73, 107–14).
10 Ibid., pp. 73–86.
11 Sahlins (1978:47–8).
12 Poole (1983:31).
13 In subsequent chapters I examine the cultural significance of cannibalism, how it is interwoven in the cultural logic of death and reproduction. In the following sections of this chapter I examine the statistical correlates of cannibalism as a means for investigating hypotheses put forth by the materialist and psychogenic explanations. This examination demonstrates that although the hypothetico-deductive approach as it has been applied to the subject of cannibalism oversimplifies complex issues, the arguments contained in this approach touch on important parameters to be elaborated upon in the later chapters.
14 Sahlins (1976:viii).
15 Arens (1979a:46).
16 Sahlins (1979:47).
17 Arens (1979b:129). The source Arens refers to in connection with this statement is Volume 5 of *The Jesuit Relations and Allied Documents* (Thwaites 1898). But this is one of forty volumes, several of which contain eyewitness descriptions. In addition to reporting their eyewitness accounts (see Chapter 6), the Jesuits write of encountering Indians carrying parts of a human body on a skewer (see, for example, Thwaites 1898, Vol. 13:79). In Volume 17 a priest writes that one of the hands of a tortured victim was thrown into his cabin

"as if giving us our share of the feast" (Thwaites 1898, Vol. 17:77). This priest also writes of a prisoner who, after torture and death, was boiling in a kettle "of which the inmates of the Fathers' cabin were invited to come and take their share" (Thwaites 1898, Vol. 17:99).

18 R. G. and Marjorie Crocombe (1968:91–2). I am grateful to Jane Goodale for bringing this reference to my attention.
19 Poole (1983); Tuzin (1983).
20 Sagan (1974:109).
21 Ibid., p. 28.
22 Ibid., p. 141.
23 Ibid., pp. 92–3.
24 Sanday (1981:171, 184–5).
25 Harner (1977:132).
26 Ibid., p. 119.
27 Ibid., p. 123.
28 Ibid., pp. 125–6.
29 Ibid., p. 127.
30 Ibid., pp. 127–8.
31 Ibid., p. 129.
32 Ibid., p. 130.
33 Harris (1977:xii).
34 Harris (1979:336).
35 Sahlins (1978:53).
36 Ibid., p. 46.
37 Ibid.
38 Ibid., p. 47.
39 Ibid., pp. 47–8.
40 Ibid.
41 Ibid., p. 47.
42 Sahlins (1976:viii, 209).
43 Sahlins (1983:74, 83).
44 Ibid., p. 83.
45 Ibid., p. 84.
46 Ibid., p. 91.
47 Weiner (1982:56).
48 Ibid.
49 Ibid.
50 Ibid., p. 61.
51 Ibid.
52 Poole (1982b:55–60).
53 Ibid., p. 61.
54 Ibid.
55 Ibid.
56 Weiner (1982:62).
57 Ibid.
58 Strathern (1982:127).
59 Weiner (1982:65).

60 Strathern (1982:127–8).
61 Poole (1982a:106).
62 Strathern (1982:128).
63 Ibid., p. 111. Regarding the relationship between the presence of large herds of domestic pigs and the absence of cannibalism in the New Guinea Highlands, it is interesting to note that in the 109 societies representing the sample employed in Tables 1–5, cannibalism is absent in all those societies relying primarily on domestic animals for food (n = 9), despite the fact that in all of these cases periods of hunger or famine are well known. A preliminary examination of these nine societies suggests the hypothesis that rituals of animal sacrifice parallel rituals of cannibalism in form and meaning. An important follow-up to this study of cannibalism will be an analysis of the meaning, symbolism, and ontological status of animal sacrifice.

Chapter 2. Analytic framework

1 Wagner (1977:395).
2 Another example of a symbolic and ritual order that does not encompass cannibalism, the Ilongot, is briefly discussed in Chapter 10.
3 Laughlin and d'Aquili (1979:280).
4 Cove (1978).
5 See the discussion by Dirks (1978:167–8) and by Laughlin and d'Aquili (1979:288–9).
6 Turnbull (1978:53).
7 Ibid., p. 72.
8 Ibid., pp. 72–3. See Rappaport (1984:237ff.) for distinction between operational and cognized environment.
9 Laughlin and d'Aquili (1979:300–1).
10 Ibid., p. 300.
11 Rappaport (1984:408).
12 Ibid., p. 410.
13 For a provocative discussion of scientific and indigenous conceptualizations of the innate from which I draw some of these ideas, see Wagner (1977:394–406). My notion of "being-in-the-world" is drawn from Ricoeur's (1979:325–6) discussion of the function of myth and symbols as "carriers of meaning" having to do "with our relationship to the world, to other beings, and to being as well." For more discussion of the role of the environment, see the discussion in Chapter 10.
14 Geertz (1973:99).
15 Fernandez (1974:122).
16 Ibid., p. 123.
17 Ibid., p. 121.
18 Wagner (1981:119).
19 Ibid. It should be noted that Wagner's notion of "invention" involves a rather different view of the nature of symbols and symbolization than the one taken here and that taken by Lévi-Strauss. See especially Wagner's theory of "symbolic obviation" (1978).

20 Lévi-Strauss (1981:603).

21 Ibid., pp. 603–4.

22 See Ricoeur (1967). My analysis and use of Ricoeur's discussion of the symbolism of evil owes much to Dunning's (1983) discussion of the dialectical structure of the subject-object polarities Ricoeur establishes in his treatment of the primary symbols and myths of evil. Although Ricoeur does not explicitly couch his analysis of the primary and mythical symbols of evil in terms of a progressive dialectic, elsewhere (1970:462–75) he compares the progressive dialectic in the Hegelian stages of self-consciousness with Freud's model of the movement of the self in psychoanalysis and in the development of the superego. Ricoeur's analysis of the progressive change in the primary symbols of evil follows the outlines of a Hegelian dialectic, as Dunning shows, but it does not parallel Hegel's discussion of the stages of consciousness in the dialectic of *Geist*. See Bernstein (1971:20) for a discussion of this dialectic.

23 Ricoeur (1967:30).

24 Ibid., p. 74.

25 Dunning (1983:347).

26 There is no English word that captures the distinctive meaning of the term *aufheben*, Bernstein says. "*Aufheben* is to negate, affirm and transcend, or go beyond" (Bernstein 1971:18). See text for Dunning's discussion of Hegel's dialectic of mediation.

27 Ricoeur (1967:101).

28 Dunning (1985:8). An obvious example of Dunning's point is Lévi-Strauss's contention, quoted above, that self-consciousness is constituted by an opposition between the self and the other apprehended as an opposition. That this type of opposition is evident in the data will become obvious below and in the chapters that follow. However, as Dunning shows, the dialectic can take other forms, also evident in the data.

29 Dunning (1985:8).

30 Ibid., p. 9.

31 Ricoeur (1967:19).

32 Ortner defines a symbol as key "insofar as it extensively and systematically formulates relationships – parallels, isomorphisms, complementarities, and so forth – between a wide range of diverse cultural elements" (1979:97).

33 Marriott (1976:111).

34 For a discussion of differential rates of growth in Papua New Guinea, see Sinnett (1977:78–84) and Malcolm (1970).

35 The dialectic of the maternal body and the individual may include an equation of humans and pigs placing pigs in the same dialectical relationship to the maternal body as humans. This dialectic is to be distinguished from the dialectic of animals and humans on several grounds. First, there is a reciprocal relationship between animals and humans in the latter case, whereas in the former there is a dependent relationship between humans and the maternal body. Second, when pigs are equated with humans in the dialectic of humans and the maternal body, pigs and humans occupy the same pole of opposition – they are not in opposition.

36 Ricoeur (1967:170). The four myths of the beginning and end of evil are: the myth of creation and primordial chaos; "the tragic theology of the god who tempts, blinds, leads astray"; the myth of the "fall" of man; and the "myth of the exiled soul" (Ibid., pp. 172–4).
37 Ibid., p. 171.
38 Ricoeur (1979:326).
39 Ibid., p. 320.
40 Ricoeur (1967:177).
41 Ibid., p. 191.
42 Ibid., p. 179.
43 Jung (1960a:45).
44 Jung (1971:455–6; 1956:137).
45 Ricoeur (1970:480).
46 Ibid., p. 474.
47 Ricoeur (1970:469).
48 Ibid., p. 470.
49 Neumann (1954:27).
50 Ibid., pp. 30–1.
51 Ibid., p. 46.
52 From the psychoanalytic point of view, the primal mother paradigms suggest a reevaluation of Paul's contention that oedipal symbolism predicates cultural forms that focus on the perpetuation of life beyond the individual's life history (see Paul 1982:7). I argue that pre-oedipal symbolism, specifically uroboric-great-mother symbolism as described by Neumann, provides another focus for organizing expressive events concerned with social regeneration.
53 Neumann (1954:309).
54 Findlay (1977:520).
55 LeClercq (1910:272–3).
56 Freud (1961b:69).
57 Ibid., p. 61.
58 Ibid., p. 66.
59 Freud (1962:157).
60 Sagan (1974:81).
61 Ibid., p. 28.
62 For another example of substitution see the discussion of Goodenough Islanders in Chapter 9.
63 Strathern (1982:121).
64 Ibid., p. 120.
65 Bloch and Parry (1982:30).
66 Strathern (1982:130) cautions against viewing cannibalism as representing an "'earlier stage' of society" because among the Gimi and Fore cannibalism is reported as having been introduced following the removal of traditional protein resources. However, this does not contradict the progression I am positing. It is possible that there were at least two ritual models available to highlanders depending on the objects of value available to them and the mode of circulating these objects through the ethnic landscape. If groups were primarily inward turning and were not engaged in, or dependent on, an exten-

sive network of exchange links, mortuary cannibalism is one model for the exchange of substance in regenerating the sources of social reproduction. If, on the other hand, groups were linked to exchange partners in other groups and depended on these links in regenerating the sources of social reproduction and for their ritual and economic status, then cannibalism is more likely to become a model that negates exchange. Cycling between these models may, in fact, characterize the highlands' historical process.

67 Dunning (1983:347). This discussion illustrates Hegel's dialectic of mediation, which, as mentioned above, Dunning argues underlies Ricoeur's analysis of the symbolism of evil. The concept of guilt in cultural anthropology is similar but not identical to Ricoeur's use of the term. As Levy (1983:131) defines it, "guilt . . . seems to imply harming someone or something through action or thought (or its lack) and invites retribution and protective atonement."

68 Ricoeur (1970:474).

Chapter 3. The mysteries of the body

1 Meigs (1984:128, 131).
2 Ibid., p. 121.
3 Ibid., p. 124.
4 Ibid., p. 3.
5 Ibid., p. xi.
6 Ibid., pp. 117–18.
7 Ibid., p. 118.
8 Ibid., pp. 118–19.
9 Ibid., pp. 58, 76.
10 Ibid., p. 115.
11 Ibid., p. 99.
12 Ibid., p. 101.
13 Ibid., p. 115.
14 Ibid., pp. 17–23, 123.
15 Ibid., pp. 121–2.
16 Ibid., p. 124.
17 Ibid., p. 110.
18 Ibid., p. 115.
19 Ibid., p. 121.
20 Meigs (1977:309).
21 Ibid., pp. 313–14.
22 Meigs (1984:71).
23 Ibid., p. 31.
24 For the kinds of relationships regulated by prohibitions on *nu* transfer, see Meigs (1984:102).
25 Ibid.
26 Ibid., p. 104.
27 Ibid., pp. 104–6.
28 Ibid., p. 106.

29 Ibid., p. 107.
30 Ibid.
31 Ibid., pp. 108–9.
32 Ibid., p. 121.
33 Ibid.
34 Ibid., p. 122.
35 Rank (1932:268).
36 Meigs (1984:61).
37 Rank (1932:268).
38 Jung (1960b:96).
39 Neumann (1954:272, 290).
40 Ibid., pp. 30–1.
41 Meigs (1984:4).
42 Strathern (1982:128).
43 Ibid., p. 128.
44 Gillison (1980:144–5).
45 Lindenbaum (1979:24).
46 Gillison (1983:33–4).
47 Gillison (1980:148).
48 Neumann (1954:46).
49 Gillison (1980:148).
50 Ibid., p. 169.
51 Ibid.
52 Ibid., pp. 147–50.
53 Ibid., pp. 151–2.
54 Gillison (1983:35–6).
55 Gillison (1980:158).
56 Gillison (1983:37).
57 Ibid., p. 38.
58 Strathern (1982:128).
59 Gillison (1983:38).
60 Ibid., p. 39.
61 Neumann (1954:47).
62 Ibid., pp. 49–52.
63 Gillison (1983:42).
64 Ibid.
65 Ibid., pp. 43–4.
66 Gillison (1980:171). The citation in the quotation is from Newman (1965:82).
67 Meigs (1984:124).
68 Ibid., p. 135.
69 Strathern (1982:127–8).
70 M. Strathern (1980:212).
71 Strathern (1982:129).
72 Ibid., pp. 119–20.
73 Ibid., p. 129.
74 Ibid., p. 112.

75 Ibid., pp. 112–17.
76 Sanday (1981:91–108).
77 See Douglas (1966:114–15) for a discussion of the body as a model of society.

Chapter 4. The androgynous first being

1 Poole (1983:7–8).
2 Poole (1982a:105).
3 Poole (1981:122).
4 Ibid., p. 145.
5 Poole (1983:9, 7).
6 Ibid., pp. 30–1.
7 Poole (1981:136).
8 Ibid., pp. 159–60.
9 Ibid., p. 124.
10 Ibid., pp. 124–5.
11 Neumann (1954:39).
12 Ibid., pp. 327–8.
13 Freud (1961c:10).
14 Poole (1983:12).
15 Ibid., p. 11.
16 Ibid.
17 Ibid., p. 10.
18 Ibid., p. 9.
19 Poole (1982a:106).
20 Poole (1981:128–9).
21 Ibid., pp. 128–30; Poole (1982a:113).
22 Poole (1981:131–2).
23 Ibid., pp. 132–3.
24 Ibid., p. 135.
25 Ibid.
26 Ibid.
27 Ibid., p. 153.
28 Ibid.
29 Ibid., p. 144.
30 Ibid., p. 133.
31 Ibid.
32 Poole (1983:17–18).
33 For the details of the ritual, see Poole (1983).
34 Hallowell (1967:88).
35 Poole (1982:120, 132).
36 Harding (1947:447).
37 Ibid., pp. 447–8.
38 Ibid., pp. 448–9.
39 Ibid., p. 431.
40 Ibid., p. 451.
41 Von Franz (1979:34).

42 Harding (1947:435).
43 Ibid., pp. 435–7.
44 Von Franz (1979:46–7).
45 Ibid., p. 48.
46 Ibid., p. 49.
47 Ibid., p. 35.
48 Lindenbaum (1983:98–9).
49 Poole (1981:122).

Chapter 5. Cannibal monsters and animal friends

1 Kohl (1860:357–8), quoted by Fogelson (1965:80).
2 Thwaites (1898, Vol. 8:31).
3 Ibid., Vol. 46, pp. 263–5, quoted in Fogelson (1965:75).
4 Hallowell (1967:256); Teicher (1960:2–6).
5 Teicher (1960:8–9).
6 Ibid., pp. 11–12.
7 Ibid., p. 16.
8 I rely here on Hallowell's definition of "manitu" (1976:382). The story is found in Teicher (1960:24).
9 Hallowell (1976:455).
10 Ibid., p. 456.
11 Ibid., p. 457.
12 Ibid., p. 458.
13 Dorson quoted by Hallowell (1976:376).
14 Ibid., p. 377.
15 Teicher (1960:23).
16 Ibid., p. 47. For the case of the mother and son, see Teicher (1960:57).
17 Ibid., p. 61.
18 Hallowell (1967:257).
19 Teicher (1960:15).
20 Fogelson (1965:74–5).
21 Ibid., p. 81.
22 Ibid., p. 87.
23 Ibid., pp. 97–8.
24 Tuzin (1983:70).
25 Ibid.
26 See Devereux (1980:122–37) for a discussion of cannibalistic urges of parents.
27 Hay (1971:8).
28 Ibid., p. 12.
29 Ibid., p. 15.
30 Ibid., p. 17.
31 Ridington (1976:108).
32 Ibid., p. 109.
33 Ibid., p. 113.
34 Ibid., p. 114.
35 Ibid.

36 Ibid., p. 115.
37 Ibid.
38 Ibid., pp. 119, 122.
39 Ibid., p. 124.
40 Ibid., p. 126.
41 Reid (1979:250).
42 Ibid., p. 251. See Adams (1981:361) for a discussion of the time depth of the Kwakiutl fishing adaptation.
43 Reid (1979:251).
44 Walens (1981:100).
45 Ibid., p. 110.
46 Ibid., p. 101.
47 Reid (1979:253).
48 Ibid., p. 256.
49 Ibid., p. 261.
50 Walens (1981:125).
51 Ibid.
52 Ibid., p. 131.
53 Ibid., pp. 131–2.
54 Ibid., p. 137.
55 Ibid., pp. 15–16.
56 Ibid.
57 Ibid., p. 162.
58 Ibid., pp. 162–3.
59 Ibid., p. 17.
60 Snyder (1975:156).
61 Ibid., p. 161.
62 Boas (1935:24).
63 Walens (1981:77).
64 Ibid., p. 154.
65 Ibid., p. 149.
66 Ibid., p. 154.

Chapter 6. The faces of the soul's desires

1 Foucault (1979:54–5).
2 Knowles (1940:189–90).
3 Tooker (1964:1).
4 Ibid., p. 7.
5 Thwaites (1898:Vol. 34:31).
6 Ibid., pp. 33–5.
7 Quoted by Hay (1971:9).
8 Ibid.
9 Wallace (1946:13–14).
10 Thwaites (Vol. 40:49).
11 Thwaites (Vol. 35:89).
12 Ibid., p. 21.

13 Tooker (1964:147).
14 A. F. C. Wallace claims that the major function of Iroquoian warfare was revenge and that the effectiveness of the league in blocking this process among the five participating tribes helped explain "the implacability and ferociousness of the Iroquois in pursuing external enemies." The establishment of peace, he says, "resulted in the displacement of revenge motivations outward, onto surrounding peoples, Indian and European alike" (Wallace 1969:46–7). To this I would add that the displacement process included cannibalism along with revenge.
15 Ibid., p. 73.
16 Thwaites (Vol. 5:286).
17 Ibid., Vol. 53, p. 225.
18 Ibid., Vol. 39, p. 219.
19 Ibid., Vol. 39, p. 221.
20 Wallace (1969:345).
21 Tooker (1964:151).
22 Wallace (1969:86–93).
23 Jung (1956:424).
24 Neumann (1954:14).
25 Ibid., pp. 96–7.
26 Tooker (1964:91).
27 Ibid., p. 90.
28 Ibid., p. 88.
29 Freud (1950:290). The image of human beings being controlled by and controlling internal states is reminiscent of Freud's (1961a:25) analogy of the ego and id as a rider and his horse. Here and elsewhere I use Freud's typology of id and ego in a metaphorical, not clinical, sense in order to convey my sense of the Iroquoian dialogue with the "wishes of the soul."
30 Wallace (1969:65).
31 Ibid., p. 66.
32 Ibid., p. 71.
33 Ibid., pp. 73–4.
34 Ibid., p. 75.
35 Ibid., p. 93.
36 Ibid., p. 79.
37 Ibid., pp. 80–1.
38 Ibid., p. 92.
39 Tooker (1964:35).
40 Ibid.
41 Ibid., pp. 35–6.
42 Ibid., p. 36.
43 Ibid.
44 Knowles (1940:181–2).
45 Ibid., p. 182.
46 Ibid., pp. 182–3.
47 Ibid., p. 184.
48 Ibid.

49 Ibid., pp. 184–5.
50 Wallace (1969:95).
51 Tooker (1964:128–34).
52 Hertz (1960:71).
53 Ibid.
54 Ibid.
55 Tooker (1964:139–40).
56 Freud (1963:178).
57 Freud (1962:141–3).
58 Devereux (1979:22).
59 Wallace (1969:29, 47).
60 See Devereux (1980:122–37) for the distinction between cannibalistic urges of parents and countercannibalistic urges of children.
61 The evidence on the participation of women in the torture of Huronian or Iroquoian victims is vague. Knowles (1940:168,174,176) describes women of other Indian groups torturing the victim. In his description of 70 cases of Windigo psychosis involving cannibalism or suspected cannibalism Teicher (1960) provides numerous examples of murder by some members of the immediate family of other members and the cannibalizing of their bodies.
62 Thwaites (1898:Vol. 39:219–21).
63 Lévi-Strauss (1969:338, 336).
64 Thwaites (Vol. 40:55).
65 Ibid.
66 Ibid., p.53.

Chapter 7. Raw women and cooked men

 1 Clunie (1977:42).
 2 See Chapter 2, note 32, for definition of key symbol.
 3 Freud (1961a:53).
 4 Clunie (1977:1).
 5 Ibid., p. 8.
 6 Ibid.
 7 Sahlins (1983:89).
 8 Ibid., p. 88.
 9 Ibid., pp. 72–3.
10 Ibid., p. 73.
11 Ibid., p. 76.
12 Ibid., pp. 80, 83.
13 Ibid., p. 83.
14 Ibid., pp. 83–4.
15 Ibid., p. 84.
16 Ricoeur (1967:177).
17 Sahlins (1983:77–8).
18 Sahlins (1981:117–19, 125). Following Weiner's (1982) discussion of banana leaf skirts as a symbol of women's wealth and a modality for reconstructing social ties, here I assume that as a principal good of ceremonial exchange

barkcloth symbolizes the weaving of the chief into a web of social and ceremonial relationships.
19 Sahlins (1981:126–7).
20 Ibid., p. 127.
21 Ibid., p. 128.
22 Quoted in ibid., p. 124.
23 Ibid., p. 118.
24 Ibid., pp. 113–15.
25 Paul (1982:7, 10). The overthrow of the primal father of the Tabua myth can
be contrasted with Paul's (1982:13–18) generative paradigm of succession
events in oedipal dramas locking junior and senior males in combat. Paul
claims that four succession roles are evident in this conflict: the order figure,
the usurper, the nemesis or avenger, and the innocent heir who, when the
drama is finished, walks onto the scene as the legitimate and guiltless (having
killed no one) successor. Having been denuded of his power by the stranger
and by the wife (the usurpers), the father in the Tabua myth avenges his loss
by claiming the right to make certain laws (the order figure). To avenge his
cannibalization and loss of his daughters, the father claims the right to kill
and eat all further castaways (substitutes for the stranger) who wash ashore
(the avenger). The castrating behavior evident in actual cannibal practice (see
below) suggests further that the Father's law regarding castaways projects
onto foreigners the castration of sexual competitors. In the Tabua myth, the
theme of castration is evident in the Father's claim that killing and eating
future castaways will prevent them from increasing in the land like Tabua's
teeth. The innocent heirs in all of this seem to be the daughters whose union
with the stranger (brother) begins a new ruling line. The active role played
by the mother and the role of the daughters, who kill no one, helps explain
the words of a Fijian ethnographer who said about his own people: "All the
chiefly clans of Fiji, they are of female ancestry" (Sahlins 1981:119).
26 Rank (1932:80).
27 Sahlins (1983:83).
28 Freud (1961c:7, 10).
29 Clunie (1977:42).
30 Ibid., p. 42.
31 Ibid., pp. 42–3.
32 Ibid., p. 33.
33 Ibid.
34 Ibid., p. 39.
35 Ibid., p. 36.
36 Ibid., p. 38.
37 Ibid., p. 33.
38 Ibid., p. 36.
39 Ibid., p. 34.
40 Ibid., pp. 19–21.
41 Ibid.
42 Ibid., pp. 35–9.
43 Ibid., p. 9.

44 Ibid., pp. 39–40.
45 Ibid., p. 40.
46 Sahlins (1983:81).
47 Ibid., p. 90.
48 Ibid., p. 91.
49 Ibid.
50 Ibid.

Chapter 8. Precious eagle-cactus fruit

1 Sahagún (1981:Bk. 2: 48–9).
2 Brundage (1972:252, 265, 118–21).
3 Ibid., pp. 22, 266.
4 Ibid., pp. 5–6.
5 Ibid., pp. 228, 250–1.
6 Ibid., pp. 254–66.
7 Carrasco (1982:201).
8 Brundage (1972:258–63).
9 Diaz del Castillo (1928:256–8).
10 Sahagún (1981: Bk. 2). Sahagún also refers to flesh eating in his discussion of the merchants (1959:Bk. 9:64, 67).
11 Sahagún (1981:Bk. 2:49).
12 Ibid., pp. 53–4.
13 Carrasco (1982:70–1) quoting from Wheatley (1971).
14 Carrasco (1981:212) quoting from Wheatley (1971).
15 Ortiz de Montellano (1982:101). This and the following discussion of the Aztec theory of the body are taken from Ortiz de Montellano's review of López Austin's book *Cuerpo Humano e Ideología;* see López Austin (1980).
16 Ibid., pp. 100–1.
17 Ibid., pp. 101–2.
18 Ibid., pp. 102–4.
19 Ibid., p. 105.
20 Carrasco (1980:307) quoting from López Austin's (1973) discussion of *hombre-dios*.
21 Davies (1980:171–2).
22 Carrasco (1982:152–3).
23 Carrasco (1982:162–3); Brundage (1972:33); Hunt (1977:59–60).
24 Nicholson (1967:131) quoted in Hunt (1977:60).
25 Brundage (1972:33).
26 Carrasco (1982:163) quoting from Diego Durán.
27 Brundage (1972:34).
28 Hunt (1977:59–60).
29 Carrasco (1982:163–5).
30 Nicholson (1971:397–8); Hunt (1977:120).
31 Nicholson (1971:398).
32 Ibid., pp. 398–9.
33 Ibid., pp. 399–400.

34 Nicholson (1971:400–1).
35 Brundage (1979:38–9).
36 Nicholson (1971:401–2).
37 Carrasco (1982:97).
38 Ibid.
39 Nicholson (1971:402).
40 Carrasco (1982:98).
41 Ibid., p. 186.
42 Brundage (1972:32).
43 Ibid., p. 131.
44 Ibid., p. 132.
45 Ibid.
46 Ibid., pp. 132–3.
47 Neumann (1954:276).
48 Sahagún (1981: Bk. 2:53–4).
49 Ibid., p. 54.
50 Sahagún (1969: Bk. 6:179–80).
51 Ibid., p. 167.
52 Ibid., p. 180.
53 Uroboric symbolism is evident in the sacrificial rites of other months as well. In these rites, men, women, boys, girls, and children are brought into bloody communion with gods and goddesses. In the first month's rites, children are sacrificed to the male and female manifestations of fertility, specifically water. During the fourth month, a fertility goddess is worshiped who is called "our sustenance," "our flesh," "our livelihood," "our strength." The fifth month is devoted to the "god of the gods," Tezcatlipoca, one of the original quadri-partite deities. During this month, a highly revered and honored imperson-ator of this god is killed by the priests and his heart raised in dedication to the sun. This is the only month in which the sacrifice suggests the killing of the father. During the eighth month, the young maize goddess, Xilonen, is killed and her heart offered to the sun. During the eleventh month, the celebration is in honor of the "mother of the gods," which means "Our Grandmother." In honor of this goddess, a female impersonator is killed, decapitated, and flayed. "A stout youth" puts on her skin and in this guise, as her impersonator, tears out the hearts of four captives. In the thirteenth month, women who represent the mountains die by heart sacrifice, after which they are rolled down the pyramid and beheaded. In the seventeenth month, a woman is killed in honor of a goddess called "Our Mother." She is stretched out upon the sacrificial stone, her heart is torn out, and she is beheaded. Afterward, her head is used in a dance. In other months, men and women are killed together, and young men kill captives in the presence of old men (Sahagún 1981:Bk. 2). In short, all members of "the family romance" display the libidinal im-pulses and the primal aggression animating the annual cycle of Aztec human sacrifice.
54 Neumann (1955:196, 203).
55 Carrasco (1982:4).
56 Ibid., p. 170.

57 Ibid., pp. 171–3.
58 Ibid., pp. 80, 89.
59 Ibid., pp. 80–1.
60 Ricoeur (1967:177).
61 Ibid., p. 191.
62 Carrasco (1982:87).
63 Ibid.
64 Carrasco (1982:87–8).
65 Ibid., p. 176.
66 Ibid., p. 137.
67 Carrasco (1982:176).
68 Ibid., pp. 176–8.
69 Ibid., pp. 193–4.
70 Brundage (1979:127).
71 Carrasco (1982:91).
72 Ricoeur (1967:246).
73 Ibid., p. 258.
74 Neumann (1954:277).
75 Neumann (1955:208).
76 Carrasco (1982:63).
77 Ibid., p. 181.
78 Ibid., p. 196.
79 Ibid., p. 202.
80 Feeley-Harnik (1981:149).
81 Richardson (1953:103).
82 Ibid., p. 149.
83 Ibid., p. 155.
84 Ibid., p. 104.
85 Hunt (1977:88–9).
86 See Turner and Turner (1978:247) for their discussion of sensory signata.
87 Sahagún (1953:Bk. 7:2).
88 Brundage (1979:40–5).

Chapter 9. The transformation and end of cannibal practice

1 Malinowski (1922:316).
2 Young (1971:187).
3 Ricoeur (1970:535).
4 See Chapter 2, note 66.
5 Freud (1961c:65).
6 Seligman (1910:vii, 7–8).
7 Malinowski (1922:332).
8 Malinowski (1935:162).
9 Malinowski (1922:316).
10 Ibid., p. 316. Malinowski's views on what he calls "the normative influence of myth on custom" are well known. He says that through the operation of "the elementary law of sociology, myth possesses the normative power of

fixing custom, of sanctioning modes of behavior, of giving dignity and importance to an institution." The importance of the kula, for example, and the rules governing all of its operations acquire through myth "their binding force" (Ibid., p. 328).

11 For the text of the myth and Malinowski's discussion, see Malinowski (1922:311–21). For Tambiah's analysis, see Tambiah (1983:180–7).
12 Malinowski (1922:78).
13 Tambiah (1983:180–2).
14 Ibid., p. 182.
15 Ibid., p. 183.
16 Ibid.
17 Ibid.
18 Ibid., p. 184.
19 Ibid.
20 Ibid., pp. 184–5. Another interpretation of this myth is that it represents a repressed oedipus complex (Spiro 1982). The fact that the murder takes place in the garden is consistent with this interpretation in that the garden in Trobriand thought is a "conscious maternal symbol" (Spiro 1982:101). Thus, the rivalry between the brothers is for the mother. Spiro's analysis is supported by the fact that the sisters, who should be living exogamously, may be living incestuously with the older brother. In this case, as Spiro suggests in reference to another myth, the sisters may symbolize the mother.
21 Tambiah (1983:187).
22 Ibid., p. 198.
23 Spiro (1982:135–6). SLS in the quotation refers to Malinowski's *Sexual Life of the Savages*.
24 Fortune (1963:151).
25 Tambiah (1983:192–3). See also Spiro's (1982:101) analysis of the garden as a "conscious maternal symbol."
26 Uberoi (1962:82).
27 Fortune (1963:74).
28 Ibid., p. 151.
29 Ibid., pp. 61–2.
30 Ibid., pp. 264–5.
31 Malinowski (1935:162).
32 Ibid.
33 Fortune (1963:77, 198).
34 Strathern (1983:84–5).
35 Ibid., p. 85.
36 Ibid.
37 Tambiah (1983:178).
38 Ibid., p. 179.
39 Quoted from Malinowski (1926:17).
40 Fortune (1963:xxv).
41 Ibid., pp. 18, 60, 103.
42 Ibid., p. 70.
43 Ibid., pp. 103, 48, 207.

44 Malinowski (1935:161–2).
45 Fortune (1963:215).
46 Weiner (1983:162).
47 Fortune (1963:216).
48 Ibid., pp. 218–19.
49 Ibid., p. 219.
50 Ibid., pp. 223–4.
51 Malinowski (1922:512).
52 Ibid.
53 Ibid., p. 513.
54 See Ricoeur (1970:535–6) for a critique of Freud's emphasis on the culture-building power of the death instinct. See also Marcuse (1955:78–105, 211, 236) for a discussion of Eros versus the death instinct in the constitution of civilization.
55 Young (1971:1).
56 Ibid., p. 3.
57 Ibid., pp. 3–4.
58 Jenness and Ballantyne (1920:35).
59 Ibid., p. 32.
60 Ibid., p. 82.
61 Ibid., p. 88.
62 Young (1971:186–7).
63 Ibid., p. 188.

Chapter 10. Conclusion

1 Geertz (1973:52).
2 Rosaldo (1977:169).
3 Rosaldo (1980:231).
4 Wallace (1969:95).
5 Ibid.
6 Ibid., p. 101.
7 Turnbull (1965:247–9).
8 Ibid., p. 250.
9 Ibid., p. 277.
10 Ibid., p. 254.
11 Ibid.
12 Ibid., pp. 254–6.
13 Ibid., p. 257.
14 Ibid., p. 259.
15 See Wagner's (1977:394–406) discussion of scientific and indigenous conceptualizations of the innate.
16 Turnbull (1965:265).
17 See Sanday (1981:23–4, 188–91) for a discussion of the feminine component of the *molimo* ceremony.
18 Moon (1970:193).

19 Lamphere (1969:302–3).
20 McNeley (1981:10).
21 Witherspoon (1977:53–5).
22 Ibid., pp. 58–9.
23 Ibid., pp. 29–30.
24 Ibid., p. 30.
25 Quoted by Witherspoon (1977:23).
26 Ibid., p. 25.
27 McNeley (1981:54).
28 Witherspoon (1977:77).
29 Ibid., p. 25.
30 Ibid., p. 194.
31 Opler (1968:377–8).
32 Witherspoon (1977:203).
33 Ibid., p. 201.
34 Ibid.
35 Ibid., pp. 17–18.
36 Ibid.
37 Reichard (1944:7–8).
38 Lincoln (1981:26).
39 Ibid., p. 30.
40 Lincoln (1981:26).
41 Mills (1959:201–2).
42 Ibid., p. 85.
43 Haile (1981:175–7).
44 Luckert (1975:190). See Morgan (1936) for discussion of Navajo "human wolves."
45 This suggestion is prompted by the opposition of human and coyote observable in the emergence myth and reconciled in the image of Changing Woman. See Moon (1970) for a synopsis of the emergence myth and see Haile (1981) for one version of this myth. See also Luckert's (1975:190) analysis of the Navajo hunter past and his suggestion that the phenomenon of human wolves echoes the Northwest Coast cannibal and wolf.
46 Luckert (1975:14). It is important to note that the Navajo were not an entirely peaceful people. They defended themselves valiantly against the Europeans, and Navajo war parties mounted raids on neighboring groups. Hill says that in general the Navajo disapproved of warfare. In most cases war parties were motivated by the desire for plunder. However, Hill notes (1936:4) that "[t]he majority were opposed to these expeditions and the local headmen did all in their power to suppress them." The people involved in offensive warfare "were always members of a single locality or at most of a district." As a nation, the Navajo never mounted warfare for conquest.
47 Turnbull (1978:73).
48 Ibid.
49 Thwaites (Vol. 35:89; 40:53).
50 Firth (1959:97–105).

51 Ibid., p. 105.
52 Turnbull (1965:259).
53 Ibid.
54 Rosaldo (1980:19).

References

Adams, John W. 1981. "Recent Ethnology of the Northwest Coast." In *Annual Review of Anthropology,* ed. Bernard J. Siegel, Alan R. Beals, and Stephen A. Tyler, vol. 10, 361–92. Palo Alto, Calif.: Annual Reviews Inc.

Arens, William. 1979a. "Letter to the Editor." *New York Review of Books* 26 (4):45–6.

1979b. *The Man Eating Myth.* New York: Oxford University Press.

Bernstein, Richard J. 1971. *Praxis and Action.* Philadelphia: University of Pennsylvania Press.

Bloch, Maurice, and Jonathan Parry. 1982. "Introduction." In *Death and the Regeneration of Life,* ed. Bloch and Parry, 1–44. Cambridge: Cambridge University Press.

Boas, Franz, 1935. *Kwakiutl Culture as Reflected in Mythology.* Memoirs of the American Folk-Lore Society. Vol. 28. New York: G.E. Stechert.

Brown, Paula, and Donald Tuzin. 1983. "Editor's Preface." In *The Ethnography of Cannibalism,* ed. Paula Brown and Donald Tuzin, 1–5. Washington, D.C.: Society for Psychological Anthropology.

Brundage, Burr Cartwright. 1972. *A Rain of Darts.* Austin: University of Texas Press.

1979. *The Fifth Sun.* Austin: University of Texas Press.

Carrasco, David. 1980. "Quetzalcoatl's Revenge: Primordium and Application in Aztec Religion." *History of Religions* 19 (4):296–320.

1981. "City as Symbol in Aztec Thought: The Clues from the Codex Mendoza." *History of Religions* 20 (3):199–223.

1982. *Quetzalcoatl and the Irony of Empire.* Chicago: University of Chicago Press.

Clunie, Fergus. 1977. *Fijian Weapons and Warfare.* Bulletin of the Fijian Museum, no. 2. Suva: Fiji Museum.

Cove, John J. 1978. "Survival or Extinction: Reflections on the Problem of Famine in Tsimshian and Kaguru Mythology." In *Extinction and Survival in Human Populations,* ed. Charles D. Laughlin, Jr., and Ivan A. Brady, 231–44. New York: Columbia University Press.

Crocombe, R. G., and Marjorie Cromcombe. 1968. *The Works of Ta'unga.* Pacific History Series no. 2. Honolulu: University of Hawaii Press.

Davies, Nigel. 1980. *The Aztec.* Norman: University of Oklahoma Press.

Devereux, George. 1979. "Fantasy and Symbol as Dimensions of Reality." In

Fantasy and Symbol, ed. R. H. Hook, 19–31. London: New York: Academic Press.

1980. *Basic Problems of Ethnopsychiatry.* Chicago: University of Chicago Press.

Díaz del Castillo, Bernal. 1928. *The Discovery and Conquest of Mexico, 1517–21.* Trans. A. P. Maudslay; ed. Genaro Garcia. London: George Routledge & Sons.

Dirks, Robert. 1978. "Resource Fluctuations and Competitive Transformations in West Indian Slave Societies." In *Extinction and Survival in Human Populations,* ed. Charles D. Laughlin, Jr. and Ivan A. Brady, 122–80. New York: Columbia University Press.

Douglas, Mary. 1966. *Purity and Danger.* London: Routledge & Kegan Paul.

Dunning, Stephen N. 1983. "Dialectical Structure in Ricoeur's *The Symbolism of Evil.*" *Harvard Theological Review* 76 (3):343–63.

1985. *Kierkegaard's Dialectic of Inwardness: A Structural Analysis of the Theory of Stages.* Princeton: Princeton University Press.

Feeley-Harnik, Gillian. 1981. *The Lord's Table.* Philadelphia: University of Pennsylvania Press.

Fernandez, James. 1974. "The Mission of Metaphor in Expressive Culture." *Current Anthropology* 15 (2):119–45.

Findlay, J. N. 1977. "Analysis of the Text." In *Phenomenology of Spirit,* by G. W. F. Hegel, 495–592. Trans. A. V. Miller. Oxford: Clarendon Press.

Firth, Raymond. 1959. *Social Change in Tikopia.* London: George Allen & Unwin.

Fogelson, Raymond D. 1965. "Psychological Theories of Windigo 'Psychosis' and a Preliminary Application of a Models Approach." In *Context and Meaning in Cultural Anthropology,* ed. Melford E. Spiro, 74–99. New York: The Free Press.

Fortune, R. F. 1963. *Sorcerers of Dobu.* New York: E. P. Dutton.

Foucault, Michel. 1979. *Discipline and Punish.* New York: Vintage Books.

Freud, Sigmund. 1950. *The Standard Edition of the Complete Psychological Works of Sigmund Freud.* Vol. 5. Ed. James Strachey. London: Hogarth Press.

1961a. *The Standard Edition of the Complete Psychological Works of Sigmund Freud.* Vol. 19. Ed. James Strachey. London: Hogarth Press.

1961b. *Civilization and Its Discontents.* New York: W. W. Norton.

1961c. *The Future of an Illusion.* New York: W. W. Norton.

1962. *Totem and Taboo.* New York: W. W. Norton.

1963. *General Psychological Theory.* Ed. Philip Rieff. New York: Collier Books.

Geertz, Clifford. 1973. *The Interpretation of Cultures.* New York: Basic Books.

Gillison, Gillian. 1980. "Images of Nature in Gimi Thought." In *Nature, Culture and Gender,* ed. Carol MacCormack and Marilyn Strathern, 143–73. Cambridge: Cambridge University Press.

1983. "Cannibalism among Women in the Eastern Highlands of Papua New Guinea." In *The Ethnography of Cannibalism,* ed. Paula Brown and Donald Tuzin, 33–50. Washington, D.C.: Society for Psychological Anthropology.

References

Haile, O.F.M., Father Berard. 1981. *The Upward Moving and Emergence Way.* Lincoln: University of Nebraska Press.

Hallowell, A. Irving. 1967. *Culture and Experience.* New York: Schocken Books.

1976. *Contributions to Anthropology: Selected Papers of A. Irving Hallowell.* Chicago: University of Chicago Press.

Harding, M. Esther. 1947. *Psychic Energy.* Bollingen Series. Princeton: Princeton University Press.

Harner, Michael. 1977. "The Ecological Basis for Aztec Sacrifice." *American Ethnologist* 4:117–35.

Harris, Marvin. 1977. *Cannibals and Kings: The Origins of Cultures.* New York: Random House.

1979. *Cultural Materialism: The Struggle for a Science of Culture.* New York: Random House.

Hay, Thomas H. 1971. "The Windigo Psychosis: Psychodynamic, Cultural, and Social Factors in Aberrant Behavior." *American Anthropologist* 73:1–19.

Hertz, Robert. 1960. *Death and the Right Hand.* Glencoe, Ill.: The Free Press.

Hill, W. W. 1936. *Navaho Warfare.* Yale University Publications in Anthropology, no. 5.

Hunt, Eva. 1977. *The Transformation of the Hummingbird.* Ithaca: Cornell University Press.

Jenness, D., and Rev. A. Ballantyne. 1920. *The Northern D'Entrecasteaux.* Oxford: Clarendon Press.

Jung, C. G. 1956. *Symbols of Transformation.* Bollingen Series. Princeton: Princeton University Press.

1960a. *On the Nature of the Psyche.* Bollingen Series. Princeton: Princeton University Press.

1960b. *The Structure and Dynamics of the Psyche.* Bollingen Series. Princeton: Princeton University Press.

1971. *Psychological Types.* Bollingen Series. Princeton: Princeton University Press.

Knowles, Nathaniel. 1940. "The Torture of Captives by the Indians of Eastern North America." *Proc. Amer. Philosophical Society* 82 (2):151–225.

Kohl, J. G. 1860. *Kitchi-gami: Wanderings round Lake Superior.* London: Chapman & Hall.

Lamphere, Louise. 1969. "Symbolic Elements in Navajo Ritual." *Southwestern Journal of Anthropology* 25:279–305.

Laughlin, Charles D., Jr., and Eugene G. d'Aquili. 1979. "Ritual and Stress." In *The Spectrum of Ritual,* ed. Eugene G. d'Aquili, Charles D. Laughlin, Jr., and John McManus. New York: Columbia University Press.

LeClercq, Father Christian. 1910. *New Relation of Gaspesia.* Toronto: The Champlain Society. Trans. and ed. W. F. Ganong. (Originally published in 1686.)

Lévi-Strauss, Claude. 1969. *The Raw and the Cooked.* Chicago: University of Chicago Press.

1981. *The Naked Man.* New York: Harper & Row.

References

Levy, Robert I. 1983. "Introduction: Self and Emotion." *Ethos* 11:128–34.
Lincoln, Bruce. 1981. *Emerging from the Chrysalis.* Cambridge: Harvard University Press.
Lindenbaum, Shirley. 1979. *Kuru Sorcery.* Palo Alto, Calif.: Mayfield.
    1983. "Cannibalism: Symbolic Production and Consumption." In *The Ethnography of Cannibalism.* Ed. Paula Brown and Donald Tuzin, 94–106. Washington, D.C.: Society for Psychological Anthropology.
López Austin, Alfredo. 1980. *Cuerpo Humano e Ideología: Las Concepciones de los Antiguos Nahuas.* Universidad Nacional Autonoma de Mexico.
    1973. *Hombre-dios: Religion y Politica en el Mundo Nahuatl.* Mexico: Universidad Nacional Autonoma de Mexico.
Luckert, Karl W. 1975. *The Navaho Hunter Tradition.* Tucson: The University of Arizona Press.
McIlwraith, J. F. 1948. *The Bella Coola Indians.* Toronto: University of Toronto Press. 2 vols.
McNeley, James Kale. 1981. *Holy Wind in Navajo Philosophy.* Tucson: University of Arizona Press.
Malcolm, L. A. 1970. "Growth and Development of the Bundi Child of the New Guinea Highlands." *Human Biology* 42:293–328.
Malinowski, Bronislaw. 1922. *Argonauts of the Western Pacific.* London: George Routledge & Sons.
    1926. *Crime and Custom in Savage Society.* London: Kegan Paul.
    1935. *Coral Gardens and Their Magic.* New York: American Book Company.
    1955. *Sex and Repression in Savage Society.* New York: Meridian Books.
Marcuse, Herbert. 1955. *Eros and Civilization.* Boston: Beacon Press.
Marriott, McKim. 1976. "Hindu Transactions: Diversity without Dualism." In *Transaction and Meaning,* ed. Bruce Kapferer, 109–42. Philadelphia: Institute for the Study of Human Issues.
Meigs, Anna S. 1984. *Food, Sex, and Pollution: A New Guinea Religion.* New Brunswick, N.J.: Rutgers University Press.
    1977. "A Papuan Perspective on Pollution." *Man* 13:304–18.
Mills, George T. 1959. *Navaho Art and Culture.* Colorado Springs: Taylor Museum.
Moon, Sheila. 1970. *A Magic Dwells.* Middletown, Conn.: Wesleyan University Press.
Morgan, William. 1936. *Human Wolves among the Navaho.* Yale University Publications in Anthropology no. 11. New Haven, Conn.
Murdock, George P., and Douglas R. White. 1969. "Standard Cross-Cultural Sample." *Ethnology* 8:329–69.
Neumann, Erich. 1954. *The Origins and History of Consciousness.* Bollingen Series. Princeton: Princeton University Press.
    1955. *The Great Mother.* Bollingen Series. Princeton: Princeton University Press.
Newman, Philip L. 1965. *Knowing the Gururumba.* New York: Holt, Rinehart & Winston.
Nicholson, Henry B. 1971. "Religion in Pre-Hispanic Central Mexico." In

References

Handbook of Middle American Indians, vol. 10, ed. Robert Wauchope, 395–446. Austin: University of Texas Press.

Nicholson, Irene. 1967. *Mexican and Central American Mythology.* London: Hamlyn.

Opler, Morris E. 1968. "Remuneration to Supernaturals and Man in Apachean Ceremonialism." *Ethnology* 7 (4):356–93.

Ortiz de Montellano, Bernard R. 1982. "The Body Dangerous: Physiology and Social Stratification." *Reviews in Anthropology* (Winter):97–107.

Ortner, Sherry B. 1979. "On Key Symbols." In *Reader in Comparative Religion,* ed. William A. Lessa and Evon Z. Vogt, 93–8. New York: Harper & Row.

Paul, Robert A. 1982. *The Tibetan Symbolic World.* Chicago: University of Chicago Press.

Poole, Fitz John Porter. 1981. "Transforming 'Natural' Woman: Female Ritual Leaders and Gender Ideology among Bimin-Kuskusmin." In *Sexual Meanings,* ed. Sherry B. Ortner and Harriet Whitehead, 116–65. Cambridge: Cambridge University Press.

1982a. "The Ritual Forging of Identity." In *Rituals of Manhood,* ed. Gilbert H. Herdt and Roger M. Keesing, 99–154. Berkeley: University of California Press.

1982b. "Symbols of Substance: Bimin-Kuskusmin Models of Procreation, Death, and Personhood." Paper presented at the annual meeting of the Association for Social Anthropology in Oceania. Photocopy.

1983. "Cannibals, Tricksters, and Witches: Anthropophagic Images among Bimin-Kuskusmin." In *The Ethnography of Cannibalism,* ed. Paula Brown and Donald Tuzin, 6–32. Washington, D.C.: Society for Psychological Anthropology.

Rank, Otto. 1932. *The Myth of the Birth of the Hero.* New York: Vintage Books.

Rappaport, Roy A. 1984. *Pigs for the Ancestors.* New Haven: Yale University Press.

Reichard, Gladys A. 1944. *Prayer: The Compulsive Word.* Monographs of the American Ethnological Society no. 7. Seattle: University of Washington Press.

Reid, Susan. 1979. "The Kwakiutl Man Eater." *Anthropologica* 21:247–75.

Richardson, Cyril Charles, ed. and trans. 1953. *Early Christian Fathers.* Philadelphia: Westminster Press.

Ricoeur, Paul. 1967. *The Symbolism of Evil.* Boston: Beacon Press.

1970. *Freud and Philosophy.* New Haven: Yale University Press.

1979. "Psychoanalysis and the Movement of Contemporary Culture." In *Interpretive Social Science,* ed. Paul Rabinow and William M. Sullivan, 301–40. Berkeley: University of California Press.

Ridington, Robin. 1976. "Wechuge and Windigo: A Comparison of Cannibal Belief among Boreal Forest Athapaskans and Algonkians." *Anthropologica* 18 (2):107–30.

Rosaldo, Michelle Z. 1977. "Skulls and Causality." *Man,* N.S. 12:168–70.

1980. *Knowledge and Passion.* New York: Cambridge University Press.

257

References

Sagan, Eli. 1974. *Cannibalism: Human Aggression and Cultural Form*. New York: Harper Torchbooks.

Sahagún, Fray Bernardino de. 1953. *Book 7 – The Sun, Moon, and Stars and the Binding of the Years*. Ed. Arthur J. O. Anderson and Charles E. Dibble. Santa Fe: School of American Research and University of Utah.

1959. *Book 9 – The Merchants*. Ed. Arthur J. O. Anderson and Charles E. Dibble. Santa Fe: School of American Research and University of Utah.

1969. *Book 6 – Rhetoric and Moral Philosophy*. Ed. Arthur J. O. Anderson and Charles E. Dibble. Santa Fe: School of American Research and University of Utah.

1981. *Book 2 – The Ceremonies*. Ed. Arthur J. O. Anderson and Charles E. Dibble. Santa Fe: School of American Research and University of Utah.

Sahlins, Marshall. 1976. *Culture and Practical Reason*. Chicago: University of Chicago Press.

1978. "Culture as Protein and Profit." *New York Review of Books* 25 (18):45–53.

1979. "Cannibalism: An Exchange." *New York Review of Books,* 26 (4):45–7.

1981. "The Stranger-King: Dumézil among the Fijians." *Journal of Pacific History* 16:107–32.

1983. "Raw Women, Cooked Men, and Other 'Great Things' of the Fiji Islands." In *The Ethnography of Cannibalism,* ed. Paula Brown and Donald Tuzin, 72–93. Washington, D.C.: Society for Psychological Anthropology.

Sanday, Peggy Reeves. 1981. *Female Power and Male Dominance: On the Origins of Sexual Inequality.* Cambridge: Cambridge University Press.

Seligman, C. G. 1910. *The Melanesians of British New Guinea*. Cambridge University Press.

Sinnett, Peter F. 1977. "Nutritional Adaptation among the Enga." In *Subsistence and Survival,* ed. Timothy P. Bayliss-Smith and Richard G. Feachem, 63–90. New York: Academic Press.

Snyder, Sally. 1975. "Quest for the Sacred in Northern Puget Sound: An Interpretation of Potlatch." *Ethnology* 14:149–61.

Spiro, Melford E. 1982. *Oedipus in the Trobriands*. Chicago: University of Chicago Press.

Strathern, Andrew. 1982. "Witchcraft, Greed, Cannibalism and Death." In *Death and the Regeneration of Life,* ed. Maurice Bloch and Jonathan Parry, 111–33. Cambridge: Cambridge University Press.

1983. "The Kula in Comparative Perspective." In *The Kula,* ed. Jerry W. Leach and Edmund Leach, 73–88. Cambridge: Cambridge University Press.

Strathern, Marilyn. 1980. "No Nature, No Culture: The Hagen Case." In *Nature, Culture and Gender,* ed. Carol P. MacCormack and Marilyn Strathern, 174–222. Cambridge: Cambridge University Press.

Tambiah, S. J. 1983. "On Flying Witches and Flying Canoes: The Coding of Male and Female Values." In *The Kula,* ed. Jerry W. Leach and Edmund Leach, 171–200. Cambridge: Cambridge University Press.

Teicher, Morton I. 1960. *Windigo Psychosis*. Proceedings of the 1960 Annual

References

Spring Meeting of the American Ethnological Society. Seattle: American Ethnological Society.

Thwaites, Reuben Gold, ed. 1896–1901. *The Jesuit Relations and Allied Documents.* 73 vols. Cleveland: Burrows Brothers.

Tooker, Elisabeth. 1964. *An Ethnography of the Huron Indians, 1615–1649.* American Ethnology Bulletin 190. Washington, D.C.: Smithsonian Institution.

Turnbull, Colin. 1965. *Wayward Servants.* New York: Natural History Press.
  1978. "Rethinking the Ik: A Functional Non-Social System." In *Extinction and Survival in Human Populations,* ed. Charles D. Laughlin, Jr., and Ivan A. Brady, 49–75. New York: Columbia University Press.

Turner, Victor, and Edith Turner. 1978. *Image and Pilgrimage in Christian Culture.* Oxford: Basil Blackwell.

Tuzin, Donald. 1983. "Cannibalism and Arapesh Cosmology: A Wartime Incident with the Japanese." In *The Ethnography of Cannibalism,* ed. Paula Brown and Donald Tuzin, 61–71. Washington, D.C.: Society for Psychological Anthropology.

Uberoi, J. P. Singh. 1962. *Politics of the Kula Ring.* Manchester: Manchester University Press.

Von Franz, Marie-Louise. 1979. *Alchemical Active Imagination.* Texas: Spring Publications.

Wagner, Roy. 1977. "Scientific and Indigenous Papuan Conceptualizations of the Innate: A Semiotic Critique of the Ecological Perspective." In *Subsistence and Survival,* ed. Timothy P. Bayliss-Smith and Richard G. Feachem, 385–410. New York: Academic Press.
  1978. *Lethal Speech.* Ithaca: Cornell University Press.
  1981. *The Invention of Culture.* Chicago: University of Chicago Press.

Walens, Stanley. 1981. *Feasting with Cannibals.* Princeton: Princeton University Press.

Wallace, Anthony F. C. 1969. *The Death and Rebirth of the Seneca.* New York: Vintage Books.

Wallace, Paul A. W. 1946. *The White Roots of Peace.* Philadelphia: University of Pennsylvania Press.

Weiner, Annette B. 1982. "Sexuality among the Anthropologists, Reproduction among the Informants." *Social Analysis* 12:52–93.
  1983. "'A World of Made is not a World of Born': Doing Kula in Kiriwina." In *The Kula,* ed. Jerry W. Leach and Edmund Leach, 147–70. Cambridge: Cambridge University Press.

Wheatley, Paul. 1971. *The Pivot of the Four Quarters.* Chicago: Aldine.

Williams, Francis E. 1930. *Orokaiva Society.* London: Oxford University Press.

Witherspoon, Gary. 1977. *Language and Art in the Navajo Universe.* Ann Arbor: University of Michigan Press.

Young, Michael W. 1971. *Fighting with Food.* Cambridge: Cambridge University Press.

Index

alchemy, 50
  and the Great Pandanus Rite, 95–9
Algonkians (*see also* Windigo mon-
    ster), 28, 31, 38, 39, 102–22
Arens, W., 9–10, 233n17
Aztec, 21, 28, 40–1, 46, 47, 48, 169–
    95, 225, 226–27, 247n53; *see also*
    Aztec human sacrifice
Aztec human sacrifice, 19, 32, 40–1,
    43–4, 47–8, 169–95; *see also* Az-
    tec; Harner, M.; Harris, M.;
    Quetzalcoatl; Sahlins, M.
  and calendrical cycle, 31, 171, 178
  and divine hunger, 51, 173, 178–9
  and folk history, 177–8, 182
  Harner and Harris on, 15–18
  and precious eagle-cactus fruit, 169,
    172, 173, 176, 178–9, 181, 182
  Sahlins on, 7, 18–22

Beaver Indians (*see also* Wechuge can-
    nibal figure), 28, 38, 39, 102–22
Bernstein, R., 236n26
Bimin-Kuskusmin (*see also* Poole,
    F. J. P.), 10, 22–5, 27, 38, 46, 47,
    83–101, 128
  and gender dialectic, 88–93
  Great Pandanus Rite of, 93–9, 122,
    130–1, 143, 214
  patterns in cannibalism of, 7–8, 26
Bloch, M., 52
Boas, F., 119
Brown, P., 3
Brundage, B. C., 178, 183, 190

Carrasco, D., 174, 176, 181, 182, 191
Clunie, F., 151
Cook, Captain James, 151–2

Cove, J., 30
cross-cultural study of cannibalism
    (*see also* hunger and famine)
  and animal sacrifice, 235n63
  classification of, 4, 8
  incidence of, 4–5
  patterns in, 4–6, 7–8, 25–6
cultural construction of self, 26, 33
culturalist interpretation of cannibal-
    ism (*see also* Sahlins, M.), x, 3,
    18–21

d'Aquili, E., 29–31
destructive aggression, 6, 7, 10–14,
    40–1, 47–8
  and Algonkian and Beaver canni-
    balism, 122
  in Aztec myth and ritual, 181–2
  in Bimin-Kuskusmin thought and
    ritual, 86, 88, 90, 97, 98–100
  and Fijian social order, 152, 161–6,
    167
  in Kwakiutl myth and ritual, 117,
    121, 122, 225
  in Massim, 206, 208, 212–13
  and Melpa witchcraft beliefs, 80–1
  and Navajo human wolves, 225–6
Devereux, G., 147, 241n26, 244n60
dialectic of chaos and order (*see also*
    dialectical opposition)
  and Aztec human sacrifice, 40–1,
    179
  and Fijian myth and cannibalism,
    40–1, 156–9, 168, 197
  and Iroquoian warfare, 51–2
  and Mbuti and forest, 219
  in myth, 41–4
  in symbol of Quetzalcoatl, 187–91

261

dialectic of mediation (*see also* dialectical opposition), 35–6, 238n67
and accommodation and integration, 41
and Kwakiutl myth and ritual, 41, 44, 53, 54
and Mbuti and forest, 219
and Navajo myth and ritual, 41, 44, 53, 54, 219–26
dialectical opposition, xi, 29, 33–41, 45–6, 48–9, 52; *see also* dialectic of chaos and order; dialectic of mediation
in Bimin-Kuskusmin ritual, 83–4, 94
and Trobriand and Dobuan paradigms, 204, 207
types of, 35–6, 42
Dobu, 196–213
and environment, 207
experience of hunger, 207
tales of, 204–5, 208–9
Douglas, M., 82, 240
Dunning, S., 35–6, 42, 236n22, 236n26, 236n28, 238n67

emotional ambivalence, 10–11, 49–51, 54
in Bimin-Kuskusmin Great Pandanus Rite, 94
and dual nature of animals, 121
and Hua theory of *nu*, 67–9
endocannibalism, 7, 43, 156, 158, 160, 167, 197, 205
endogamy ("turning back")
and Bimin-Kuskusmin cannibalism, 24–5
and Gimi and Hua cannibalism, 59, 79
and Trobriand Myth of Flying Canoe, 203
environment, role of, in cannibalism, xii–xiii, 8, 20–1, 26, 27, 29–31, 38, 40, 52; *see also* hunger and famine; materialist explanation of cannibalism
and ecological language, 229–30
and Kwakiutl Man Eater, 120, 122
in Massim, 206–7, 209–12

and Windigo monster, 105, 109, 122
exocannibalism, 7, 43, 197
eyewitness reports of cannibalism, 9–10
and Bimin-Kuskusmin mortuary cannibalism, 10, 27

Feeley-Harnik, G., 193
Fernandez, J., 32–3
Fiji, 28, 43, 151–68, 197; *see also* Fijian cannibalism
Fijian canibalism (*see also* Fiji; Sahlins, M.), 22, 32, 40–1, 47–8, 51, 195
and divine hunger, 152, 165, 166–7
extent of, 166
Sahlins on logic of, 154–5
and torture rituals, 165–6
Firth, R., 228–9
Fogelson, R., 109–10
Fortune, R., 202, 204, 205, 207
Freud, S., xi, xiii, 10, 44, 45, 47, 49–50, 86, 116, 146, 151, 159, 160, 161, 167, 196, 198, 230, 236n22, 243n29

Geertz, C., 3, 32
Gillison, G., 72–8
Gimi (*see also* Gillison, G.), 27, 46, 47, 59–82, 84, 134, 147
and gender dialectic, 77
mortuary cannibalism of, 81
Goodenough Islanders (*see also* Young, M.), 27, 31, 196–213, 237n62
end of cannibalism among, 210–11

Hallowell, A. I., 95, 106, 108, 109, 110
Harner, M., 15–17, 20
Harris, M., 15–18, 20
Hay, T., 110, 111, 128
Hegel, G. W. F., 35–6, 45–6, 48, 53, 236n22, 236n26, 238n67
Hua (*see also* Meigs, A.), 27, 38, 46, 47, 59–82, 84, 121, 128
diet of, 60–1
mortuary cannibalism of, 81, 214

Index

hunger and famine, xii, 4–5, 8, 25; *see also* environment, role of, in cannibalism; materialist explanation of cannibalism
  Aztec famine and drought, 16, 21, 41, 183
  and cannibalism cross-culturally, x–xi, xii, xiii, 3, 4–6, 8, 25, 26, 55
  Huron perception of, 149–50, 228
  Ik experience of, 30, 227–8
  and intensification of rituals of cannibalism, 20, 41, 183
  in Iroquoian endocannibalism, 129
  Kwakiutl experience of, 40, 118–19
  in Kwakiutl myth and ritual, 116–17
  in Massim, x, 205, 207, 209–12
  in Tikopia, 228–9
  and Windigo monster, 105–6, 107–8, 109–10
Hunt, E., 178, 179, 194

identification, xi, 45, 48, 227
  in Gimi mortuary ritual, 77
  in Hua cannibalism, 69
  with Iroquoian gods in dreams, 136–9
  in Kwakiutl Cannibal Dance, 113, 117–18
  in Melpa birth ritual, 80
  in *Totem and Taboo,* 146
Ik (*see also* Turnbull, C.), 30, 227–8, 230
Ilongot headhunting, 215–17, 219, 230
individuation, xii, 45, 47, 48, 70
  in Bimin-Kuskusmin ritual, 96, 122
  in Gimi gender ritual, 60
  in Hua gender ritual, 60, 70
  in Iroquoian myth and torture ritual, 135, 149
  in Kwakiutl Cannibal Dance, 121–2
Iroquois, 28, 46, 47, 51, 52, 125–50, 159, 217
  creation myth of, 43, 130–6
  and experience of grief, 143–6, 216–17
  and focus of desire in torture rituals, 143–7, 148

torture rituals of, 32, 41, 49, 126–7, 139–43

Jenness, D., 209–10
Jesuit Relations, The, 9, 126–7, 129
Jung, C. (*see also* Neumann, E.), xi, xiii, 44, 46–7, 70, 133, 230

Kohl, J. G., 109–10
Kwakiutl, 28, 38, 39, 40, 54, 102–22, 225
  Bella-Coola Cannibal Dance of, 6–7
  Cannibal Dance of, 41, 44, 53, 117–18
  and cannibal monster, 46, 47, 117
  and Man Eater, 102, 113–20, 122
  and myth of transformation, 44

Lamphere, L., 219–20
Laughlin, C., 29–31
Lévi-Strauss, C., 33, 148–9, 236n28
Lincoln, B., 223–4
Lindenbaum, S., 6, 72–3, 100
López Austin, A., 174–6

Malinowski, B., ix, 199, 200, 205, 207, 208–9, 248–9n10
Marriott, M., 37, 99
Massim, Islands of, ix–x, 196–213
materialist explanation of cannibalism (see also Harner, M.; Harris, M.), x, xiii, 3, 8, 14, 15–18, 26, 183–4, 229
maternal uroboros
  and Aztec thought and ritual, 46, 47, 184–6, 191–2, 247n53
  in Bimin-Kuskusmin thought and ritual, 38, 46, 47, 85–6, 96
  and dual nature of animals, 121
  in Fijian Tabua myth, 159–61, 167, 168
  in Gimi belief, 46, 47, 59, 73–4, 76–8, 134
  in Hua myth and ritual, 38, 46, 47, 59, 70–1, 78, 121
  in Iroquois myth and ritual, 46, 47, 133–5, 147

maternal uroboros (*cont.*)
  and Kwakiutl cannibal monster, 46,
    47, 117
  symbol of in cannibalism, 47–8
Mbuti (*see also* Turnbull, C.), 29, 215,
    217–18
  dependence on forest of, 218–19,
    229–30
Meigs, A., 60–70, 78
Melpa (*see also* Strathern, A.), 24–5,
    29, 52, 59, 72, 80–1, 122, 197
  cordyline ritual of, 80
  and gender ideology, 79–80
method of analysis, xi–xiii, 3–4, 10,
    27
mythical basis of cannibalism, xi, 25,
    41–4
  and Aztec creation myth, 40, 43,
    179–81
  and Fijian Tabua myth, 43, 152–4,
    167

Navajo, 29, 41, 53, 54, 214–31,
    251n45, 251n46
  and bloodless sacrifice, 222
  compared with Aztec, 225, 226–7
  cosmogony of, 220–6
  and myth of emergence, 44, 251n45
  and warfare, 251n46
Neumann, E., 46–7, 48, 71, 73, 76,
    85–6, 133–5, 184–6, 191, 237n52
Nicholson, H. 179

oedipal conflict
  in Fijian Tabua myth, 159–61
  in Hua theory of *nu*, 67, 69
  in Iroquoian creation myth, 134,
    159
  in Iroquoian torture ritual, 146
ontological basis of cannibalism, xi–
    xiii, 15, 26, 31, 32–6, 38, 41, 44,
    46, 50, 55, 215, 227, 229–31; *see
    also* dialectical opposition; predi-
    cation of consciousness
  Aztec ontology, 174–6
  Beaver ontology, 111–12
  Bimin-Kuskusmin ontology, 38,
    84–8, 95, 100, 101, 128
  Gimi ontology, 59, 84

Hua ontology, 38, 59, 60–6, 84,
    128
Iroquoian ontology, 128
Kwakiutl ontology, 114–15, 119
Navajo ontology, 41, 219, 225
and ontological symbols, xi–xii,
    36–41, 44–6, 51, 55, 84, 120, 227
Ortner, S., 236n32

Parry, J., 52
Paul, R., 160, 192, 237n52, 245n25
phallicism, 47–8, 215
  in Aztec human sacrifice, 47–8, 184
  in Fijian warfare and cannibalism,
    47–8, 162–3
  and Gimi, 77, 81
Poole, F. J. P. (*see also* Bimin-
    Kuskusmin), x, 7–8, 10, 23–4,
    26, 83, 84, 93, 100
predication of consciousness, xi–xii,
    26, 32–41, 45–6, 50, 54–5, 120,
    121
  in Bimin-Kuskusmin thought and
    ritual, 93, 99
  in Hua thought and ritual, 61–5
  in Iroquoian thought and ritual,
    128, 135, 136–9
  in Navajo myth and ritual, 225
projection, x, xii, xiii, 6, 7–8, 9, 34,
    41, 48, 51–2, 55, 71, 82, 197, 215
  in Aztec human sacrifice, 51, 174
  in Bimin-Kuskusmin thought and
    ritual, 86–8, 91–2, 96
  and displacement of endocannibal-
    ism, 128
  and divine hunger, 130
  in Fijian cannibalism, 51, 167
  and Ilongot headhunting, 217
  in Iroquoian warfare and torture,
    51, 129, 217
  and Mbuti and forest, 229–30
psychodynamics of cannibalism, 44–
    51; *see also* destructive aggression;
    identification; individuation; ma-
    ternal uroboros; oedipal conflict;
    phallicism; projection; psycho-
    genic explanation of cannibalism
  and death instinct, 49–50, 54, 86,
    135, 151, 167, 198, 209, 212–13

and Eros, 49–50, 54, 86, 135, 198, 207–9, 212–13, 215, 224–5
and lordship and bondage, 48–9, 149–50
psychogenic explanation of cannibalism (*see also* Sagan, E.), x, 3, 8, 10–15, 26

Quetzalcoatl (*see also* Aztec human sacrifice), 186–92
in Aztec creation myth, 179–81
duality of, 187, 191, 198
fall of, 191–2
as model of *hombre-dios,* 176
and myth of return, 186
and prohibition of human sacrifice, 170, 171, 188–90, 193

Rank, O., 70, 159, 160
Rappaport, R., 31, 235n8
Reid, S., 113–14, 115
reproduction (*see also* social reproduction in rituals of cannibalism), 20–5, 26
of Aztec universe, 19
of cosmological categories, xii
in Hua mortuary cannibalism, 67
Ricoeur, P., xi, xiii, 33–5, 36–7, 41–4, 45–6, 53, 120, 136, 156, 168, 186, 187, 191, 196, 198, 199, 230, 235n13, 236n22, 237n36, 238n67, 250n54
Ridington, R., 111–13
Rosaldo, M., 215–17, 230

Sagan, E., 10–14, 50, 110
Sahagún, B., 16, 169, 172, 246n10
Sahlins, M., 5, 7, 8, 9, 15, 18–22, 28, 43, 152–3, 157, 159, 160, 166, 174
Sanday, P. R., 4, 13, 81, 250n17
Seligman, C. G., 198–9
Siriono, 30
social bonding, patterns of, 226–31
social other, formulation of, xiii, 26, 33, 36–7, 44–5, 51–2, 54, 55, 62, 83, 93, 95
and animal-spirit-other, 121
social reproduction in rituals of canni-

balism, 20–5, 26, 32, 38, 55, 81, 121, 197, 214–15; *see also* reproduction
in Aztec human sacrifice, 19, 32, 172, 194–5
in Bimin-Kuskusmin ritual, 22–5, 96–7, 101
definition of, 22
in Fijian myth and cannibalism, 22, 155, 168, 195
in Hua cannibalism, 59, 67, 78, 80
in Trobriand mortuary ritual, 22–4
Spiro, M., 202, 249n20, 249n25
Strathern, A., 24–5, 52, 59, 71–2, 75, 79, 80, 81, 205–6, 213, 237n66
Strathern, M., 79–80
substitution in cannibal practice, 51–2, 197, 213; *see also* transformation of cannibal practice
and endo- or exocannibalism, 43, 197
in Fijian Tabua myth, 160
and Fore equation of pigs and humans, 6
in Gimi past cannibal ritual, 75, 79
in Iroquoian sacrificial rites, 149
and Melpa substitution of pigs for persons, 24–5, 29, 52, 59, 72, 80–1, 197

Tambiah, S., 199–200, 201–2, 203, 206
Teicher, M., 105, 108, 109, 110, 244n61
Tooker, E., 126
transformation of cannibal practice, 51–4, 197, 211, 213; *see also* projection; substitution in cannibal practice
Trobriand Islanders, 22–4, 54, 196–213
and cannibalistic consciousness, 206
and experience of hunger, 205, 207, 212
myths of, ix–x, 29, 54, 196, 199, 200–3, 204, 212
Turnbull, C., 30, 218, 227–8
Tuzin, D., 3, 5, 10, 110

Uberoi, J. P., 203
unconscious, role of
  in Windigo syndrome, 110–11
  and wishes of the soul, 136–9

Von Franz, M., 98

Wagner, R., 33, 235n13, 235n19,
  250n15
Walens, S., 114, 116, 117, 118, 119–
  20
Wallace, A. F. C., 28, 128, 131, 137,
  139, 147, 243n14

Wechuge cannibal figure (*see also* Beaver Indians), 39, 102, 111–13,
  115–16
  as metaphor for broken taboos, 120
  transformation to, 112–13
Weiner, A., 22–3, 24, 208, 244–5n18
Wheatley, P., 174
Windigo monster (*see also* Algonkians), 31, 39, 102, 104–11
  as metaphor for consuming natural
  forces, 120
Witherspoon, G., 221, 224–5

Young, M., 209, 211